Removing the Commons

Removing the Commons

A Lockean Left-Libertarian Approach to the Just Use and Appropriation of Natural Resources

Eric Roark

LEXINGTON BOOKS
Lanham • Boulder • New York • Toronto • Plymouth, UK

Published by Lexington Books
A wholly owned subsidiary of The Rowman & Littlefield Publishing Group, Inc.
4501 Forbes Boulevard, Suite 200, Lanham, Maryland 20706
www.rowman.com

10 Thornbury Road, Plymouth PL6 7PP, United Kingdom

British Library Cataloguing in Publication Information Available

Library of Congress Cataloging-in-Publication Data

Roark, Eric, 1979-
Removing the commons : a Lockean left-libertarian approach to the just use and appropriation of natural resources / Eric Roark.
pages cm
Includes bibliographical references.
ISBN 978-0-7391-7468-5 (cloth) -- ISBN 978-0-7391-8540-7 (pbk.) -- ISBN 978-0-7391-7469-2
1. Commons. 2. Natural resources, Communal. 3. Right of property. I. Title.
HD1286.R63 2013
333.7--dc23
2013022648

∞™ The paper used in this publication meets the minimum requirements of American National Standard for Information Sciences Permanence of Paper for Printed Library Materials, ANSI/NISO Z39.48-1992.

Printed in the United States of America

Contents

Acknowledgments vii

Introduction ix

1 The Shared World 1

2 Natural Resources and Artifacts 27

3 Lockean Left-Libertarianism 41

4 Property Rights and Access to the Self 67

5 The Use of Natural Resources Within the Commons 89

6 The Appropriation of Natural Resources from the Commons 135

7 Global Poverty and Environmental Degradation 149

Appendix: Defining Use 171

Bibliography 175

Index 181

Acknowledgments

When I began writing, *Removing the Commons* my original plan was for the book to be a revision of my dissertation that I completed at the University of Missouri in 2008. But things took a different path. The more I reflected about the removal of the commons, the more I realized that an upheaval—rather than a revision—of my dissertation was in order. This book is the result of that upheaval. I have many teachers, friends, and colleagues to thank not merely for encouragement and ideas during the process of upheaval but also for instilling in me the intellectual curiosity to be willing to call in the intellectual bulldozer and build anew rather than painting over rotten wood. It is not easy to tear down what you have built, but it was much easier with the type of intellectual support that I have been fortunate enough to have.

Before I even understood the basic way in which the academic world functioned, Mary Ann Tétreault showed me that it is possible to be a world-class scholar and world-class teacher at the same time. Through the lens of political economy she opened a world of thinking and imagination that has never left my side. Kathleen Waggoner served as my mentor through the last two years of my undergraduate education. Her relentless dedication to students and uncompromising standards served as a constant challenge to better myself and never settle for good enough. Both of these influences allowed me to call in the intellectual bulldozer as my only genuine option.

While this book is an upheaval of my dissertation, it would also not have been possible without the experiences and thought that went into that work. I owe a special debt of gratitude to Peter Vallentyne who not only served as my dissertation advisor but also taught me just about all that I know about political philosophy. His wealth of knowledge, caring, commitment, and patience with graduate students fostered a wonderful environment in which to live the philosophical life. Additionally, Brian Kierland, Michael Otsuka,

Robert Johnson, Joseph Bien, and John Howe were all active and extremely helpful members of my dissertation committee from which the ideas in this book were born. Reflecting back, I would be remiss not to thank Bina Gupta for her mentorship as I learned how to be a philosopher. She opened my mind to Eastern thought and, as such, a new way of looking at the world. While I do not specifically reference Eastern thought in this book, it is never far from my mind's eye and a significant factor as to why I was able to embrace the intellectual bulldozer that allowed me to carve out this book.

I am indebted to the philosophy department at Florida International University for proving me with travel funds to speak about the idea of applying the Lockean Proviso to the use of unappropriated resources. The hospitality and intellectual rigor of the department shown to me on my visit were greatly appreciated. Also, I thank Bill Kline at the University of Illinois-Springfield and I.H.S. (Institute for Humane Studies) for proving me with a forum to discuss self-ownership and left-libertarianism as I was developing the ideas in this book.

There are also a number of people who provided me with very helpful feedback and encouragement on drafts of this work for which I am deeply indebted. Alan Tomhave, John Trerise, Peter Vallenyne, David Schmidtz, and an anonymous reviewer offered valuable feedback during the writing process. The ideas in this book would not be as fruitful without their help. Of course, any mistakes in this book are my own. Jordan Pennington helped with proofreading and editing. Jordan's conscientiousness and attention to detail are second to none, and I have no doubt he will be a success at whatever path in life he opts to pursue. Any grammatical mistakes are likely the result of my not taking his sage advice.

Chapter 5, "The Use of Natural Resources Within the Commons" draws upon material published in: Eric Roark, "Applying Locke's Proviso to Unappropriated Natural Resources," *Political Studies*, 60:3 (2012): 687-702. Copyright 2012, and used with kind permission of Wiley-Blackwell.

The staff at Lexington Books, especially including Jana Hodges-Kluck, is to be commended for making the publication process extremely enjoyable. My only concerns during the writing process were with my ideas and ability to express them, not with procedural matters of publication—an ideal situation for any writer.

Last, but of course not least, I thank my parents who always encouraged me to think for myself even at the expense of parental convenience and to my wife, Leah, who constantly reminds me without having to tell me that kindness is the greatest virtue.

Introduction

On May 19, 1980, members of the Love Canal Homeowners Association took two federal EPA workers (one a public relations official and the other a doctor) hostage. Lois Gibbs, president of the Homeowners Association, recalls the moment the hostages were taken:

> I looked at both of them and told them that they were hostages of the "Love Canal People." I told them no harm would come to them, but that if they left the office, I could not be responsible for what the crowd, now numbering 500 people would do. We had no guns, no weapons, but for their own protection I advised them to stay in our office. We had plenty of food, all homemade, and they could use our phone as they wished. My office was so packed with reporters and residents no one could walk through it. I had no idea of what one did when holding hostages. I thought to myself: Why didn't I watch television more carefully! [1]

It is amazing that the hostage-taking of federal workers at Love Canal (a small neighborhood in the southeast corner of Niagara Falls, New York) has not gotten more attention since it is represents one of the most effective single instances of civil disobedience, or something akin to civil disobedience, in U. S. history. It was highly effective because the hostage takers had their demands met in full and because, again amazingly, no legal actions whatsoever from the government (state or federal) were ever brought against anyone who participated in the hostage-taking.

And what did this brash small group of predominately non-violent, law-abiding, middle-aged, middle-class, civically minded parents from Upstate New York who belonged to the local homeowners association demand? They demanded that the federal government relocate them and their families from the environmental disaster zone that had been created by years of dumping thousands of tons of toxic chemicals. By this point, almost no one wanted to buy a house in Love Canal, and many of the working class homeowners, unable to sell their homes and escape Love Canal, could not afford to pay both the mortgages on their homes in Love Canal, and buy or rent another home somewhere else. They were stuck. The Love Canal neighborhood had long lived with suspiciously disproportionate amounts of serious heath ailments, birth defects, and miscarriages. As Lois Gibbs tells it, "The entire community seemed to be sick!"[2]

For roughly a decade (between 1942-1953), Hooker Chemical and Plastics Company and its subsidiaries used their property in Love Canal as a place to dump thousands of tons of toxic chemicals. The Hooker Company, it is fair to note, broke no laws in doing this because at the time there were effectively no laws pertaining to the dumping of toxic chemicals. According to a New York Times story Occidental Chemical Company, which acquired Hooker Chemical after dumping had ended, alleged in court documents that the United States Army had itself dumped thousands of tons of toxic waste at the Love Canal site during the 1940s, but the federal government has denied any dumping or destruction of documents related to dumping.[3]

The dumping of toxic chemicals stopped in 1953 when Hooker Chemical sold its land (dumpsite) to the city of Niagara Falls for one dollar. Hooker Chemical, in an effort to mitigate legal liability at the time of the sale, made clear to the city that the land should be closed off to protect people and animals. But despite these warnings, the city of Niagara Falls built the 99th Street School directly above the newly purchased, highly contaminated land. The prospect of building on land that cheap must have been too good to pass up. In 1978, the state of New York declared a health emergency and closed down the 99th Street School as well as some adjacent property around the school.

The final straw for Lois Gibbs and the Love Canal People came two days before the hostages were taken, when blood tests analyzed by the federal EPA revealed that some of the residents of Love Canal had undergone "chromosomal breaks" (almost certainly from toxic pollutants) and were subject to significantly higher risk for a host of serious health conditions. The soon-to-be hostages were sent from Washington to discuss the results and impacts of the chromosomal study with the community. But for many Love Canal residents, the time for talk was over. They needed out of Love Canal, and they needed out fast. Lois Gibbs describes how hours before the public relations official from the EPA came to speak with the residents of Love Canal, the idea of taking hostages gained traction.

> I heard one of the residents saying that we should take the EPA representatives hostage. "Let's see how much they like being in this neighborhood. If we can't leave and we have to die here, then they can, too!" The other residents agreed

> that it was a good idea. Within minutes, the idea spread through the crowd, and as if the crowd was a single mind, everyone decided to hold the EPA officials hostage when they arrived. By now there were 300 people out front. As they talked to one another, they stimulated each other's anger.[4]

The hostage standoff ended with the release of the two EPA officials moments before the expiration of an FBI demand to release the hostages or face the use of physical force.[5] Neither hostage was harmed. Two days after the release of the hostages, President Carter met the demands of Lois Gibbs and the Love Canal People and provided temporary funding to allow all the residents of Love Canal to relocate. A few months later, President Carter signed legislation that provided funding for the permanent relocation of all residents in Love Canal.

There are numerous lessons to be learned from the Love Canal environmental disaster. One lesson, made resolutely clear by the taking of hostages, is that even people who participate in bake sales and candy drives can take very drastic action when they feel as if their health and safety (and that of their children) are placed at grave risk. The Love Canal People felt as if they were fighting for their lives, and they acted accordingly.

Another lesson, more germane to the central concern of this book, is that the impetus of the environmental disaster at Love Canal can be found in the maltreatment or misuse of the environment. The residents of Love Canal were subjected to serious threats to both their physical safety and financial security because of the ways that others used natural resources. The destruction of the environment and desperate grips of poverty that confront so many seem, for the most part, to be two disassociated problems with separate origins that demand different solutions. But this initial impression is misleading. Both the primary cause and solution to these serious moral problems are found in the same locus. The *misuse*, broadly understood, of *natural resources* has caused and continues to accelerate both the ruin of the earth *and* the desperate poverty faced by so many.

Throughout this work, my overarching goal is to offer a plausible and promising moral solution to both of these problems by defending a Lockean left-libertarian account of the just use and appropriation of natural resources that properly recognizes the moral stake that all agents have in respect to natural resources. (An agent is simply an autonomous being whose actions are guided or instructed by moral judgment. In what follows I generally opt to use the term "agent" as opposed to "person" to avoid philosophical complications inherent in the language of personhood.)

The first chapter begins the process of articulating the moral stake that all agents have in respect to natural resources by defending the claim that *everyone has an initial equal moral claim to natural resources* and that the best way to understand this claim is that "natural resources initially belong to everyone." This is not an unfamiliar position. The claim that natural resources initially belong to everyone (or a closely related thesis) has been defended historically by such notable thinkers as Hugo Grotius, Samuel Pufendorf, John Locke, Herbert Spencer, Pierce-Joseph Proudhon, and Henry George.[6] The view has found contemporary support in the writings of Alan Gibbard, Brauch Brody, G.A. Cohen, James Grunebaum, Will Kymlica, Hillel Steiner, Philippe Van Parijs, Peter Vallentyne, Michael Otsuka, Joseph Mazor, and Eric Roark.[7] These thinkers maintain that initially natural resources exist within some type of shared common arrangement, often referred to as "the commons." The problem with most analyses of the commons is that the moral conditions governing the *use* of natural resources within the commons are frequently ignored or quickly passed over to "cut to the chase" of uncovering the moral conditions governing how such resources are *appropriated.* The working assumption is typically that agents within the commons are at liberty to use natural resources (perhaps within some vague constraints of *fair use*) with usually little or no attention given to what these conditions of fair use amount to or the implications that might result from such constraints. Philosophers who are sympathetic to the idea that natural resources initially belong to everyone typically do not give adequate attention (or in most cases any attention) to the moral conditions that govern the *use* of natural resources within the commons.

John Locke, for instance, even after a careful and influential discussion of the commons in his *Second Treatise of Government* (1690), ignores the possibility that moral conditions govern the use of natural resources within the commons. Nearly three hundred years later, Alan Gibbard acknowledged that some moral conditions governing the use of natural resources in the commons exist.[8] But after this acknowledgment, Gibbard devotes the bulk of his attention to discussing how unanimous consent from everyone is required for the *appropriation* of natural resources from the commons and the implications that this requirement of universal consent has for contemporary private property rights. G. A. Cohen's discussion of the commons grants, and builds from, the plausible assumption that agents are at liberty to use natural resources within the commons but then quickly transitions to the idea (an implausible idea which he ultimately rejects) that agents jointly-own all natural resources within the commons.[9] Cohen, like Locke and Gibbard before him, never adequately addresses the moral conditions that govern the *use* of natural resources within the commons.

Political philosophers have traditionally transitioned much too quickly from the recognition that initially the world was held by all agents in some sort of shared common fashion to an analysis of how the private appropriation of the world might be morally established. Of course, not all thinkers are equally guilty of this charge. Hugo Grotius, for instance, offers a rare and sharp discussion of the moral conditions that govern the use of natural resources within commons and the relationship between use—or possession, as Grotius often puts it—and private property.[10] Grotius argued, for instance, that the first agent to take possession of some thing had the liberty to use the unclaimed thing and consume it to satisfy physical necessity.

There is generally, however, a significant step missing from the analytical bridge that leads from the use of natural resources within the commons to the appropriation of natural resources from the commons. That step is the considered examination of the moral conditions governing the use of natural resources within the commons. One recurring theme of this book is that it is not possible to offer a plausible account of how agents appropriate (come to have private property in respect to) natural resources from the commons without first comprehensively addressing the moral conditions governing the use of natural resources within the commons. Appropriation (as will be discussed at greater length in the fourth chapter) is the exercise of a moral power to *alter* the initial normative situation (some type of common use arrangement) found within the commons. The nature of appropriation as a type of alteration is important because it suggests that before we can assess how something can be altered we must first establish the conditions that exist prior to the alteration. We must first establish the conditions governing how agents may use natural resources in the commons before determining the conditions by which an agent may alter this initial normative situation and privately appropriate a natural resource from the commons all for herself. Use first, then appropriation.

The crucial role that natural resources and things derived from natural resources play in the lives of agents is explored in the second chapter. Natural resources play a substantial role in fostering the survivability, well-being, and autonomy of agents. This point is made vividly clear in cases like the Love Canal disaster where the effects of pollution ruin natural resources such as clean air and water that agents depend upon to survive. An agent's access to natural resources also plays a major role in protecting her against exploitation by others. An agent in desperate need of food, clean water, or other life-preserving natural resources for herself or her child is likely "willing" to do just about anything asked by another in order to secure these resources, making her easy prey for those who wish to exploit. Ensuring that agents have non-trivial access to (or rights in respect to) natural resources goes a long way in reducing morally objectionable exploitation.[11]

Lockean left-libertarianism will be offered and examined in the third chapter as a plausible theory of justice by which to evaluate the moral conditions that govern the use of natural resources within the commons and the appropriation of natural resources from the commons. The endorsement of a Lockean-inspired theory of justice affirms the moral status of agents as *equal* and *independent* and marks a commitment to the liberal traditional of natural (moral) rights that protect *all* agents from the aggression or harm of others.

John Locke persuasively defended this rights based approach to justice in his *Second Treatise of Government.*[12] (Henceforth all references to Locke's thought will be drawn from his *Second Treatise* unless otherwise noted.) The support of a Lockean-inspired theory of justice is not meant to signify a dogmatic championing of Locke's entire corpus of political thought.[13] Locke was, for instance, mistaken about the moral conditions governing the appropriation of natural resources from the commons and ignored the moral conditions that govern the use of natural resources within the commons. But despite some substantial disagreement with portions of Locke's thought, his rights-based approach to morality serves as a promising cornerstone for a plausible and compelling theory of justice that is squarely focused on the moral status of agents as *equal* and *independent.*

The *libertarian* component of the endorsed theory of justice primary concerns the endorsement of a controversial moral right—the right of *full self-ownership.* Self-ownership will be explored in chapters three and four, but at this early point it suffices to say, taking a lead from Daniel Attas that, "self-ownership asserts that each person is his own property."[14] Self-ownership is controversial, and many political philosophers who are sympathetic to a Lockean-based (or, for that matter, any) liberal theory of justice reject full or nearly full self-ownership and hence would reject a libertarian theory of justice.

The reasons for the partial or wholesale rejection of self-ownership are numerous. Some of these rejections surround the rejection of private ownership generally (this rejection typically comes from Marxists and not liberals). Others reject self-ownership because it is often viewed as an impediment to worthwhile egalitarian goals given that traditional accounts of self-ownership hold that agents privately own and hence may keep all, or nearly all, of the income that they earn from their labor. Still others reject self-ownership because of its implications toward suicide, voluntary slavery, drug use, or consenting sexual acts between adults. Despite the understandable leeriness that many have toward self-ownership I will defend full, though not absolute, self-ownership in the third and fourth chapters. In these chapters, I hope to establish that full self-ownership is a necessary component of an agent's moral status as independent. I also strive to show that a thoroughgoing conception of full self-ownership poses no moral threat to a host of significant egalitarian goals such as the eradication of global poverty.[15]

Against the backdrop of agents with moral rights (including rights of self-ownership) the Lockean-inspired theory of justice used throughout also endorses four central claims that Locke makes about property in respect to natural resources. These claims are: (1) *initially natural resources belong to everyone in common,*[16] (2) *appropriators of natural resources from the commons have a duty to " leave enough and as good " for others,*[17] (3) *agents may (under the right moral conditions) unilaterally, that is to say without the consent or permission of others, use natural resources within the commons,*[18] and (4) *agents may also unilaterally appropriate (again under the right conditions) natural resources from the commons.*[19]

The first two Lockean claims above can be taken in tandem to provide the moral foundation for the *leftness* of the adopted Lockean left-libertarian theory of justice. Left-Libertarians, unlike their more popular right-libertarian partisans, draw substantial egalitarian implications from the initial shared common condition of natural resources. As briefly discussed earlier, one plausible way to think about the initial shared common condition of the world is that "natural resources initially belong to everyone." To appropriate a natural resource from the commons that initially belongs to everyone has the strong potential to injure (all) others that have an initial moral stake in the world and, as such, generates a duty owed to others by those who appropriate from the commons.

Locke, by invoking what Robert Nozick described as the *Lockean Proviso*, maintains that those who appropriate natural resources from the commons must "leave enough and as good" for others.[20] The Lockean Proviso serves as an egalitarian check against an agent from injuring others by taking "too much" of the commons and leaving others with little or nothing. Locke's proviso will be clarified and explored at greater length in chapters three, five, and six. The important point here is that Locke's proviso on appropriation serves as a way to protect the moral stake that *all* agents initially have in natural resources which could be undermined or threatened by the "over appropriation" of natural resources from the commons by *some*.

The fourth chapter expands upon the proposed Lockean left-libertarian theory of justice by discussing the far-reaching and broad nature of property rights. Special attention in the chapter is placed upon the relationship between self-ownership and the private ownership of natural resources. There I will argue that self-owners have a right against others from *impeding access to their selves*. This will prove to have important implications concerning the use and appropriation of natural resources.

Then, in chapter five, I discuss the moral conditions that govern the use of natural resources within the common. Here I utilize the familiar Lockean Proviso to guide my discussion of the duties that those who *use* natural resources within the commons owe to others. The Lockean Proviso has almost always been exclusively applied to the appropriation of natural resources from the commons.[21] This is not altogether unexpected since Locke originally introduced the idea to address worries related to appropriation. I show in chapter five that the use of natural resources within the commons can be every bit as injurious to others as the appropriation of natural resources from the commons and, as such, the moral impetus for maintaining that appropriators of natural resources have a duty to leave others "enough and as good" is no less strong or morally relevant for users of natural resources.

After unearthing the moral conditions that govern the use of natural resources within the commons, chapter six turns toward the topic of appropriation. In a similar vein as chapter five, chapter six strives to uncover the moral conditions that govern the appropriation of natural resources from the commons. My attention to issues concerning the moral conditions governing the use of natural resources within the commons prior to evaluating the appropriation of these resources from the commons is deliberate. This ordering of topics is fashioned upon the earlier discussed idea that the use of natural resources within the commons has a type of moral primacy over the appropriation of these resources from the commons.

The seventh and final chapter is devoted to discussing the implications that the developed Lockean left-libertarian approach to the use and appropriation of natural resources has for environmental degradation and global poverty. I make the case in the final chapter that the established Lockean left-libertarian account of justice can provide a plausible and promising moral approach to the eradication of global poverty and prevention of environmental ruin while at the same time preserving the full self-ownership of agents.

NOTES

1. Lois Gibbs, *Love Canal: The Story Continues* (Gabriola Island, Canada: New Society Publishers, 1998) 175.
2. Ibid., *Love Canal*, 34.
3. Andrew Yarrow, "U.S. Denies Role in Toxic Dumping," *The New York Times* (Feb 2, 1992) www.nytimes.com/1992/02/02/nyregion/us-denies-role-in-toxic-dumping.html.
4. Gibbs, *Love Canal*, 174.
5. Ibid., 180-181.
6. See Hugo Grotius, *The Free Sea* (New York: Oxford University Press, 1916); Hugo Grotius, *The Rights of War and Peace*, ed. A.C. Campbell (New York: M Walter Dunne, 1901); Samuel Pufendorf, *On the Law and Nature of Nations*, ed. Craig L. Carr (Oxford; Oxford University Press, 1994); John Locke, *The Second Treatise of Government*, ed. Thomas Peardon (New York: Macmillan, 1986); Herbert Spencer, *Social Statics* (London: John Chapman, 1851); Pierce-Joseph Proudhon, *What is Property*, trans. Benjamin Tucker (New York: Dover, 1970); Henry George, *Progress and Poverty*, (New York: Robert Schalkenbach Foundation,1955).
7. See Alan Gibbard, "Natural Property Rights," *Nous* 10 (1976): 77-86; Brauch Brody, "Redistribution without Egalitarianism," *Social Philosophy and Policy* 1 (1983): 71-87.; G.A Cohen, "Self-Ownership, World-Ownership, and Equality," in *Justice and Equality Here and Now*, ed. Frank Lucash (Ithaca, NY: Cornell University Press, 1986): 108-135.; James Grunebaum, *Private Ownership* (New York, Routledge and Kegan Paul, 1987); Will Kymlica, *Contemporary Political Philosophy* (London: Oxford University Press, 1990); Hillel Steiner, *An Essay on Rights* (Cambridge: Blackwell Publishers, 1994); Philippe Van Parijs, *Real Freedom for All* (London: Oxford University Press, 1995); Peter Vallentyne, "Left-Libertarianism and Liberty," in *Debates in Political Philosophy*, eds. Thomas Christiano and John Christman (Cambridge: Blackwell Publishers, 2009): 137-151.; Michael Otsuka, *Libertarianism Without Inequality* (London: Oxford University Press, 2003); Joseph Mazor, *A Liberal Theory of Natu-*

ral Resource Property Rights (Ph.D. dissertation: Harvard, 2009); Eric Roark, "Applying Locke's Proviso to Unappropriated Natural Resources," *Political Studies* 60 (2012): 687-702.

8. See Gibbard, "Natural Property Rights".

9. See Cohen, "Self-Ownership, World-Ownership, and Equality".

10. Grotius, *The Rights of War and Peace*, 86-116.

11. For an excellent analysis of exploitation, see Alan Wertheimer, *Exploitation* (Princeton: Princeton University Press, 1996).

12. *Second Treatise*, §6.

13. For an excellent and thorough discussions of Locke's political thought, see John Simmons, *The Lockean Theory of Rights* (Princeton: Princeton University Press, 1992); John Simmons, *On The Edge of Anarchy: Locke, Consent, and the Limits of the State* (Princeton: Princeton University Press, 1993).

14. Daniel Attas, "Freedom and Self-Ownership," *Social Theory and Practice* 26 (2001): 1.

15. For other attempts to reconcile self-ownership with egalitarian-minded considerations, see Cohen, "*Self-Ownership, World-Ownership, and Equality*"; Steiner, "*An Essay on Rights*"; Van Parijs, "*Real Freedom for All*"; Otsuka, "*Libertarianism without Inequality*"; John Christman, *The Myth of Property: Toward an Egalitarian Theory of Ownership* (Oxford: Oxford University Press, 1994).

16. *Second Treatise*, §25-27, 34.

17. Ibid., §27, 33-34.

18. Ibid., §25-26.

19. Ibid., §28.

20. Robert Nozick, *Anarchy State and Utopia* (New York: Basic Books, 1974), 175.

21. For exceptions to this, see Eric Roark, *Using and Coming to Own: A Left-Proprietarian Treatment of the Just Use and Appropriation of Common Resources* (Ph.D. dissertation: University of Missouri-Columbia, 2008); Eric Roark, "Applying Locke's Proviso to Unappropriated Natural Resources," *Political Studies* 60 (2012): 687-702; Eric Mack, "The Natural Rights of Property," *Social Philosophy and Policy* 27 (2010): 53-78. Mack in the above referenced work discusses a scenario in which a "Trickster" who only uses and does not appropriate natural resources might be said to violate the Lockean Proviso by hiding natural resources with a spray that makes them undetectable to others. Mack, however, seems to be uncommitted whether this potential violation of the Lockean Proviso would constitute a wrong action. Instead, Mack builds upon the Trickster example as a strategy to establish a natural right to acquire private property (engage in appropriation) arising from self-ownership.

Chapter One

The Shared World

When children go off to primary school they typically learn a great number of morally valuable lessons. This book, at core, is about one of these lessons. At school, children learn that no matter how much they desire to have a coveted train, doll, book, or swing all to themselves, it is only right that they share the toys with other classmates. The toys belong in some fashion to all the children in class, and as such, they should be shared between all the classmates so that everyone can enjoy and benefit from them.

Regardless of a person's views about ethics and political philosophy, there is substantial agreement with the moral idea of sharing things that are *held in common*. The alternatives to sharing these types of things are strikingly bad. The biggest or strongest child ought not be able to push other children out of the way and monopolize the use of the best or most desired toys. Might does not make right. Likewise, the quickest child to get to the toys and claim them as "mine" ought not be able to monopolize the best toys. Quick does not make right. It is difficult to imagine any serous moral alternative to the idea that the toys in the classroom ought to be shared, in some fashion, by all the classmates. Classroom toys, however, are just one applied instance of the general moral principle that *things held in common ought to be shared.*

It is often difficult for both children and adults to share things that are held in common, but the alternative to sharing these types of things is unfairness and injustice. Our kindergarten teachers had it right, though the idea of sharing things that are held in common will turn out to be more complicated than was explained to us when we were five. Nonetheless, the basic moral idea of sharing things that are held in common should be kept in mind to serve as a guidepost through the occasional weeds of heavily wooded philosophical argument.

It might seem like an odd comparison, but the way in which children ought to treat toys is similar to the way in which agents ought to treat natural resources. In the case of child's play, the toys belong to no child in particular and instead should be seen as held by all the children in some common arrangement for the enjoyment and benefit of everyone in class. The same basic reasoning applies to describe the proper relationship between moral agents and the initial stock of natural resources. Natural resources initially belong, in some shared sense, to everyone. One central claim that shall motivate the remainder this project is that *moral agents have an initial equal moral claim in respect to natural resources.*[1]

The notion that moral agents have an initially equal moral claim in respect to natural resources is highly plausible because an agent cannot appeal to anything that she has done or any sort of hereditary right that she has to establish a greater initial claim over natural resources than any other agent can legitimately claim. All agents stand in the same initial moral relationship to natural resources. *No* agent is morally, or for that matter causally, responsible for creating or establishing in any way whatsoever land, fresh water, the oceans, the atmosphere, crude oil, wild berries, or any other natural resource. Natural resources are simply established or given by Nature or God. Appealing to an agent's industriousness, labor, or other aspects of her agency cannot demonstrate that she possesses any greater *initial* claim to natural resources than any other agent because natural resources are not brought about as a result of labor or any aspect of agency.

Agents are, of course, capable of using labor to *alter* natural resources and thereby create artifacts *from* natural resources. An agent can, for instance, exhibit her agency as she saws a tree into lumber in order to construct a cabin. Altering natural resources to create artifacts will be discussed at more length in the second chapter, but for now it is important to highlight that while an agent can exhibit agency in respect to creating *from* a natural resource, she cannot do this in respect to bringing about a natural resource. The changes or alterations that an agent makes to a natural resource are not obviously relevant to the *initial* claim that the agent (and everyone else) has in respect to the natural resource that she altered. An anxious and independent child might arrive very early to her first day of school and, before her classmates arrive, put together a train track from shared class materials. But the mere act of constructing the train track does not alter, in some *ex post facto* sense, the initial equal moral claim that all the classmates have to the materials that were used to construct the train track.

Further, no one is born a moral king with some sort of greater initial moral claim over natural resources than any other agent. John Locke soundly and decisively beat to death, more than three centuries ago, in his *First Treatise of Government*, the view advanced by Robert Filmer that a king owned the entirety of the earth and had absolute dominion over his subjects because he claimed to be a direct descendant of the Almighty's first son, Adam.[2] No agent, Locke persuasively argued, has any moral right or birth claim to a greater initial moral claim to the earth than any other agent.

If an agent's actions or birth right are not suitable reasons to explain why she has a greater initial moral claim to natural resources than any other agent, then it is difficult to see what type of reason(s) could accomplish such a feat. Absent any convincing reasons, and I am highly skeptical any such reasons exist, that would differentiate the initial moral claim that agents have in respect to natural resources, it stands to reason that *all* agents possess the *same* initial moral claim in respect to these resources. I shall often describe the claim that agents have an initial equal moral claim to natural resources with the language that, "natural resources initially belong to everyone." For simplicity, *everyone* is to be understood as *all agents*. To be clear, "belongs" is invoked in a weak sense here. It merely implies that all agents possess the same non-trivial claim in respect to natural resources. It does not imply, for instance, that all agents initially possess some type of private ownership claim in respect to natural resources.

One could levy the charge that while there is plausible appeal with the idea that agents have an initial equal moral claim in respect to natural resources, the language that "natural resources initially belong to everyone" *sneaks* in an egalitarian element into the discussion and does not necessarily follow from the initial moral principle. It is true that the description does not necessarily follow from the underlying moral principle, but it is not true that the description nefariously sneaks in an egalitarian element. It is not a stretch of language or an obfuscation to maintain that if all agents have an initial equal claim in respect to some thing, then that thing initially belongs, in at least some weak fashion, to all agents. The plausibility of the claim that natural resources initially belong to everyone can be appreciated by considering the alternatives to the claim.

If natural resources do not initially *belong to everyone*, then they either initially *belong to some* (or in greater proportion to some than others), or initially *belong to no one at all*. As already discussed the idea that natural resources initially belong only to some agents, or in greater proportion to some agents, is not, as Locke persuasively argued, a serious alternative. There is no plausible reason to think that some agents have a greater initial claim with respect to natural resources than other agents. This leaves only the possible alternative that "natural resources initially belong to no one." This alternative description is logically consistent with the general moral principle that agents possess an initial equal moral claim in respect to natural resources. It is possible for agents to have an equal claim to nothing. Logical consistency will not help adjudicate whether the initial equal moral claim with respect to natural resources should be described as, "natural resources initially belong to everyone" or as "natural resources initially belong to no one."

The primary difference between the idea that "natural resources initially belong to everyone" and that "natural resources initially belong to no one" is how each description treats the *moral stake* that agents have in respect to natural resources. If natural resources initially belong to everyone, then everyone has a definite initial moral stake in the world that confers upon them certain moral protections. It is *prima facie* morally objectionable, for instance, to deny an agent reasonable access to, or benefit from, a thing that belongs, even in a shared sense, to her. A city mayor, for instance, is not at moral liberty to prevent her political rival from having an afternoon picnic with his family in a public city park. The public park belongs in some shared sense to everyone in the city including the political rival and his family, and it is *prima facie* wrong to deny anyone access to and benefit from that which belongs, in a shared sense, to her.

The same moral protections captured in the notion that natural resources initially belong to everyone cannot be presumed to exist if natural resources initially belong to no one at all. If natural resources initially belong to no one, then it is not clear if anyone has any initial moral stake with respect to natural resources at all. Put another way, if natural resources do not initially belong, in any sense, to an agent, then she does not seem to have any obvious legitimate complaint if other agents monopolize, overuse, or destroy the initial stock of natural resources. After all, these resources never belonged, in any fashion, to her or anyone else. Under such an assumption, it is as if natural resources are simply *up for grabs* for agents to do with as they please. But given the extremely important role that natural resources play in the lives of agents, it is implausible to maintain that agents lack any initial moral stake in respect to natural resources and is hence highly implausible to maintain that natural resources initially belong to no one at all.

Imagine, for instance, that an agent—call her Newcomer—enters the world after other agents have taken private ownership over *all* natural resources, including even the very paltry amount of natural resources that Newcomer needs to survive. Grant, for the sake of argument, that these property owners have full liberal property rights over natural resources that allow them unfettered control over the resources as well as any income derived from the resource. Herbert Spencer offers a similar thought experiment in his *Social Statics* where he considers a scenario in which "the entire planet may lapse into private hands."[3] Given that some thinkers, such as Robert Smith, have advocated for, or are sympathetic to, the wholesale private ownership of all or nearly all natural resources, this is not nearly as far-fetched an example as it might first appear to be.[4] If natural resources "initially belong to no one," and others possess absolute and full liberal private property rights over all natural resources, then Newcomer lacks any obvious grounds to object to her complete lack of any moral stake in the world, even a stake that allows for her subsistence.

Others could simply, by invoking their liberal property rights, refuse to let Newcomer use any natural resources at all, an exclusion that would result in Newcomer's death. Alternatively, others could strike a deal with Newcomer that she *voluntarily* agrees to become a slave (or something very close to a slave) in exchange for some share of *their* natural resources. Still yet, the private owners of the world could be benevolent and simply give Newcomer some share of natural resources that enable her to survive or even flourish.

The common element in the above scenarios is that the private owners of natural resources possess an *absolute dominion* over Newcomer because they have absolute and full liberal rights in respect to all natural resources and, as such, can dictate the terms by which Newcomer can gain access to the world and with it access to her self. Newcomer's lack of any moral stake in the world fails to afford her adequate moral protection. The absolute dominion that others are at liberty to exhibit over Newcomer given her lack of any moral stake in the world is at odds with any plausible account of the moral respect and consideration due to Newcomer. Newcomer's *life* and *liberty* is contingent upon being able to strike a bargain with others that gives her access to some share of natural resources. But no plausible defense, for good reason, of moral rights in the Lockean tradition maintains that an agent's morally fundamental rights are *contingent* upon the willingness of others to bargain or exhibit good will. A defense of the wholesale ownership of the world where other agents will come into the world and find themselves with no moral stake in the world is inconsistent with the ability of agents to exercise unilateral dominion over their own lives.

In Newcomer's case, morality demands some exception be made or proviso established to allow her access to a share of natural resources that afford her protection against others dictating the terms of her life. Even an advocate of the wholesale private ownership of natural resources would likely assent under intellectual pressure to carve out such an exception to ensure that Newcomer does not perish or become a slave merely because she arrives to the world later than others. Why the presumed willingness to make such an exception? The likely answer is because the moral importance of an agent's ability to be free from the dominion of others trumps the moral importance assigned to unencumbered private property rights in respect to natural resources.

Newcomer's plight demonstrates two important ideas. First, there ought to be a degree of uneasiness brought about by the restrictions on the liberty (and in some cases, life) of some that can result when others have robust private property rights over natural resources. This is not to say that all forms of private property over natural resources ought to be rejected, but it is to say that robust private property rights over natural resources should be cautiously approached as they have the strong potential to greatly undermine the ability of agents who lack substantial private property in natural resources to exercise substantive autonomy and live a life of their choosing. Second, Newcomer's plight, while extreme, demonstrates the folly with the view that natural resources do not initially belong, in any interesting moral sense, to anyone. If we are to take the view seriously that *all* agents have moral rights that protect their ability to direct their own lives free from the dominion of others, then it follows that *all* agents must have some initial non-trivial moral stake in respect to natural resources.

Israel Kirzner stands out as a strong critic of the view that, initially "natural resources belong to everyone." Kirzner argues in favor of a "finders-keepers ethic" in which natural resources belong to whomever *discovers* them. He states his position as follows:

> In order to introduce plausibility into the notion of finders-keepers, it appears necessary to adopt the view that, until a resource has been discovered, *it has not*, in the relevant sense to the rights of access and common use, *existed at all.* On this view it seems plausible to consider the discoverer (of the hitherto "non-existent" resource) as, in the relevant sense, the *creator* of what he has found. It becomes then fairly easy to understand how the finder can be held justly entitled to keep that which he has "created."[5]

Kirzner thinks that natural resources do not exist, in the relevant moral or economic sense, until an agent discovers, and thereby *creates*, them.[6] An undiscovered natural resource is on the same moral par, for Kirzner, as a non-existent natural resource. If natural resources do not exist, in a morally relevant sense, until they have been discovered, then the idea that initially natural resources belong to everyone is flawed.

Kirzner's position that natural resources fail to exist, in a morally relevant sense, until an agent *creates* them via discovery is clever and inventive, but it ultimately fails for a number of reasons. One of the problems with Kirzner's view is the difficulty with drawing a distinction between merely *noticing* and *discovering* a natural resource. The first agent to merely notice a natural resource cannot be said, even metaphorically, to have created the resource and has no greater claim to the resource than any other agent. The first agent to have noticed the Grand Canyon did not in any fashion create it and, as such, has no greater claim to the Grand Canyon than other agents based upon a claim of creation. Kirzner is aware of this problem and accepts that "the first man to land on Mars can hardly claim title to it as its 'creator.'"[7]

An agent who first notices a natural resource has no greater claim to the resource than other agents. Kirzner can admit this is true, while still maintaining that the creation of natural resources via discovery implies that, in at least some cases, natural resources do not initially belong to everyone. The example of phytoplankton possess a serious problem for Kirzner's view that an agent who discovers a natural resource is, in the relevant moral sense, the creator of the natural resource. Phytoplankton also possess a serious challenge to Kirzner's view that undiscovered natural resources are essentially on the same moral par as non-existent natural resources.

Imagine a world in which all agents depend upon marine life for their subsistence. Phytoplankton in this world, much like in the actual world, allows marine life to exist. Grant that agents who depend upon phytoplankton for their subsistence do not know that it exist or the important role that it plays in contributing to the delicate marine ecosystem that provides them with food. We might imagine that these agents are in the same epistemic position in respect to phytoplankton as were agents in the actual world just decades ago. Then one day a super-genius builds a microscope and discovers phytoplankton. This agent's discovery in no way implies that she "created," in any morally relevant sense, phytoplankton. One reason to think that the super-genius did not create phytoplankton is because other agents were already using it to subsist. An agent cannot create, even metaphorically, natural resources that other agents are already making use of. The example of phytoplankton puts to rest any necessary or tight connection between discovering and *creating* a natural resource.

Kirzner's argument still has some life left even after both the distinction between noticing and genuine discovery and the problem of phytoplankton are taken into account. This is because Kirzner can still appeal to natural resources that were genuinely discovered, as opposed to noticed, that no one was making use of before the discovery. (Although it should be clear that the implications from Kirzner's argument, even if true, have been withered away substantially and might not apply to the vast majority of natural resources in our actual world.) Here we might imagine a miner who finds a gold nugget buried deep under a riverbed. The miner has genuinely discovered the gold nugget, and no one was benefitting from the nugget before her discovery of it. In this case, Kirzner would suggest that the gold nugget was, for moral and economic purposes, created *ex nihilo* by the miner who discovered it. And if we add the premise that agents are entitled to keep what they create, then the miner is entitled to a greater share (maybe even the entire share) of the gold nugget that she has created. If this is true, then we have reason to think consistent with Kirzner's view that natural resources that are genuinely discovered and that no one else was making use of at the time of discovery do not initially belong to anyone but instead belong to whoever discovers them.

Kirzner's position depends upon a subtle and problematic epistemic premise. His line of reasoning depends upon the principle that some thing, such as a natural resource, cannot belong to an agent in a moral sense until she knows that it exists. This is why, for Kirzner, gold nuggets lack any moral significance until they are discovered. No one knows about the nugget, so it does not belong, in any moral sense, to anyone. The problem with

Kirzner's line of reasoning is that a thing can belong to an agent or set of agents, in the relevant moral sense, even if they do not know the thing exists. Whether a natural resource or some other thing belongs to an agent does not depend upon her knowing that the thing exists.

An agent, for instance, could purchase a dwelling that contains gold coins in the attic that no agent knows of and that no extant documents reference. Even though the new homeowner has no idea that the gold coins were in the attic, it is plausible that, holding aside other moral considerations, the coins belong to the agent who purchased the house. The agent need not know about the coins in order for them to belong to her. Now imagine that the agent who bought the house throws a house-warming party and invites her neighbors to tour the house. One of her neighbors is particularly snoopy and finds his way to the attic where he "discovers" the gold coins. The snoopy neighbor slyly asks the homeowner if she has had a chance to check the attic for insulation, and the homeowner replies, "No, I have not even been up there yet and never plan on going up to the attic." The sly neighbor takes this as his cue to simply take the gold coins for himself and sell them for a hefty price. The sly neighbor says to himself, "I am the discoverer of these gold coins and have thereby created them, in the morally relevant sense, *ex nihilo*. Since I am the creator of these coins, they belong to me as part of my creation."

The sly neighbor's reasoning goes wrong in the same way that Kirzner's reasoning goes wrong. Both incorrectly assume that in order for some thing to belong to an agent they must know that it exists. Kirzner would apply this reasoning to a gold nugget buried under a riverbed, and the sly neighbor would apply this reasoning to gold coins in another's attic. Once we see the folly in thinking that an agent must know that something exists in order for it to belong to her, then it is not difficult to see how a finders-keepers ethic as it concerns natural resources is flawed. Natural resources, even those that are undiscovered and no one is yet benefitting from, belong to everyone.

One important limitation of the analysis thus far is worth stressing. Simply noting that natural resources initially belong to everyone does not specify the precise parameters of an agent's initial moral stake in respect to natural resources. There is no intuitively obvious way to understand the claim that natural resources initially belong to everyone. There is a good deal of work that must be done to determine the most plausible way to interpret both the claim that natural resources initially belong to everyone and the moral implications that follow from this claim. This task of clarifying how to best understand the claim that natural resources initially belong to everyone will occupy the better part of this project, but at this early stage the important idea is that any plausible interpretation of the idea will imply that all agents possess the same initial non-trivial moral stake in the world.

In the classical liberal and libertarian traditions, John Locke stands out as a staunch defender of the view that initially the world belongs to all agents in some shared common fashion. Locke tells us that God has given the world to mankind in common.[8] The world in its initial state is described by Locke as "the commons," the set of all natural resources that initially belongs to all agents in some shared common fashion. Locke's endorsement of the commons follows a long natural law tradition, including thinkers such as Grotius and Pufendorf, of maintaining that the world was originally given (by God) to *everyone*. Hugo Grotius, a major proponent of this natural law tradition maintained, roughly eighty years before Locke, that the seas belonged in some shared sense to everyone and that no one or nation had the moral authority to deny others access to the seas.[9] The commons can be loosely compared with the notion of public spaces or publically designated common areas such as public sidewalks, parks, and roadways. These publically designated areas also belong to "mankind in common," or at least to members of the public in some legally designated fashion

Locke quickly moved from a description of the commons to a moral account of how agents can come to morally acquire private property (appropriate) from the commons. Locke moved so quickly away from his description of the commons that he exerted no direct attention toward examining the moral conditions that govern the way in which agents may use natural resources within the commons. Locke does note that, "The earth and all that is therein is given to men for the support and comfort of their being."[10] And in the *First Treatise* Locke maintains that, "Man has a right to use of creatures . . . to preserve his being. And thus man's property in the creatures was founded upon the right he had to make use of those things that were necessary or useful for his being."[11] This offers some hint to what Locke might think about the moral conditions governing the use of the commons, but it is only a hint that Locke never develops.

Prior to discussing the commons, however, Locke spent a good deal of time detailing the moral conditions governing how agents may permissibly treat each other. Locke outlined his natural rights approach to morality by maintaining "no one ought to harm another in his life, health, liberty, or possessions."[12] Locke, perhaps surprisingly, does not address the possibility that his natural rights approach to morality is directly applicable to the moral conditions governing the use of natural resources within the commons. This is because how an agent treats or uses a natural resource within the commons can often directly "harm another in his, life, health, liberty, or possessions." An agent's pollution or overuse of the commons, for instance, can be every bit as detrimental to the life, health, liberty, and possessions of another as any punch to face.

To borrow an example inspired by Robert Nozick, imagine that an agent acting within the commons decides to pollute and thereby destroy the sole water source of a desert community.[13] (Nozick's example involves an agent who appropriates the sole water source within a community.) The agent's action of polluting a shared natural resource directly harms others in their life, heath, liberty, and arguably (shared) possession of drinkable water. To invoke Lockean language, the destruction, or attempted destruction, of the sole water source places the destroying agent in a "state of war" with others. The action of destroying the sole water source *aggresses* against others with all the vigor of any bodily trespass. This aggression (or "act of war," as Locke would refer to it) is important to highlight because it marks the point at which non-consensual force may be used against an agent. Locke maintained an agent may permissibly use force, including deadly force, against another who "tries to destroy him" or "attempts to get another man into his absolute power."[14] The intentionally destructive pollution of the sole shared water source certainly qualifies as an attempt to destroy others; as such, an agent may use *force* to prevent another from using the water source in a destructively polluting fashion.

There is no serious moral objection (aside from general objections to the use of force from pacifists) to the use of force to prevent the malicious destruction of the sole water source. An agent who destroys, or attempts to destroy, the sole water source has aggressed against others and, as such, has forfeited or otherwise alienated the natural right that would otherwise normally protect her against the non-consensual use of force by others. The destroyer of the shared water source has, to use the parlance of contemporary political philosophers, breached an enforceable duty of justice.

The same reasoning can be applied to the actions of an agent who overuses or frivolously uses natural resources within the commons. Consider an agent, once again acting within the commons, who uses water that is in critically short supply to water a patch of grass so that it looks appealing knowing full well that others will perish of thirst because the water that would have kept them alive is now soaking into the roots of grass seed. In such a case, the use of extremely scarce water to "water the grass" so that it looks appealing should be viewed as an act of aggression against others. There is little, or perhaps no, moral difference between an agent who destroys the sole water source in a community and an agent who frivolously uses the sole water source in a way that deprives others of an opportunity to subsist. The frivolous use of the sole water source should, like the instance of destructive use, be viewed as a breach of an enforceable duty of justice against others. As ideas proceed, particularly in the fifth chapter, I will consider a number of additional examples to better motivate this worry about the *unjust use* of natural resources within the commons.

It is difficult to say what led Locke to neglect the extension of his natural rights approach to a discussion of the moral conditions that govern the use of natural resources within the commons. It could have been that he set his attention so squarely toward the moral conditions governing the appropriation of natural resources from the commons that he did not give the issue much consideration. He might have thought that the appropriation of all or most of the commons was inevitable and, as such, it was not worth his attention to discuss the moral conditions that govern the use of natural resources within the commons. Whatever the reason, the general lack of attention that Locke gave to the moral conditions governing the use of natural resources within the commons is an omission that set the stage for the centuries old tradition among the vast majority of political philosophers to ignore, downplay, or deny the existence of such conditions and instead focus exclusively on the appropriation of natural resources from the commons. This oversight is significant because examples such as the destructive or frivolous use of a sole water source demonstrate it is implausible to maintain that there are not significant moral conditions that govern how agents ought to *use* natural resources within the commons. The fifth chapter is devoted to shoring up this gap by addressing the question: *what are the moral conditions that govern the use of natural resources within the commons?* The sixth chapter then builds from this analysis with an examination of the much more familiar question: *what are the moral conditions that govern the appropriation of natural resources from the commons?*[15]

The two questions above are intertwined but not in the way that might be suspected given the emphasis that political philosophers have generally placed on the appropriation of natural resources from the commons. Progress can be made on the first question without evaluating or appealing to the second question. Discussions of the moral conditions that govern the use of natural resources within the commons need not appeal to the appropriation of natural resources from the commons. An agent that either rejects the appropriation of natural resources from the commons outright or has never given the idea serious consideration may still be deeply concerned with determining the moral conditions that govern the use of natural resources that are shared within the commons. A Marxist, for instance, might not ultimately be concerned with appropriation from the commons because of her rejection of private property generally, but she might be quite interested in the moral conditions governing the use of the commons. Evaluating the moral conditions governing the use of natural resources within the commons is not dependent upon any assessment of appropriating these resources from the commons.

It is doubtful, however, that substantial progress can be made on the second question without addressing the first question. Before determining the moral conditions under which an agent may privately acquire (appropriate) natural resources *from* the commons it stands to reason that first the moral conditions governing the use of natural resources within the commons must be established. This is because the moral power to appropriate and come to privately acquire a natural resource from the commons is *dependent* upon the morally legitimate claims or rights that others have to use (or rights that others not use in certain ways) natural resources within the commons. Put another way, the sense in which natural resources initially belong to everyone must be settled before venturing out to establish how an agent may come to privately acquire natural resources from the commons. Note that this is true even if one maintains that there are *no* moral conditions that govern the use of natural resources within the commons, a position that I have argued is implausible. The idea here is not that the moral conditions governing the use of natural resources within the commons must be addressed *in a certain fashion* in order to adequately address how these resources may be appropriated from the commons. The point instead is that use must be adequately addressed *in some fashion* before appropriation is given its due consideration.

The moral conditions governing the use of natural resources within the commons has a primacy over the moral conditions that govern the appropriation of these resources from the commons. This "primacy of use" influences the overall direction of this book. In most places throughout this book, for instance, concerns surrounding the moral conditions governing the use of natural resources within the commons will be addressed before any like concerns of appropriation are considered. Political philosophers who have examined the appropriation of natural resources from the commons without first discerning the moral conditions governing the use of these resources in the commons find themselves in the same precarious position of a football player who has rumbled down the field to score what he thinks is a touchdown only to look back and see that he fumbled the ball a few yards before crossing the goal line.

Robert Nozick's influential account of appropriation illustrates the type of philosophical fumble described above. The basic idea behind Nozick's account of appropriation is that an agent justly engages in an appropriation of natural resources from the commons if and only if her appropriation does not worsen what the empirical condition of other agents would have been in the commons had the appropriation not occurred.[16] An appropriation of natural resources from the commons is morally permissible, according to Nozick, so long as the appropriation does not leave others worse off than they would have been within the empirical conditions of the commons. Nozick suggests that the empirical conditions within the commons are fairly bad, and as such, it will generally not be onerous of appropriators to satisfy the moral demand not to worsen the empirical condition of others. The ease at which Nozick suggests agents can appropriate from the commons plays a major role in his defense of free-market capitalism and the economic inequalities resulting thereof.

The trouble with Nozick's account of appropriation is that he, like Locke, neglects the existence of non-trivial moral conditions governing the use of natural resources within the commons. Nozick presumes, throughout his discussion of appropriation, that there are no moral conditions that govern the use of natural resources within the commons. The only support that Nozick offers for this presumption is that natural resources within the commons are initially (privately) unowned and given this unowned status are presumably not subject to be used in an unjust fashion.[17] Nozick does not entertain the possibility that natural resources within the commons might initially belong to everyone in an unowned but shared fashion that confers agents with some type of initial non-trivial moral stake in the world.

Nozick's lack of attention to any moral conditions that govern the use of natural resources in the commons is important because it enables him to propose an empirical, as opposed to moral, baseline to determine if an appropriation from the commons harms others. If moral conditions governing the use of the commons exist as they very plausibly do, then the analysis of whether an appropriation from the commons is just must address, at least, whether the appropriation violated the on-going moral conditions governing the use of natural resources within the commons. Absent the existence of any moral conditions governing the use of natural resources within the commons, Nozick's suggestion of an empirical baseline to determine if an appropriation worsens the condition of others would be plausible. But, as has been examined, the absence of such moral conditions (which underpins the plausibility of Nozick's empirical baseline) is deeply flawed.

By ignoring the moral conditions that govern the use of natural resources within the commons Nozick asks the wrong question. He asks: *when does an appropriation of natural resources from the commons make others worse off as compared with what their empirical (actual) condition would have been within the commons?* Given that moral conditions do, in fact, govern the use of natural resources within the commons, he should have asked: *when does an appropriation of natural resources from the commons make others worse off as compared with what their condition would have been within the commons wherein the moral conditions governing the use of natural resources are taken into consideration?* If there are moral conditions that govern the way in which natural resources in the commons may be used—and there is very strong reason to think that there are—then these conditions should not be excluded from the moral assessment of whether an agent's appropriation makes another worse off.

Nozick's neglect of the primacy of use, however, is not a deviation from the standard treatment of appropriation since at least Locke. Nozick's treatment of appropriation was critiqued at this early stage because of its influence, not because it is uniquely guilty of failing to take into account the moral conditions governing the use of natural resources within the commons. One of the primary reasons why the moral conditions governing the use of natural resources within the commons and the "primacy of use" have been in large part dismissed or neglected in roughly the past half century is due to an appeal to the "tragedy of the commons." The tragedy of the commons occurs when natural resources within the commons are overused and agents engage in a race to use and thereby deplete natural resource before others can get a chance to do the same.[18] The tragedy of the commons can also be thought of as a collective action problem in which agents acting individually in self-interested fashion do worse for themselves by overusing the commons than they would for themselves if they acted collectively and found a way to preserve natural resources for sustainable uses.

This presumed tragic depletion of natural resources within the commons has generally persuaded contemporary political philosophers to set their sights on worries associated with the appropriation of natural resources from the commons as opposed to use within the commons. The commons are often treated as a "lost cause" that we should move away from as quickly as possible. Some political philosophers have argued, and many others are sympathetic to the view, that appropriation serves as a type of solution or remedy to the tragedy of the commons.[19]

The tragedy of the commons will receive additional attention later, but a dilemma at this early stage will make clear why it does not derail an attempt to uncover the moral conditions that govern the use of natural resources within the commons. This dilemma can be put as follows: either the tragedy of the commons is meant to be an empirical description of what agents in the commons will actually or usually do, or it is meant to be a normative or moral assessment of what agents in the commons ought to do.

If the tragedy of the commons is merely meant to be a descriptive assessment of what agents in the commons actually do, then it will not undermine the central normative concerns in this work. It is worth pointing out that a number of thinkers have rejected the idea that agents within the commons will generally engage in behaviors that bring about a tragedy of the commons.[20] But for the sake of argument let us grant that agents in the commons will often overuse natural resources and in so doing create a tragedy of the commons. Any resulting tragedy of the commons only serves to impress upon the importance of determining the moral conditions that govern the use of natural resources in the commons, it does nothing to render the moral concern moot or unimportant.

The example of assault helps to illustrate this point. It is very common for agents to aggress against and thereby assault others. This is an unfortunate but accurate description of the world. This frequent behavior can be deemed the "tragedy of aggression." But the tragedy of aggression is an empirical description of the world and does not offer any reason whatsoever to ignore the moral conditions that govern the way in which agents may permissibly use force against others. If anything, the tragedy of aggression makes such a moral assessment all the more pressing. Likewise, if the tragedy of the commons is understood as a descriptive assessment of how agents treat natural resources within the commons, it poses no challenge to the investigation of the moral conditions governing how agents ought to treat such resources within the commons.

The second horn of the dilemma suggests that the tragedy of the commons is a moral, as opposed to descriptive, assessment of the commons. This moral understanding of the tragedy of the commons maintains that the overuse of natural resources within the commons is morally permissible. The significant flaw with this moral assessment of the commons is that it depends upon the assumption that natural resources within the commons are merely "up for grabs" to whoever can get to them first and that overuse and other morally problematic types of use in the commons are morally permissible. But there is very strong reason to reject this assumption. The previous example of the frivolous or overuse of the sole water source in a desert community to water grass for aesthetic reasons while others perish of thirst offers good reason to think that natural resources within the commons should not be viewed as merely up for grabs to whoever can get to them first. The tragedy of the commons cannot be defended as a moral state of affairs. In the very least, it should be clear that the idea that natural resources within the commons are merely up for grab to whomever gets to them first should be viewed as a dubious position that would need a rigorous defense and not a view that ought to be assumed without defense. The tragedy of the commons, understood in either a descriptive or moral sense, does nothing to unravel the compelling case for uncovering the moral conditions governing the use of natural resources within the commons.

An examination of the moral conditions governing the use of natural resources within the commons is not derailed by the tragedy of the commons, but nonetheless *locating* the commons takes some effort. Where are the commons? Are the commons merely a theoretically abstract idea or hermeneutical linguistic device? For most agents, the experience of the contemporary world is one in which the commons have been displaced with increased privatization. The nearly exhaustive and pervasive private ownership over natural resources, particularly land, often obscures efforts to morally examine, or for that matter imagine, the moral conditions that govern the use of natural resources within the commons.

There is no doubt that the commons have been historically subject to increasing private enclosure. This privatization of the commons makes thinking about the moral conditions that govern the use of natural resources within the commons or appropriation of natural resources from the commons a challenging and seemingly abstract pursuit. But before examining the private enclosure of the commons it is worth pointing out that many aspects of ordinary life mimic common-like arrangements and that large parts of the commons have not undergone robust private enclosure.

Consider how much of ordinary life, for most agents, is governed by "common-like" arrangements. Many agents live in shared residential settings such as fraternities, sororities, or shared apartments. When an agent drives on a public roadway or walks on a public sidewalk or bikes on a public bike path, she is using a shared common (or public) space. Upon arriving at work, many agents use a shared break-room with colleagues. When doing laundry, an agent might go to a laundry mat where she uses shared washing machines and dryers. On the weekend or in the evening, an agent might visit a public library where she checks out a shared book or visit a public park where she uses a shared shelter to prepare a meal. An agent might free herself from the rigors of work and take a vacation to a state or national park or preserve on shared land and stay in a hostel with shared lodging accommodations. These examples are just a small sampling of the many aspects of ordinary life in which agents participate and live within shared common-like arrangements.

While sharing important similarities with the commons, the roadway, sidewalk, break-room, library, and park are not the commons. The actual commons are the initial set of all natural resources, and the examples above are agent-made artifacts that were established, usually within legal parameters, so that certain goods may be effectively shared between agents. A thirsty philosopher looking for a free cup of coffee from a corporate break-room that she is not affiliated with is likely to be escorted out by security. Common-like arrangements, despite their differences from the commons, offer extremely helpful and familiar ways to think about the commons. They represent a way of a making the idea of the commons less abstract and more firmly related to ordinary life.

When a colleague or roommate fails to clean up the break-room or apartment after she makes a mess, or when someone refuses to return or defaces a library book, or when an agent vandalizes a public park, these acts draw justifiable moral condemnation because in all these cases an agent harmed others by *misusing* and devaluing something that belonged to a group of agents in some shared sense. The same general reasoning regarding the misuse of a shared place or thing can be extended as a model to think about how agents might act impermissibly in respect to shared natural resources within the commons. Throughout I will often make reference to common-like arrangements, particularly the library, as a way to motivate and make inroads into an analysis of the moral conditions that govern the use of the commons.

Aside from common-like arrangements there are still, despite the predominate privatization of the commons, mass amounts of natural resources that still effectively exist within the commons. The atmosphere and the oceans are, for the most part, privately unowned and exist in roughly the same common state as they always have. There are some international agreements such as the Law of the Sea treaty, of which the United States is not a signatory, that set some terms on how the oceans maybe be used, but the oceans today still, for the most part, remain in the commons.[21] These natural resources, however, often go unnoticed because they are not salient in the ordinary lives of most agents. The oceans are, for most, not an observable part of daily life for many, and the atmosphere is so ubiquitous that it frequently becomes part of the backdrop and is easily overlooked. Of course, this is not always true; the oceans might be very salient to an agent if overfishing prevents her from catching a subsistence share of fish, and the atmosphere will be a very salient natural resource to an agent who must visit the emergency room because polluted air has triggered an asthma attack. I will have more to say about the oceans and the atmosphere in the next chapter where I delve deeper into a discussion of natural resources and in the final chapter where I focus on issues of global poverty and pollution. Here I simply want to emphasize that the atmosphere and the oceans represent instances in which the commons are still very much with us today in non-trivial ways.

Despite numerous common-like arrangements that often pervade ordinary life and examples such as the oceans and the atmosphere that effectively remain as part of the commons, it can nonetheless be difficult to think of natural resources, particularly land, without a fence or some other mark of exclusion accompanying the thought. Even the very notion of civil society is often strongly linked with thoughts of exclusion and private property. Rousseau, for example, infamously observed in his *A Discourse on the Origin and Foundation of the Inequality of Mankind* that:

> The first man who, having enclosed a piece of ground, bethought himself of saying, "This is mine," and found people simple enough to believe him, was the real founder of civil society. From how many crimes, wars, and murders, from how many horrors and misfortunes might not anyone have saved mankind, by pulling up the stakes, or filling in the ditches, and crying to his fellows: Beware of listening to this imposter: you are undone if you once forget that the fruits of the earth belong to us all, and the earth itself to nobody.[22]

Rousseau continues by offering an interesting speculative anthropology about the origins of private property and other forms of social inequality. That account is interesting and worth considering for its own merit, but for our purposes Rousseau's insights serve to reinforce the Lockean idea that the world initially belonged in common to everyone and that the appropriation and private ownership of natural resources was an alteration to this initial state of affairs.

The history of the modern Western world, particularly since the enclosure movement in England and the ensuing Industrial Revolution, is largely one in which natural resources are treated as and assumed to be privately owned commodities to be taken from the commons and placed under the domain of a private owner(s). It is difficult to imagine by looking around the contemporary world that prior to the sixteenth century land in many parts of England was under an "open field system" (as opposed to a private ownership system) in which a member of the commons could simply use land for mowing hay, grazing animals, or other productive activity. The open-field system is often criticized on the grounds that without the private ownership of land, economic inefficiency and the overuse of land (the hallmark of the tragedy of the commons) mark the inevitable consequences. The evidence for such criticisms, however, is murky, mixed, and not nearly as compelling as it is often taken to be. Margaret McKean, for example, offers a compelling case for the claim that the collective management of land, as opposed to a system of private property, does not necessarily lead to the overuse of land or greater economic inefficiency than a system of private property.[23]

Peter Kropotkin, a late-nineteenth-century socialist and anarchist, makes the case that a system of private property does not necessarily have any immunity to the charge of waste and economic inefficiency. He asks:

> How can the peasant be made to believe that the bourgeois or manorial land belong to the proprietor who has a legal claim, when the peasant can tell us the history of every bit of land for ten leagues around? Above all, how make him believe that is useful for the nation that Mr. So-and-So keeps a piece of land for his park when so many neighboring peasants would only be so glad to cultivate it?[24]

Kropotkin makes a strong point with his second question that an instance or system of private property can fail to benefit the great majority of agents and can also be highly economically inefficient. Merely having any system of private property in place is not a magic bullet to greater overall prosperity or economic efficiency. The specific rules governing appropriation from the commons will establish the desirability of privatizing the commons. As Jeremy Waldron forcefully points out, it is important to distinguish between having a system of rules governing property at all from any particular system of property.[25] Additionally, the desirability of having *some* rules governing property should not necessarily compel deference to a system of private property as opposed to other systems of property. Rules governing property can take many different forms including common use models, collective property models, private property schemes, and combinations of the three. There is little reason to think that any of these models of property is intrinsically better able to foster economic prosperity than the others. Instead, the model of property that works best in any given economic situation will likely involve a complex interplay of culture, prevailing social norms, and localized economic conditions.

The open field system in England began to crumble toward the beginning of the sixteenth century as the enclosure movement gained momentum. English legislation allowing for the private enclosure of the commons can be found as early as the thirteenth century, but it was not until the sixteenth century that the English Parliament demonstrated the will to enact and enforce the widespread enclosure of the commons. Early in the sixteenth century the English Parliament passed a series of laws that allowed the commons to be enclosed and come under private ownership. These laws allowed the government to increase its coffers through a more centralized and easily identifiable tax base. The enclosure movement also allowed a privileged few to benefit from the enclosure of once common land so that grazing animals such as sheep could be enclosed and their wool more easily harvested.

J. M. Neeson chronicles how for many, the enclosure movement meant misery, destitution, and a pervasive sense of loss.[26] Historians differ on the exact numbers, but many forced evictions occurred as families who had lived on a plot of common land for many generations found themselves instant *trespassers* on newly enclosed private land. The English saw a good number of riots owed to the enclosure movement, and many in the English Parliament were uneasy with the negative social ramifications owed to the enclosure of the commons and actively stood in opposition to enclosure. The enclosure movement, nonetheless, slowly gained traction, and the privatization of the commons become the rule, rather than the exception, in England.

Many viewed, and many still view, the enclosure movement in England as little more than a massive theft, a governmentally-orchestrated taking of the commons to be put in the hands of a few for the gain of a wealthy elite and the building of the government's tax base. E.P. Thompson makes a strong case for the claim that enclosure meant the loss of rights had by commoners and signified a general shift of wealth and resources from commoners to those in the upper class, which resulted in class antagonism and increasing social inequality.[27] George Orwell was another strong critic of enclosure. He devoted a section of one of his "As I Please" columns to the enclosure of the commons and its lasting social impacts in England. In his August 4, 1944 column, Orwell expressed displeasure that the railings, once removed to gather scrap iron for the war effort, had been reestablished around various London squares. He writes:

> I see that the railings are returning—only wooden ones, it is true, but still railings—in one London square after another. So the lawful denizens of the squares can make use of their treasured keys again, and the children of the poor can be kept out.[28]

An unnamed correspondent then challenged Orwell's dismay at the reestablishment of the railing around the London squares. Orwell in his August 18, 1944 "As I Please" column quotes the unnamed correspondent as asking and commenting, "Are the squares to which you refer public or private property?

If private, I suggest that your comments in plain language advocate nothing less than theft and should be classed as such."[29]

Orwell seized the opportunity of this challenge to launch an assault on the enclosure movement and the ill effects that he maintains it had brought to England. Orwell does not shy away from the description of his position as one of theft; instead he languishes in the thought as he writes, "If giving the land of England back to the people of England is theft, I am quite happy to call it theft."[30] In defense of this "theft," Orwell offered the following scathing account of the enclosure movement:

> In his zeal to defend private property, my correspondent does not stop to consider how the so-called owners of the land got hold of it. They simply seized it by force, afterwards hiring lawyers to provide them with title-deeds. In the case of the enclosure of common lands, which was going on from about 1600-1850, the land grabbers did not even have the excuse of being foreign conquerors; they were quite frankly taking the heritage of their own countrymen, upon no sort of pretext except that they had the power to do so.[31]

But Orwell did not contain his disdain of the enclosure movement to a point about historical injustice. He continues by lamenting about the harms that have been caused by enclosure by describing the "few thousand families" that currently own "nearly every square inch of England" as follows:

> These people are just about as useful as tapeworms. It is desirable that people should own their own dwelling houses, and it is probably desirable that a farmer should own as much land as he can actually farm. But the ground-landlord in a town area has no function and no excuse for existence. He is merely a person who has found out a way of milking the public while giving nothing in return. He causes rents to be higher, he makes town planning more difficult, and he excludes children from green spaces: that is literally all he does except to draw his income. The removal of the railings in the squares was a first step against him. It was a very small step, and yet an appreciable one, as the present move to restore the railings shows.[32]

Orwell is not launching a full-scale assault on private property; instead he directs his ire toward the way in which the system of private property in England developed in line with the enclosure movement to afford tremendous benefit to a few at the expense of most.

The enclosure movement also received critical attention from Karl Marx. Marx devoted chapter 27 of *Das Kapital* titled "Expropriation of the Agricultural Population from the Land," to chronicling and discussing enclosure.[33] Enclosure, for Marx, could not be meaningfully detached from the Industrial Revolution that would begin auspiciously in early seventeenth-century England. The Industrial Revolution required a great deal of laborers that were willing to engage in what was fairly unpleasant and often highly dangerous labor. As a general rule, desperate agents with awful alternatives such as starvation would be the best candidates to fill the first factories of the Industrial Revolution.

It is plausible to view the enclosure of the commons as a contributing factor to substantial amounts of rural poverty and desperation in England that allowed for a steady and receptive supply of factory workers needed to fuel the Industrial Revolution. Marx's account of the factory worker who is alienated from her labor and ultimately alienated from her humanity needs some catalyst to explain why anyone, absent slavery or other forms of coercion, would agree to such awful terms. The enclosure movement offered Marx this historical catalyst in the very location that the Industrial Revolution began. It is an oversimplification to maintain that enclosure was the only historical event that led to the economic conditions that allowed for the ample supply of factory workers necessary for the Industrial Revolution. The enclosure of the commons, however, was one notable reason that partially explains the desperation that swayed many to submit to the toils of early industrial life.

Something akin to an enclosure movement also occurred in the American West during the nineteenth century. Land in the American West during the first half of the nineteenth century was generally treated as the commons *until* someone put up a fence, began to mine, or otherwise exhibited some intent to make land her own private property. The California Gold Rush during the mid-nineteenth century marked a rush by many to be "first-claimer" over a spot of land and to stake a private claim to gold. Legal property rights in California during the Gold Rush were complicated by the fact that California had changed hands from Mexico to the United States in 1848 and did not become a state until 1850, right at the heart of the Gold Rush. A miner in California during the Gold Rush era generally possessed a legal stake over a mining claim so long as she was the *first* to make the claim and was *actively laboring* on the claim that she had made. The discovery of gold in California inspired a rush to claim the commons that helped foster values such as adventurousness and entrepreneurship that have had an enduring impact on American culture.[34] Between 1848-1858, the Gold Rush had transformed Northern California from a place in which just about all the land was a part of the commons to a place in which the legal private control of land and other natural resources was the rule rather than the exception.

California was not the only place in the American West to see a dramatic shift from commonly held land (open range land) to a codified system of private ownership. In many Western states there were bloody conflicts between farmers and ranchers who had staked private claims to land and "open-range cattlemen" who moved cattle (sometimes through claimed land) across the vast Western expanse. The invention of barbed wire in the late nineteenth century created a cost-effective way to enclose land for agricultural production and often forced open-range cowboys and their cattle to be directed away from land claims. The invention of barbed wire also had a substantial impact on agricultural production in the American West.[35]

The fencing of land was so pervasive in Texas as ranchers tried to protect grazing land for their own cattle that open-range cowboys would frequently face the mass death of their cattle as fencing prevented their cattle from accessing grazing areas. This scarcity of grazing land created by enclosing land claims with barbed wire fencing lead to the "fence cutters war" in which open-rangers and those sympathetic to them cut and destroyed large amounts of barbed wire fencing.[36] According to Bob Alexander, by 1883, the practice of cutting barbed wire was prevalent across most of Texas.[37]

Open-range cowboys have largely gone the way of the dodo in the American West, but the historical conflicts between the "cowboys" and the "barbed wire folk" over the use and ownership of natural resources continue to play themselves out with different modern actors. Environmentalists and conservationists frequently play the role of the open-range cowboys who are often skeptical of large private land holdings and generally maintain that land should be kept public and publically managed. This is not to say that most conservationists would agree with the way in which the U. S. federal government (or state governments for that matter) has managed public lands under its control in the American West. The role of the "barbed wire folks," alternatively, is frequently played by private interests in the American West that are able to make substantial profits from exclusive claims over land, timber, and other natural resources. It is the same battle for control over scarce natural resources with different modern soldiers.

My primary motivation for briefly discussing a few historical instances in which the commons have been privately enclosed is not to suggest that all private property is illegitimate or that all natural resources should remain in the commons in perpetuity. The motivation instead is three-fold. First, considering various instances of private enclosure offers a historical reason to explain why it is often difficult to look around the contemporary world and locate the commons. Land, for most agents, is a very salient natural resource, and the vast majority of it has been removed from the commons and placed under private control. Reviewing various enclosure movements simply highlights the historical process by which this transition has occurred.

Second, various enclosure movements inform us that the private ownership of natural resources is not mandated by an unalterable and inevitable law of economics or social order. Enclosure can be done, undone, or could have never been done at all. The private enclosure of the commons, I shall argue, is morally permissible under the proper conditions, but the enclosure of the commons is no more inevitable than its antithesis of non-enclosure. The enclosure of the commons is instead a socially, politically, and legally directed course of action that is directed and guided by agents.

Lastly, it is important to appreciate that the private ownership of natural resources and those things derived from natural resources has the strong potential to afford significant advantages to some at the expense of others. As Allan Gibbard reminds:

> If a person owns a thing, his ownership enhances is liberty, but it does so at the expense of the liberty of others. Ownership of a thing gives a person the right to exclude others from its use, and that right, though it adds to the freedom of the owner, detracts from the freedom of those others.[38]

Later the concept of ownership will be examined at much greater length, but for now it is important to see that the private enclosure of natural resources affords some a great deal of freedom specifically *at the expense of* the freedom of others. If private ownership did not restrict the freedom of some, then it would be of no benefit to the private owner. *Private ownership is valuable to those who have it strictly because it restricts the freedom of others.*

This chapter was primary concerned with making a compelling case for the claim that all agents enjoy an initial equal moral claim to natural resources and that the best way to understand this claim is that "natural resources initially belong to everyone" in some shared fashion. The commons, the initial set of shared natural resources, was then introduced as a way to think about the world prior to private enclosure. I devote the next chapter to clarifying what natural resources and artifacts (things derived from natural resources) are as well as exploring the relationship between the two. The next chapter will also highlight the role that natural resources play in the lives of agents. The attention directed toward considering the significant role that natural resources play in the lives of agents serves to sharpen the importance of determining the moral conditions that govern the use of natural resources within the commons and appropriation of these resources from the commons.

NOTES

1. The analogy that I draw between natural resources held in common and school toys held in common is illustrative thought, admittedly, and is far from perfect. Ultimately the toys are privately owned by the school district and this makes them different from natural resources in the commons. I invoke the analogy merely as an illustrative starting place and not to formulate a perfect analogy.

2. John Locke, *Two Treatises of Government*, ed. Paul Laslett (New York: Cambridge University Press, 1998).

3. Herbert Spencer, *Social Statics*, 114-115.

4. Robert Smith, "Resolving the Tragedy of the Commons by Creating Private Property Rights in Wildlife," *Cato Journal* 1 (1981): 439-468.

5. Israel Kirzner, "Entrepreneurship, Entitlement, and Economic Justice," *Eastern Economic Journal* 4 (1978): 17-18.

6. Kirzner also argues that an agent can discover and thereby create a use for a resource that entitles her to the profits from such a discovery. An agent, for instance, might discover that

Aloe vera has medicinal uses as opposed to merely being a shrub. Before the discovery, *Aloe vera* might sell for pennies per plant but after the discovery of the new use the plant is worth much more. Kirzner argues that the agent who discovered and thereby created this new economic value is entitled to the profit created by her discovery.

7. Ibid, 18.
8. Locke, *Second Treatise*, §25-27, 32,34.
9. See Grotius, *The Free Sea*.
10. Locke, *Second Treatise*, §26.
11. Locke, *First Treatise*, §86
12. .Locke, *Second Treatise*, §6.
13. Nozick, *Anarchy, State and Utopia*, 179-180.
14. Locke, *Second Treatise*, §16-17.
15. Note that appropriation is generally taken to mean "coming to privately own" or original acquisition from the commons. As such there will not be a focus toward how agents come to privately own natural resources through transfer, rectification, or means other than original acquisition.
16. Nozick, *Anarchy, State, and Utopia*, 174-182.
17. Ibid., 178.
18. For the seminal treatment of the "tragedy of the commons," see Garrett Hardin, "Tragedy of the Commons," *Science* 162 (1968): 1243-1248.
19. See Smith, "Preserving Wildlife"; also see David Schmidtz, "When is Original Appropriation Required," *Monist* 90 (1990): 504-518 where he argues that appropriation is required in some cases as a way to fulfill the Lockean Proviso.
20. See Elinor Ostrom, *Governing the Commons: The Evolution of Institutions for Collective Action* (Cambridge: Cambridge University Press, 1990); Margaret McKean, "Success on the Commons: A Comparative Examination of Institutions for Common Property Resource Management," *Journal of Theoretical Politics* 4 (1992): 247-281.
21. The entire Law of the Sea Treaty may be found at www.unlawoftheseatreaty.org/
22. .Jean Jacques Rousseau, *Discourse on the Origin and Basis of Inequality*, trans. G.D.H. Cole (New York: E.P. Dutton, 1950) 234-35.
23. See Margaret McKean, "Success on the Commons".
24. Peter Kropotkin, *Anarchism: Its Philosophy and Ideal* (London: Freedom Pamphlets, 1909) 9-10.
25. Jeremy Waldron, *The Right to Private Property* (Oxford: Clarendon Press, 1988).
26. For a defense of this position see J.M. Neeson, *Commoners: Common Right, Enclosure, and Social Change in Europe, 1700-1820* (Cambridge: Cambridge University Press, 1996).
27. See E.P. Thompson, *The Making of the English Working Class* (New York: Vintage, 1966).
28. George Orwell, *The Collected Essays, Journalism and Letters of George Orwell Volume III*, eds. Sonia Orwell and Ian Angus (New York: Harcourt, Brace, and World, 1968) 200.
29. Ibid., 207.
30. Ibid.
31. Ibid.
32. Ibid., 207-08.
33. See Karl Marx, *Capital Volume I: A Critique of Political Economy*, ed. New Left Review (London: Penguin, 1992).
34. For a discussion of the relation between the Gold Rush and American values see Henry W. Brands, *The Age of Gold: The California Gold Rush and the New American Dream* (New York: Random House, 2003).
35. The relation between the invention of barbed wire and agricultural economic development has been recently explored by Richard Hornbeck, "Barbed Wire: Property Rights, and Economic Development," *The Quarterly Journal of Economics* 125 (2010): 767-810.
36. See Wayne Gard, "The Fence-Cutters," *The Southwest Historical Quarterly* 51 (1947): 1-15.
37. Bob Alexander, *Rawhide Ranger, Ira Allen: Enforcing Law on the Texas Frontier* (Denton, TX: University of North Texas Press, 2011) 106-107.

38. Gibbard, "Natural Property Rights," 77.

Chapter Two

Natural Resources and Artifacts

To this point, only an intuitive conception of natural resources through the use of examples has been put forward. But given the central role that natural resources play throughout this work, more discussion focusing on natural resources and artifacts (those things derived from natural resources) is in order. A categorization of the physical world reveals the ubiquitous nature of natural resources. *Every* physical object can be placed within one of three categories: (1) beings with moral standing, (2) natural resources, or (3) artifacts.[1] There is nothing in the physical world, remarkable as it might be, that falls outside of these three categories.

An agent is a paradigmatic example of a being with moral standing, that is to say, a being that must be given moral consideration. An agent is generally understood as an autonomous being whose actions are guided or instructed by moral judgment. Not all human beings are moral agents. A two-day-old neonate or a human operating under mass psychotic delusion, for instance, is not an agent. Moral standing, however, need not be limited to agents. Philosophers disagree substantially about what conditions must be met before a being possesses moral standing. A Kantian, for instance, would likely argue that rationality is both necessary and sufficient for a being to possess moral standing. Most utilitarians, alternatively, would suggest that sentience is necessary (perhaps also sufficient) for a being to possess moral standing. Libertarians, on the other hand, do not have a standard view about the conditions that must be met before a being possesses moral standing.

General disagreement among ethicists in respect to the conditions governing moral standing abounds in cases involving non-human animals, people with severe mental illness or mental disability, fetuses, and infants. It is an open question, for example, whether a trout is a being with moral standing or a natural resource. My inclination is to treat a trout as a natural resource but to treat a chimpanzee and other primates as beings with moral standing, but I will not argue this position here. Cases of infants, persons with severe mental disabilities or severe psychological problems, and non-human primates offer reasons for thinking that the class of beings with moral standing should plausibly be extended beyond that of agents. Nonetheless, beyond the clear case of agents there is legitimate philosophical disagreement surrounding the types of beings that possess moral standing, and I do not seek to settle this disagreement here. Throughout, for the sake of simplicity, I shall assume that agents possess moral standing and leave open the question of whether non-agents, of various types, possess moral standing.

Aside from beings with moral standing, the world also possesses natural resources. A natural resource, according to Peter Vallentyne, is "a non-agent resource in the world that was not created by any (non-divine) person and exists in its *non-improved* form."[2] Natural resources are non-improved as opposed to non-altered. An agent walking along a path in the woods alters the path but does not improve the path. In such a case, the wooded path remains a natural resource even though it was altered or disturbed in some fashion. The same would be true if an agent polluted and hence made worse a natural resource such as in a case of dumping a toxic chemical into a waterway. In this case, the agent has altered the natural resource, but has not improved it, and, as such, the waterway would remain a natural resource, albeit a polluted one. Examples of natural resources include but are not limited to the following the sun, land, the oceans, the atmosphere, minerals, a running spring of water, forests, a cave shelter, wild berries, and deposits of fossil fuels such as natural gas and crude oil.

Before natural resources underwent improvement(s), the picture of *all things* in the physical world would end here with natural resources and beings with moral standing. Agents, however, have improved natural resources in vast and varied ways. Hence the need for a third category of physical objects: artifacts.

Artifacts are resources that have undergone improvements of a value-additive nature by agents.[3] When an agent improves a natural resource, she *creates* an artifact. Thus, when an agent cuts down a tree and *builds* a log cabin from the tree, the log cabin is an artifact as opposed to a natural resource. If lightning, however, had struck the tree in precisely the "right way" and a qualitatively identical "log cabin" was produced by the strike, then this lightning-created log cabin would be a natural resource as opposed to an artifact. Artifacts are created by agents who take action to improve natural resources and are never simply given by nature or God.

The cedar tree always precedes the cabin from which it was built. For this reason, it is impossible to comprehensively and historically evaluate the moral conditions governing the use and appropriation of an artifact without first accomplishing this task with respect to the natural resource(s) that constitute the artifact in question. In order to determine if an agent legitimately privately owns a cabin that she constructed from a cedar tree, it must first be established if she acted in a morally permissible fashion when she altered the cedar tree that she used to build the cabin. If an agent were to create a cabin from natural resources that she illegitimately obtained or otherwise did not have the moral power to use in her construction of the cabin, then any private ownership claim that she makes in respect to the cabin should be seen as dubious. *A comprehensive moral analysis surrounding the property rights of an artifact must include a moral analysis of the historical origins of the natural resources from which the artifact was created.*

Despite the moral inseparability of artifacts from the natural resources that constitute them, the claim that natural resources initially belong to everyone should not be presumed to apply to artifacts. An agent who builds a log cabin plausibly has a stronger moral claim, *caeteris paribus*, to the cabin than do others who did not build the cabin. The agent who built the log cabin stands in a different moral relationship to the cabin than do other agents who did not labor to create the cabin. It is unfair, holding other considerations constant, that someone who did not labor on the cabin should have a moral claim to the cabin on par with the agent who expended her time, labor, and talents to build the cabin. In the case of an artifact, a presumption of a greater moral stake or claim for the artifact's creator is plausible.

One might have a degree of trepidation with the idea that natural resources initially belong to everyone in some equal sense while artifacts (or artifactual value) belong, in whole or disproportionate part, to the producer of the artifact, especially since all artifacts are produced from natural resources. There is nothing inconsistent, however, with the idea that agents can have an initial equal claim to some thing and then through differential contributions of labor come to have unequal shares in what is produced from the thing. Consider a case of inheritance to illustrate this idea. Four siblings might inherit at the same time an equal share of an old mansion. Three of the siblings over the next twenty years give the mansion little thought and exert virtually no effort in respect to maintaining the property, while one of the siblings spends every free weekend that she has tending to the property and fixing it up. All four siblings began with an initial equal claim to the mansion, but twenty years later the sibling that put her time and effort into improving the mansion has a greater moral claim to the *improved value* that she has added to the mansion. All four siblings still have a claim to the mansion as such, but only the sibling who improved the mansion can make a legitimate claim to the improved value that she added to the mansion.

The ideas developed by Henry George in his highly influential *Progress and Poverty* offer a promising way to approach how the initially equal moral claim that everyone has to natural resources can be separated from the differential claims that agents often have to artifacts. George maintained that land

and other natural resources belong to everyone and ought to be treated as common property but that an agent owns the products of her labor and any improved value that she adds to natural resources.[4] George developed this idea by arguing that an agent should be recognized as the private owner of a natural resource such as land if and only if she pays the competitive rental value of the natural resource or, as will be more closely examined in the fifth chapter, if she pays the competitive value of rights in respect to a natural resource such as land.[5]

This rent, George suggested, would be collected as a tax that would generally be distributed back to everyone on a per capita basis. This tax on natural resource appropriation would go back to everyone because everyone has an initial equal claim to the natural resource(s) being taken as private property. George emphasized that a tax on the competitive rental value of land (and presumably other natural resources) ought to be the *only* tax levied by a government.[6] His endorsement of mandating that private property owners pay the competitive rental value of land and other natural resources is comparable, through far from analogous, to property taxes levied in most modern liberal democracies. What makes George's idea unlike *typical* tax schemes is that he emphatically rejects other forms of taxation and insisted that the rent collected (tax) ought to go directly back to the very agents to which *it is owed* and not merely to fill some innocuous governmental coffer.

An agent consistent with George's ideas, however, who produces an artifact, may keep *all* the value that she adds to natural resources. The creator of the log cabin, for instance, must pay the competitive rental value of the trees and any other natural resources that she uses to construct the cabin and any land under or around the cabin claimed as private property, but once this payment is made she is entitled to the full value that her production adds to natural resources. Georgism will be discussed at greater length later as a plausible and promising approach to address the moral conditions that govern the use of natural resources within the commons and appropriation of these resources from the commons. The idea is invoked here to outline a method by which it is conceptually possible to separate the initial equal moral claim that agents have in respect to natural resources from the disproportionate claims that agents often have in respect to artifacts.

The presumption that agents often have differential claim in respect to artifacts, however, should not be viewed as a reason to eliminate the pressing need to evaluate the moral conditions surrounding the natural resource base of an artifact. An agent might expend a great deal of time and labor to grow beautiful roses that improve the value of a plot of land. If, however, she does this on her neighbor's property while her neighbor is out of town and without permission from her neighbor, then her labor and time do not yield a moral claim to anything.

Although there is a general presumption that the agent(s) who created an artifact has a greater moral claim over the artifact or its improved value than others, there are a number of general cases in which agents plausibly possess an *equal moral claim in respect to artifacts*. Consider an artifact, for example, that was *abandoned* by its private owner. If an artifact is abandoned it seems as if no one has any greater claim over the abandoned artifact than anyone else. Everyone, it seems, has the same moral claim to the couch that is left on the curb for garbage pick-up. Abandoned artifacts revert to possessing the same moral status as natural resources in the commons.

Aside from instances of abandonment, universal gifting also plausibly marks a means by which agents could gain an equal moral claim in respect to an artifact. Everyone plausibly has an equal moral claim over an artifact that is gifted to everyone by its private owner. The private owner of a log cabin can conceivably completely alienate her private property rights over the cabin and give the cabin to everyone. If this were to occur, then all agents have an equal moral claim with respect to the cabin, just as they *initially* had over the cedar trees used to construct the cabin. Something akin to a limited universal gift occurs when an art collector bequests a famous work of art to a museum, or series of museums, with the stipulation that the work must be open to public viewing for some designated amount of time.

Other examples of artifacts in which everyone, or at least everyone in a certain defined public group, has an equal moral claim can be found in public spaces. The manicured lawns or benches at a maintained public park are examples of "public artifacts." An agent might be allowed to reserve a park pavilion for a private social gathering and exclude uninvited agents for a few hours, but every member of the public ought to be governed by this rule of reservation and can have their turn at exclusion if that is their desire. Of course, the community of agents that controls the park might also reject the idea of reserving a private space within the park. The important point is that as public artifacts are concerned the moral claims of everyone in the community can be thought of as the same and in this way these types of artifacts are on moral par with natural resources in the commons.

Artifacts (or the increased value added by the production of an artifact) that are *illegitimately produced* are also plausibly on the same moral par as natural resources within the commons. Here I leave open exactly what "illegitimately produced" amounts to, but generally it can be taken to mean producing an artifact in a fashion that violates a moral duty owed to others. Consider again the case of an agent who deliberately violates her neighbor's property rights by producing beautiful roses on her neighbor's property without the permission of her neighbor. What should be said about the normative status of the illegitimately added improved value brought about by the production of the roses? One promising proposal is that everyone has an equal moral claim to the improved value of the illegitimate action, excluding the agent who took the illegitimate action. No agent, similar to the conclusion drawn about natural resources, has any greater moral claim to the improved value resulting from the illegitimate production of artifactual value than any other agent.

It could be maintained that the owner of the property where the roses were planted should reap all (or a greater share of) the added improved value from the illegitimate rose production, but it is not clear why the property owner where the illegitimate action took place is any more entitled to the improved value of the artifact than any other agent. The property owner is, after all, no more responsible for the production of the added improved value than anyone else. The only agent responsible for the production of the improved value did so in an illegitimate fashion and hence should not be able to benefit from the wrong act. If the agent who illegitimately produced the roses damaged or in any way harmed the property owner where the roses were produced then she should fully compensate the owner and rectify her wrong action, but this is a different matter than assessing the normative status of the improved value created by the wrong act

It is worth highlighting the significant practical implications that could result from the suggestion that the value added through illegitimate artifact production should belong to everyone absent the agent who did the wrong act. The added value brought about from illegitimate production given the mass amounts of illegitimate production that has occurred historically could amount to an immense amount of value in the world that belongs to everyone. Before any sweeping practical implications are drawn, there are complicated issues concerning history and moral culpability that confront the suggestion that the value added to artifacts through illegitimate production ought to belong to everyone. Many of these complicating factors were sidestepped by the rose example in which history played little role and culpability was clear. An artifact, for instance, might be constructed or altered over hundreds or even thousands of years and in the process change hands among many agents. The historical scars on an artifact from illegitimate production might be as obvious as a fresh gunshot wound or they might better resemble a slight blemish on an otherwise "morally clean" historical record.

A full treatment of issues surrounding concerns of history and moral culpability as they relate to illegitimate artifact production would demand a great deal more analysis that I will offer here, but a few cursory points are in order. The historical concern is much more onerous as a practical, rather than a moral, concern. It will often be very difficult to tell given the incomplete and disputed historical record just how much of an artifact's value is the result of illegitimate production. The straightforward moral rule ought to be that legitimately added value belongs to the producer while illegitimately added value belongs to everyone, but sorting out when value has been legitimately or illegitimately added can be a practical mess.

It is this practical mess brought about by determining the degree and scope of historical injustice that led Robert Nozick to conclude, "A *rough* rule of thumb for rectifying injustices might seem to be the following: organize society as to maximize the position of whatever group ends up least well-off in society."[7] Nozick, perhaps surprisingly, adopts the egalitarian sensitive difference principle developed by John Rawls in his *Theory of Justice* as a rough attempt to rectify past historical injustice.[8] The issue at hand is not exactly the same as rectifying past injustices generally; instead, our concern is with figuring out what ought to be done with the value that was added to artifacts via illegitimate production. As a rough rule, however, taking Nozick's lead and applying Rawls's difference principle could be the best practical solution to address what should be done with the vast amount of value that has been added via illegitimate production.

Issues of moral culpability also complicate what to do with value added by illegitimate production. In the original rose case, the running assumption was that the producer knew that her actions were wrong. What if, however, the agent who illegitimately produced roses on her neighbor's property did her due diligence and researched where her property line was but because of an error in legal paperwork mistakenly planted the roses in her neighbor's yard? In this revised case it seems clear that the rose producing agent acted in a morally non-culpable fashion.

There are a number of competing solutions that could be advanced with respect to what should be done with added value produced in an illegitimate but non-culpable fashion. These solutions could range anywhere between the producing agent reaping all of the improved value to the producing agent getting none of the improved value, as was proposed in the case of culpable illegitimate production. Both of these solutions veer too much in one extreme or the other. A plausible middle-ground position would maintain that the added value in the case of non-culpable illegitimate production belongs to *everyone*, including the agent who engaged in the non-culpable illegitimate production. An agent who engages in illegitimate production, even in a non-culpable fashion, should not have a full claim to the fruits of the wrong but blameless act, nor should she be denied an equal moral claim to the added value of the illegitimate production.

The examples of abandoned artifacts, universally gifted artifacts, public artifacts, and illegitimately produced artifacts demonstrate that an artifact can be, just as natural resources initially are, an object in which everyone has an equal moral claim. For clarity's sake, these types of artifacts can be referred to as *common artifacts*. Any conclusions that are drawn about the moral conditions governing the use of natural resources within the commons or appropriation of natural resources from the commons should generally be presumed to apply to common artifacts as well.

Now that the nature of and distinction between natural resources and artifacts has been considered, it is worth taking stock of the incredibly important role that natural resources and artifacts play in the lives of agents. It is difficult to overstate the importance of access to natural resources (or things derived from natural resources) in the lives of agents. (I assume here that being able to use or appropriate a natural resource exhausts the manner in which an agent can have access to a natural resource.) The importance can be seen by considering the ways in which access to natural resources contributes to the *survivability*, *well-being*, and *autonomy* of agents.

Agents need to be able to use natural resources in order to survive. An agent, for instance, might use a cave shelter to survive by protecting herself from the elements, or she might use the wood from a tree to construct a dwelling for the same purpose. In the most straightforward sense without the use of natural resources, breathable air and drinkable water for instance, agents would quickly perish. Here it is worth asking whether the consumption of a natural resource, for instance, eating an apple, constitutes a using or an appropriation or perhaps both. Does an agent appropriate a natural resource in virtue of her consumption of it? An agent who consumes an apple certainly does use the apple. But it is much less clear that merely consuming the apple constitutes an appropriation of the apple. Later I will make the case that consumption is neither necessary nor sufficient for an agent to appropriate, that is, acquire private property in, a natural resource.

We need not, however, go so far as the survivability of agents to see the importance and far-reaching implications surrounding access to natural resources. The use or appropriation of land, clean air, nutritious food, and so forth is undoubtedly an important element to the well-being of agents.[9] An agent's life goes well, or has a much better chance of going well, when she can use or appropriate the natural resources or things derivable from natural resources that she desires to use or privately own. If, for instance, Sarah enjoys sailing, then her life goes better when she has access to a sailboat and a nice spot for sailing.

In some cases the use of a natural resource or an artifact derived thereof is adequate for a significant increase in well-being, but in other cases the appropriation of these things might be needed for an agent to experience a significant increase in well-being. Using a trail at a public park, for example, might offer an agent a significant increase in well-being. An agent might not have any desire to privately own the trail; she might even desire not to privately own the trail. The private ownership of a toothbrush, however, would offer most agents a greater degree of well-being than having to share a communal toothbrush with others.

The ability to use or appropriate natural resources or artifacts derived thereof also allows an agent to better engage in autonomous or self-determining action. We saw an example of this in the last chapter involving Newcomer. An agent who lacks (or has very limited) access to natural resources will have a very restricted set of ways in which she can determine the course of her life. Millions of women in rural Africa, for example, spend long hours everyday gathering water so that they and their children may live.[10] These women have little choice but to carry heavy containers filled with many gallons of water many miles while often dodging the threat of sexual violence along the way just so they may access the water necessary for survival. The very limited access to water in many parts of rural Africa clearly plays a significant role in limiting the ability of millions of women to determine the course and direction of their lives. I do not mean to suggest that all the impediments confronting the self-determination of most women in rural Africa would suddenly evaporate if access to drinkable water was no longer very limited, but so long as women must spend the bulk of their day gathering water, their lives will be better described as water-determined, rather than self-determined.

Access to natural resources also has important implications concerning the exploitation of agents. An agent plausibly needs access to a certain minimal amount of natural resources as a form of protection against being exploited by others. This idea is humorously illustrated in episode 128 of *The Simpsons*. In that episode, Montgomery Burns, the rich and greedy owner of a nuclear power plant, devises a plan to construct a machine that will block out the sun and in doing so force the people of Springfield to purchase more electricity created from his nuclear plant. Burns's plan was to exploit others by intentionally restricting their ability to access the sun—a natural resource that belongs to everyone.[11]

Such examples are unfortunately not limited to cartoons. As chronicled in the documentary film *The Corporation*, the government of Bolivia, in an agreement to placate the demands of the World Bank, agreed in 1997 and 1999 to privatize the nation's water supply. This privatization of the water supply included *rainwater*. Bolivians, many already living in extreme poverty and earning roughly two dollars a day, found themselves paying up to one-quarter of their income for water after the privatization deal went into effect.[12] The privatization of all water in such a way that strips some of the world's poorest agents of one-quarter of their income was perhaps an idea too cruel and exploitative for even Mr. Burns. Given the initial equal moral claim that all agents have in respect to natural resources such as rainwater, an agent's basic access to these natural resources, particularly those that allow for subsistence, should not be bargained away *by others* striking political and economic deals. Such bargains are a clear and direct affront to the moral claim that all agents have in respect to natural resources.

Pollution and environmental degradation demonstrate in stark terms that the way an agent uses natural resources can also negatively impact the survivability, well-being, and autonomy of others. There is an expansive body of scientific literature that strongly indicates various polluting actions of agents have, and continue to, deteriorate the atmosphere in ways that are detrimental for health and ultimately survival. Climate change brought about by increased carbon pollution, for instance, poses substantial threats to agricultural production as well as existential threats, caused by the melting of Arctic ice, to agents and their homelands near sea level. There is wide agreement within the international scientific community that the earth is warming at an alarming rate and that this warming is due, in large part, to the actions of agents. This widespread international scientific agreement can be found by reviewing the *Climate Change 2007*, fourth assessment report of the United Nations International Panel on Climate Change (IPCC).[13] The IPCC report details the unequivocal evidence of global warming from over 6,000 peer reviewed scientific studies. The report concludes that it is very likely that most of the increased warming since the middle of the twentieth century is due to anthropogenic greenhouse gas concentrations.

The direct impact that agents can have toward global warming is old news to the scientific community. As early as the late nineteenth century, scientists were developing the view that increased carbon in the atmosphere would result in a "greenhouse effect" that could raise global temperatures. Svante Arrhenius, for instance, discussed in 1896 how carbon dioxide contributed to the "greenhouse effect" and how the greenhouse effect could impact the earth's climate.[14]

Climate change is, without any serious scientific doubt, a worry that deserves a great deal of attention and a clear instance in which agents pose harms and threats to the well-being of others via the use of natural resources. Worries about atmospheric pollution, however, are frequently limited to discussion of climate change, and this is a mistake that neglects other serious and immediate harms caused by atmospheric pollution. The RAND corporation, for example, estimates that between 2005-2007 roughly 30,000 people in California, of which a third were children suffering from asthma, were hospitalized or treated in an emergency room because of excessive levels (levels beyond what is legally allowed by state and federal regulation) of ozone and particulate pollution.[15] The case of an asthmatic child who must bear the cost of another's polluting action is a paradigmatic example of how the actions of some can create negative externalities for others. To add insult to injury the negative externality is being created by the degrading use of a thing—the atmosphere—that belongs as much to the asthmatic child as it does to the owners of the polluting power plant.

Growing concerns about poor air quality are an international problem. The notoriously bad air quality in large parts of China, for instance, hit a boiling point during January of 2013 when normally healthy residents in Beijing were advised to strictly limit their time outside, and sights of people wearing masks to filter out pollutants were the rule rather than the exception in the city. The level of air pollution became so pronounced in Beijing that poor visibility from heavy smog prompted airlines to cancel flights to the city. But flights are not the only fatality of heavy pollution in China. According to data from the "2010 Global Burden of Disease Study" published in *The Lancet* (a British medical journal) air pollution contributed to the premature death of more than 1.2 million Chinese people—and more than 3 million people around the world.[16]

The pollution of the oceans also yields serious threats to agents. Within the past hundred years, the oceans have been increasingly polluted, often from "run-off" pollution owed to polluted rivers and other ocean tributaries. Many inhabited coastal regions are now inundated with oceanic "dead zones" on which chemical pollutants have led to conditions in which marine life cannot survive. These dead zones, which now include over 400 designated areas, are particularly prevalent in the Baltic Sea, the Gulf of Mexico, the Black Sea, the East China Sea, and along the upper Atlantic coast of the United States.[17] This oceanic pollution is not only destructive to marine life, but also to agents who depend on the ocean to provide their subsistence. Ocean caught fish, for instance, are increasing contaminated with high levels of mercury and other heavy metals directly related with human illness, disease, and death.[18] Aside from the pollution of ocean waters and marine life, unsustainable overfishing of the oceans also poses substantial threats to agents. Industrial fishing methods as well as new technologies have greatly contributed to the unsustainable overfishing of the oceans.[19]

The World Wildlife Fund's 2012 Living Planet Report highlights the current dire state of the global environment. The report concludes that at *current* levels of consumption, people are using 50 percent more resources than the Earth can provide on a sustainable basis, and by 2030 even two planet Earths will not be enough to support the sustainable consumption of people.[20] The Earth is being exhausted of its resources in the same way that a desperate retiree dips into the principal of his retirement account until one day he discovers that he has bled his account dry.

Some agents suffer and die, and no doubt agents in the future will suffer and die, because of the ways that other agents use the atmosphere and the oceans (natural resources that belong to everyone). This state of affairs should strike anyone as fundamentally immoral and presses upon the need to establish the moral conditions that govern how agents may use natural resources within the commons or appropriate these resources from the commons. As briefly noted in the last chapter, the atmosphere and the oceans are not only natural resources but are natural resources that, for the most part, constitute a present-day commons. There are international agreements that generally govern some uses of the oceans such as the Law of the Sea Treaty, but these agreements do not serve to privately enclose the oceans or otherwise generally remove it from the commons. Further, nation-states frequently claim sovereignty over the air space (some part of the atmosphere) above their territorial lands, but such claims function to serve as a military warning and not normally to privately enclose the atmosphere.

It is incredibly difficult to predict how and in what ways the ever-diminishing quality and supply of natural resources will impact the ability of agents to live and live well as the future unfolds. But as the examples of atmospheric and oceanic pollution indicate, and so much more could have been said, we can look at the world in its present state and see the dramatically harmful impacts that pollution has already had and continues to have on the lives of agents. Non-renewable natural resources are being consumed, depleted, or degraded at a relatively high rate. At the same time, the demand to use and consume natural resources is exploding on a global scale with billions of agents in developing countries exceedingly anxious to consume resources at a rate comparable to their wealthier neighbors. The basic trend is fewer, or increasingly degraded, natural resources for more agents to use. Technological advancement, global development trends, global population, and conservation efforts will shape the urgency and severity of the impacts brought about from a degraded and diminishing stock of non-renewable natural resources. The basic picture, however, of "less and more degraded resources for more agents" should pique an interest toward the moral conditions surrounding the use and appropriation of natural resources, an interest that ultimately leads back to the commons.

To this point I have argued that the moral principle that ought to guide the evaluation of the moral conditions governing the use of natural resources within the commons and appropriation of these resources from the commons is that "natural resources initially belong to everyone." The next chapter builds upon this guiding moral principle by developing and defending a Lockean left-libertarian theory of justice. The Lockean left-libertarian theory of justice that I defend is built upon the pillars of the *equal* and *independent* moral status of agents. This equal and independent moral status, I will argue, affords all agents with rights that protect them against others from exercising dominion over their self (or will) as well as rights that properly recognize the equal claim that all agents initially have in respect to natural resources.

NOTES

1. There are non-physical things in the world that this trichotomy does not deal with. Abstract objects, for instance, such as ideas and propositions are not dealt with in this material analysis.

2. Vallentyne, "Left-Libertarianism —A Primer", 5.

3. Brian Kierland offers the following counterexample to the above definition of an artifact. Consider that an agent makes a statue in a way that devalues the clay (say it is very valuable clay before it has hardened). Is the statue an artifact or a natural resource? Admittedly, this is a good challenge to the above definition of an artifact. Intuitions probably differ here but

I am inclined to call the statue a natural resource. Aside from this clash of intuition concerning what counts as an artifact Kierland's example might suggest that we should have two categories of artifacts, (3a) value-added artifacts, and (3b) non-value added artifacts. I am inclined not to recognize the second set of physical objects as artifacts, but if one is compelled by Kierland's example the above typology is worth exploring.

4. George, *Progress and Poverty*, 328-338.

5. Ibid., 403-407.

6. Ibid., 406.

7. Robert Nozick, *Anarchy, State, and Utopia*, 231.

8. This is an odd admission by Nozick given that he strongly challenges Rawls's distribution theory of justice (*Anarchy, State, and Utopia*, 183-231) for roughly forty pages before he endorses the difference principle (the cornerstone of Rawls's distributive theory of justice) as a rough but promising way to rectify historical injustice.

9. There is a good deal of disagreement among philosophers about how to understand the concept of well-being. There are three major accounts of well-being: hedonistic, desire-based, and "objective list" accounts. Additionally, Gary Chartier has also recently proposed a plausible natural law understanding of well-being in his (2013) *Anarchy and Legal Order*, pp. 7-43. All three major accounts and Chartier's new natural law account are reasonable ways to understand well-being, and all four maintain that in just about all cases an agent's use or appropriation of natural resources is an important component of, or contributing factor to, her well-being. One of the only exceptions to this would be an agent who does not desire to use natural resources perhaps because she no longer desires to live.

10. See the United Nations 2006 Global Development Report, *Beyond Scarcity: Power, Poverty, and the Global Water Crisis.* The full report can be found at http://hdr.undp.org/en/reports/global/hdr2006/

11. "Who Shot Mr. Burns? (Part 1)," *The Simpsons*, first broadcast May 21, 1995 by FOX, Directed by Jeffrey Lynch and written by Bill Oakley and Josh Weinstein.

12. *The Corporation*, directed by Mark Achbar and Jennifer Abbott, (2003; New York: Zeitgeist Films, 2004), DVD.

13. The synthesis report of the *IPCC Fourth Assessment Report: Climate Change 2007* can be found at www.ipcc.ch/publications_and_data/publications_ipcc_fourth_assessment_report_synthesis_report.htm

14. Svante Arrhenius, "On the Influence of Carbonic Acid in the Air and upon the Temperature on the Ground," *Philosophical Magazine and Journal of Science* 41 (1896): 237-276.

15. John Romley, Andrew Hackbarth, Dana Goldman, *RAND Corporation. The Impact of Air Quality on Hospital Spending*, 2012. The full report can be found at www.rand.org/pubs/technical_reports/TR777.html

16. This data was published by *The Lancet* Dec. 13, 2012, and can be found at www.thelancet.com/themed/global-burden-of-disease

17. See Robert Diaz and Rutger Rosenberg, "Spreading Dead Zones and Consequences for Marine Ecology," *Science* 321 (2008): 926-929.

18. See Carl Sindermann, *Ocean Pollution: Effects on Living Resources and Humans* (Boca Raton, FL: CRC Press, 1996).

19. See Callum Roberts, *The Unnatural History of the Sea* (Washington D.C.: Shearwater Books, 2007); Callum Roberts, *The Oceans of Life*, (New York: Penguin, 2012).

20. The World Wildlife Fund's 2012 *Living Planet Report* can be found at http://wwf.panda.org/about_our_earth/all_publications/living_planet_report/2012_lpr/.

Chapter Three

Lockean Left-Libertarianism

There are many theoretical frameworks that could be used to evaluate the moral conditions that govern the use of natural resources within the commons or the appropriation of natural resources from the commons. These moral conditions could be approached from communitarian, utilitarian, liberal, Marxist, Aristotelian, conservative, libertarian, or other theoretical frameworks. Each of these frameworks can be further demarcated into many variants of each general theory. The theoretical framework that I will employ to examine the moral conditions governing the use of natural resources within the commons and the appropriation of these resources from the commons will be that of *Lockean left-libertarianism*. The primary goals of this chapter are (1) to outline a version of Lockean left-libertarianism that is primarily focused on the *equal* and *independent* moral status of agents and (2) offer compelling reasons why the endorsed version of Lockean left-libertarianism is a plausible and promising theory of justice.

Two preliminary points are in order. First, Lockean left-libertarianism is not the only plausible theory of justice. There are at least half a dozen theories of justice and an even greater number of variations to these theories that have been given plausible interpretations. I am drawn to the belief that Lockean left-libertarianism is a plausible and promising theory of justice and I hope to offer some compelling reasons in this chapter to bolster that claim, but I do not attempt a full comparative defense of the view here. A full and robust comparative defense, of any theory of justice, would take (at least) a much longer book and goes well beyond the scope of my aims here.

Second, given that there are a number of plausible theories of justice other than the Lockean left-libertarianism that I defend, any of these plausible theories could be called upon to evaluate the moral conditions governing the use of natural resources within the commons and appropriation of natural resources from the commons. *Offering thorough and meaningful attention to the concerns that drive this project does not require adherence to the version of Lockean left-libertarianism that I defend in this chapter.* It should be treated as a welcome advancement whenever someone addresses the use of natural resources within the commons or the appropriation of natural resources from the commons with *any* plausible theory of justice. It would be much better if the marketplace of ideas determined that these issues ought to be addressed with a theoretical framework other than the proposed Lockean left-libertarian approach rather than the issues wither away from neglect.

Not only are there many theoretical approaches that can be used to examine justice but the concept of justice itself is open to a number of different meanings. Vallentyne, for instance, cites five ways in which political philosophers understand justice. These include moral permissibility of legal structures, legitimacy (in the sense of the impermissibility of forcible interference by others), fairness, comparative fairness, and the duties that we owe to each other.[1] This list of various ways in which political philosophers understand the concept of justice (which is not meant to be exhaustive) makes clear that there is no universal consensus or anything approaching a universal consensus about how to best understand the concept of justice.

Just as there are a number of plausible theoretical approaches to justice, the above five ways to understand the concept of justice are all plausible ways to understand what justice amounts to. Taking the lead from my approach concerning various theoretical approaches to justice, I will not seek to argue that one concept of justice is more plausible than another. It might turn out that there are multiple concepts of justice. There might, for instance, be legitimacy-justice, fairness-justice, duty-justice, and so forth. I have no strong views about whether justice should be treated as one (highly contentious) concept or whether the label of justice is a description that embodies multiple concepts.

In what follows I will understand justice to mean *the duties that agents owe to each other*. It is plausible to think that justice is highly connected with the duties that agents owe one another. It is not uncommon, for instance, to speak about (or simply associate) an injustice occurring when an agent disregards the duties that she owes to others, e.g. breaks a promise to another or assaults another. By understanding justice as the duties that agents owe to each other, an emphasis is placed on a respect for the individual and, in particular, the legitimate grievances that she can lodge against the actions of others. Further, I will understand the duties that agents owe to each other to be a matter of respecting the rights of others. An agent, therefore, acts justly when she respects the rights of others and unjustly when she violates the rights of others.

Rights, then, will play a central role in the proposed duty-focused notion of justice, but what are rights? A right, in its most identifiable sense, is a *constraint* on the actions of others that protects the holder of the right. Robert Nozick helpfully suggests that when a person is protected by a right, "a line or (hyper-plane) circumscribes an area in moral space around an individual."[2] Rights are *protections* that specify the *constraints* upon the ways we may treat others and the ways others may treat us.

Taking a lead from Wesley Newcomb Hohfeld's influential discussion of rights, however, a detailed analysis of rights goes beyond the idea that a right serves as a constraint (or claim) against other(s).[3] Hohfeld demarcates his analysis of rights into four categories: *claims*, *liberties*, *powers*, and *immunities*. What Hohfeld describes as a *claim* is usually associated with having a right or what is frequently labeled as a *claim right*. If Tim has a *claim right* that others not deprive him of a "fair share" of natural resources, then others have a *duty* not to deprive Tim of a "fair share" of natural resources. Duty, as such, can be taken to mean *limitation*. (Going forward, unless specified otherwise the mention of a right should be taken to mean a claim right.)

If others lack a claim against an agent in respect to some action, then the agent has a *liberty* in respect to that action. Often this is labeled as a *liberty right*. If others, for instance, have no claim against Tim's use of a subsistence share of natural resources within the commons, then Tim is at liberty to use a subsistence share of natural resources within the commons. Tim, in this case, would not have a duty to refrain from using a subsistence share of natural resources within the commons and, as such, has a liberty to do so. Agents possess a liberty right to do whatever actions are not excluded by the claims of others. Put another way, agents possess liberties to do whatever actions are not barred by duties that they have to others.

A power is the ability to *alter* an existing normative situation.[4] Sally can exercise a moral power by promising Bill that she will no longer use a car that they both previously shared together. This promise could, plausibly, alter the existing normative situation that Sally and Bill previously had with respect to property rights over the car. Consent represents another common way in which an agent can exercise a moral power. Grant, for the sake of argument, that Sally has a claim right in respect to her body that prevents others from using her body without her permission. Sally can alter this initial normative situation by giving her permission (consent) to Bill that he may kiss her. The act of consent in this case alters the duty that Bill normally has to not kiss Sally without her permission. Bill, given Sally's exercise of a power, is at liberty to kiss her, whereas before Sally' exercise of a power—in the form of her granting consent—he had a duty not to kiss her.

It is important to point out that *the appropriation of natural resources from the commons is the exercise of a moral power as opposed to a claim right or liberty*. This is because the appropriation of natural resources from the commons marks an alteration to a previously existing normative situation. Natural resources do not initially exist as anyone's private property;

instead, they initially exist within some shared common fashion. Only through appropriation (an alteration to this normative situation) do agents come to privately own natural resources. This point is not overly controversial as virtually anyone who has written about appropriation takes it to be an action that alters some previous normative situation. The only clear way around the view that appropriation involves the exercise of a moral power would be to maintain that *no* normative conditions concerning natural resources exist within the commons and, as such, appropriation is not the exercise of a power because it does not alter an existing *normative* situation. This way around the suggestion that appropriation involves the exercise of power is, however, a dead end. Examples presented in the first chapter concerning the destructive use and overuse of natural resources within the commons offer very strong reason for the rejection of the claim that no normative conditions exist in the commons prior to appropriation from the commons.

An *immunity* protects an agent against the exercise of a power by other(s). Bob, for instance, has an immunity against Sally exercising a moral power and simply expropriating as her own private property a car that they jointly privately own. The car belongs to both Sally and Bill, and as such, Bill has an immunity that protects him against Sally exercising a power to alter this existing normative situation and simply taking the car as her own.

It is plausible that agents have certain immunities from others appropriating natural resources, in at least certain ways, from the commons. If Jill and Marcy share the commons together, then each of them plausibly has an immunity against the other exercising a moral power and taking parts of the commons as her own private property without leaving some "fair share" for the other. It would be unjust for Jill to simply take the best parts of the world all for herself and leave Marcy only the scraps of what is left. Given the initial equal moral stake that both Jill and Marcy have in respect to natural resources, such a taking by Jill violates a duty that she owes to Marcy. Marcy plausibly has an immunity that prevents Jill from taking natural resources from the commons as her own in the fashion that she has.

One of the virtues of Hohfeld's analysis aside from needed clarity that it adds to talk of rights is that it lends itself well to various normative considerations. A Hohfeldian treatment of rights can be applied to either legal or moral rights, as well as other types of rights that could exist such as social, cultural, or religious rights. Unless otherwise specified, my usage of rights should be understood as "moral rights." Thus, when the ideas of claims, liberties, power, and immunities are invoked, they can be read as moral claims, moral liberties, moral powers, and moral immunities. This focus on moral rights is driven by the overarching concern of examining the *moral* conditions that govern the use of natural resources within the commons and the appropriation of these resources from the commons. If, however, the task at hand was altered to examine the legal conditions, cultural conditions, or religious conditions that govern the use of natural resources within the commons and appropriation of these resources from the commons, then a Hohfeldian framework could still be employed to specify a duty-based approach to justice. This approach to justice, however, would presumably employ different normative considerations than the moral approach offered here.

A Hohfeldian analysis suggests that a claim right held by an agent against others is correlated with a duty owed by others. This tight connection between claim rights and duties is plausible because it is difficult to see what a claim against others could mean if it did not imply a duty (limitation) on the part of others. The extent to which duties and rights are correlated with one another is, however, controversial among political philosophers. [5] As Hillel Steiner points out some, though not all, of the controversy involving the correlativity of rights and duties is caused by a misunderstanding of rights or, perhaps better put, a misapplication of Hohfeld's analysis.[6] A claim against another agent always (or nearly always) entails a duty by that other. The moral authority, however, to exercise a power entails no duty by others. There is no need to encroach too far into the philosophical controversy surrounding the correlativity of rights and duties and stake any firm commitment. What is important for present purposes is that claim rights are very plausibly highly correlated with the duties of others. As such, the duties that agents owe to one another as a matter of justice involve respecting the moral claims (rights) of others.

Moral duties are *inter-personal* in nature and, as such, track with the moral claims of other agents. They are actions owed to other agents in virtue of the rights held by other agents and hence not actions owed to either ourselves or to no one at all in some impersonal fashion. In a world with only one person, no just or unjust action can occur because justice is owed *to other* rights-holders. When an agent is charged with acting unjustly this is a charge that ought to include a "list" of other agent(s) who suffered a violation of right(s). If such a "list" cannot be given or a rights violating action cannot be specified, then the charge of acting unjustly should be seen with deep skeptical ire.

At least two important questions crop up here about rights. First, what is it that rights protect? And, second, how stringent are the moral protections offered by rights?

There are a number of plausible answers that have been offered to the question of what it is that rights protect. For instance, rights could protect choices, interests, desires, some combination of these possibilities, or perhaps nothing at all. The concept of a right is open to any of the above suggestions, and any answer to the question of "what is it that rights protect" must be argued for and not merely settled by examining the concept of a right. The concept of a right does not tell us what it is that rights protect. For simplicity, when discussing rights I will typically speak of rights in a permission-giving or permission-receiving fashion which will normally imply that rights are choice-protecting (or will-preserving) as giving or receiving permission is often associated with one's will or choices.[7] When an agent—in a free, informed, and voluntary fashion—tells her doctor hands off, the doctor is no longer at liberty to treat the agent, even if it is in the interest of the agent to be treated because treating the agent against her will fails to respect the agent's ability to direct the course of her life. In this case, the agent has exercised a power (by way of her dissent) to alter the terms of the doctor-patient relationship that she earlier entered into.

Noting that rights serve as constraints on the actions of others tells us nothing regarding the *stringency* of these constraints. For instance, rights could serve as merely *weak pro-tanto* constraints that are easily, perhaps very easily, morally outweighed by other considerations or, alternatively, rights could serve as *absolute* constraints that can never be overridden by other considerations. Or still yet, rights may be subject to thresholds so that they have *no* moral force when the benefits to others of transgressing a right are sufficiently great. Still further, it could be that rights can be outweighed by competing moral considerations but still carry *some* moral force. It is just that this moral force is outweighed or trumped by other moral considerations. The concept of a right does not inform us as to the proper answer regarding how the stringency of a right ought to be viewed. A constraint on the actions of others, after all, can be extremely weak or absolutely unbendable.

There is a moral tightrope to walk when considering how stringent rights ought to be. If a right is absolute, then others have an absolute duty to adhere to the right. This absolute treatment of rights seems too stringent because it *never* allows for a slight infraction of another's rights even when such an infraction might yield tremendous benefit to another. But at the same time, if rights are to offer agents significant moral protection against others then they must have force even when their neglect would yield great gains to others.

Property rights provide a good illustration of this point. If the property owner of the only food source in town has an absolute right that others not use his property (food) without his permission, then others have a duty never to use his food without his permission when they are starving to death, even when they have offered to buy the food at a price that gives a hefty profit to the owner of the food. This example suggests that property rights ought not to be viewed as absolutely unbendable constraints. The agents who are starving to death plausibly have a liberty to take the food that they need to subsist, at least under certain conditions. This is a view shared by Grotius, who argued that "extreme necessity seems to form an exception" to the property rights of those who have appropriated from the commons.[8] Grotius defended this view on the grounds that any moral reasons that justify appropriating natural resources from the commons could not trump or supersede the claim that agents have to the use of natural resources to provide for their basic necessity.

Yet at the same time, if property rights (or other types of rights) are to offer significant moral protections to agents, they must serve as very strong constraints. The owner of the food does have rights that protect him against others taking his property without his permission in almost all cases but plausibly not every case. This treatment of rights serving as very strong, as opposed to absolute, constraints is prevalent among libertarian thought. Robert Nozick, for instance, addresses the stringency of rights by suggesting that (maybe) a person's rights should be overridden to avoid "catastrophic moral horror," where catastrophe moral horror is left vague.[9]

The proliferation of rights, like the stringency of rights, is also inevitably linked with the duties or limitations of others. Rights are good things to have so the uncritical thought goes, and the stronger the rights the better. But rights are much more of a double-edged sword than is often acknowledged in ordinary discourse. This is because a duty or limitation always, or nearly always, accompanies a right. Rights are desirable to an agent because they establish the constraints on the actions of *others*, but rights are undesirable in that they set constraints or limitations on *her*. The more rights that agents possess, the more corresponding duties (limitations) that agents must observe. The "best" pragmatic position, though it is not a moral position given that agents possess equal moral rights, is that of a king who has all sorts of rights but owes no duties to anyone. It is the pull of this pragmatic desire to be a moral king that makes the Ring of Gyges presented by Glaucon in the second book of Plato's *Republic* such a tempting option to most readers. Appreciating the duties that accompany rights suggests that merely proliferating rights for the sake of *freedom* is a self-defeating proposition. One promising strategy to avoid the proliferation of rights that also inevitably leads to the proliferation of duties is to limit rights to a small core set that afford agents highly stringent constraints against others.

To this point in the chapter the discussion of rights has been, for the most part, limited to examining the concept of rights, offering the basic components of a Hohfeldian analysis of rights, and considering issues related to what it is that rights generally protect, as well as the stringency of rights. I now turn toward a Lockean approach to offer content to the moral protections that rights afford agents. In particular, I shall expand upon the cursory treatment, offered in the introduction and first chapter, of Locke's natural rights approach by impressing and building upon the *equal and independent* status that Locke ascribes to agents. It is the equal and independent moral status of agents that serve as the cornerstones of a compelling left-libertarian theory of justice.

Locke makes clear that the natural rights that he ascribes to all agents is due to the moral status of agents as being equal and independent. Locke writes:

> The state of nature has a law of nature to govern it, which obligated everyone; and reason which is that law, teaches all mankind who will but consult it that, being equal and independent, no one ought to harm another in his life, health, liberty, or possessions.[10]

The equal moral status of agents demands the presumption that agents initially enjoy the same set of rights (claims against others).[11] The moral rights of all agents are the same whether they are a pauper or a prince. All agents, this is to say, ought to be afforded the same moral protections against others. (There might be exceptions to this thesis of moral equality, although I have no exceptions in mind. Even if exceptions exist, they would have to be rigorously defended against the presumption that all agents are moral equals and entitled to the same moral protections against others.) One important implication that follows from the view that agents all possess the same moral rights is that all agents correspondingly possess the same moral duties, at least where these duties are correlated with a claim right held by another.

In addition to being moral equals (possessing the same set of moral rights), agents are also *independent*. An agent is independent in the sense that, once she reaches the age of reason, she enjoys a sovereignty or dominion over herself, which entails that no one and no state has moral authority or power over her absent her consent to the contrary. Locke makes this clear when he writes:

> The natural liberty of man is to be free from any superior power on earth, and not to be under the will or legislative authority of man, but to have only the law of nature as his rule. The liberty of man in society is to be under no other legislative power but that established by consent in the commonwealth, nor under the dominion of any will or restraint of any law but what that legislative shall enact according to the trust put in it.[12]

Locke bolsters the same point later in the *Second Treatise* when he argues, "Men being, as has been said, by nature all free, equal, and independent, no one can be put out of this estate and subjected to the political power of another absent his own consent."[13]

The independent status of agents should not be viewed as disconnected from the moral equality of agents. The independent status of agents, instead, follows directly from the equal moral status of agents. This is because if we grant that all agents are moral equals—that is to say, possess the same moral rights—then no agent can be presumed to have moral authority or dominion over any other agent. If all agents possess the same moral claims against each other, then any claim that an agent makes against another can likewise by made against her by the other. *From equality rises the independent status of all agents*. Far from being in opposition with one another, equality and freedom from the subjugation of others are natural compliments to one another.

Since Isaiah Berlin's 1958 lecture, "Two Concepts of Liberty," there has been a good deal of philosophical interest in the distinction between "freedom to" (positive liberty) and "freedom from" (negative liberty), much of the discussion too nuanced to afford due consideration here. The moral status of agents as independent was couched above as a type of *freedom from* the subjugation of others. The reason for the focus on freedom from or negative liberty as the best way to describe an agent's independent moral status is twofold. First, the account of justice offered takes rights to be, primarily, claims against others and, as such, is more amenable to freedom from rather than freedom to. On a more substantive note, a good case can be made for the claim that freedom to engage in an activity such as self-mastery or engage in a democratic process is predicated upon freedom from certain types of interference or subjugation from others. In this way, freedom from the subjugation of others marks a more foundational concern than freedom to. The issues are complicated here, but as a general rule freedom to is generally an outgrowth (often a valuable outgrowth) of freedom from.

Two questions arise here. The first: what does it mean to be subjugated, in non-consensual fashion, to the will or dominion of other(s)? The second: what rights are necessary to protect an agent from being subjugated, in non-consensual fashion, to the will or dominion of other(s)? Addressing these questions in turn will clarify what it is that serves to undermine the moral status of an agent as independent and what moral protections are needed to guard against such threats.

There are clear cases when an agent is subject, in non-consensual fashion, to the domination of another agent. In Stephen King's novel *Misery*, for instance, an obsessed fan of a writer serendipitously finds her object of obsession in a snowy mountain crash.[14] She nurses her object of obsession back to health only to then keep him against his will and torture him by (among other brutal acts) cutting off his foot and cauterizing the wounded leg with a blowtorch. A physical assault against or kidnapping (imprisonment) of another represents paradigmatic cases in which an agent is subjugated to the will of another.

Some forms of dominion, however, over another are less obvious than the methods depicted in *Misery*. An agent, for instance, can be subject to the will or dominion of another without any direct bodily interference. An agent could be subjected to powerful cult-like psychological persuasion or brainwashing that places her will under the control of another, or she could be hypnotized and persuaded to act in ways that she would not normally act.[15]

In such cases an agent, through psychological manipulation, is subjugated to the will of another.

In less bizarre cases a fraud, deception, or invasion of privacy could also serve to subjugate the will of another. Eric Mack offers the following example to illustrate how deception can serve to place an agent under the dominion of another:

> Suppose that Josh is on the beach that is about to be submerged by a rising and dangerous tide. He is thinking of escaping by running down the beach—across a point that will very soon be flooded—to the only staircase leading up the surrounding cliffs. Before he sets out, however, he sees Bekah gesturing to him and lowering a rope ladder to him from a neat point on the cliffs. Relying upon the ladder still being there when he arrives at it, Josh heads toward it and forgoes the chance of crossing over to the foot of the staircase. As he approaches the rope ladder, Bekah pulls it up and waves.[16]

Bekah's deception of Josh, by her act of manipulation, places him under her control and in so doing threatens his moral status as independent.

In a less drastic case, imagine that Bekah promises Josh that if he fixes her car, she will pay him two hundred dollars. Josh fixes the car and Bekah gives him counterfeit money before leaving the country never to be seen by Josh again. Josh would have never wasted his time and labor fixing the car if he knew he was going to be paid with counterfeit money. Bekah's deception manipulated Josh into being an object of her will. We can ask: is Bekah's paying Josh with counterfeit money any worse than if she had made him fix the car at gunpoint? Josh would have probably been more frightened if Bekah had drawn a gun and demanded his labor, but in an important sense both actions share the moral similarity that they manipulate an agent into serving the will of another. In both cases, Bekah subjugates Josh's will and in so doing seriously undermines his independent moral status.

Aside from cases involving physical force and psychological manipulation, an agent can be subjugated to the will of another though the deprivation of resources. Imagine that Bekah hoards all the natural resources required to manufacture a cancer drug for an excruciatingly painful and terminal form of cancer that Josh suffers from. It is impossible for more of the drug to be manufactured absent the natural resources that Bekah has secured, and there is no other effective treatment for Josh's cancer. Bekah has taken an action or series of actions that serves to place Josh under her absolute dominion. If Josh wants to live and avoid an excruciatingly painful death, then he is subject to Bekah's will. Bekah determines the course of Josh's life no less than if she had strapped a bomb to his chest and commanded that she will not detonate the bomb so long as he dances or do whatever action she decides.

Henry George offers a poignant example to illustrate that a lack of access to natural resources can serve to subjugate an agent to the will or dominion of another in a way similar (if not identical) to the conditions of chattel slavery. He writes:

> Place one hundred men on an island from which there is no escape, and whether you make one of these men the absolute owner of the other ninety-nine or the absolute owner of the soil of the island, will make no difference either to him or to them. In the one case, as the other, the one will be the absolute master of the ninety-nine—his power extending even to life and death, for simply to refuse the permission to live on the island would be to force them into the sea.[17]

An agent directs her life in the world with some set of natural resources and artifacts derived thereof, not apart from it. The ninety-nine agents trapped on the island in which they have no moral claim are no less subjugated to the will of another than is the writer in *Misery*, the members of a cult, the unwitting victim of hypnotism, the deceived mechanic, and the cancer victim.

The common kernel running through the preceding examples is that an agent is subjugated to the will of another when her life is *other-determined* as opposed to *self-determined.* In order to avoid being subjugated to the will of another, an agent needs to be able to direct, in a non-trivial fashion, her life free from the interference or manipulation of others. No doubt there are borderline cases in which it is not clear if an agent is self-determining or other-determined. Additionally, there will be unclear cases in which it is difficult to determine if an agent is other-determined because she offered her valid consent to a particular state of affairs or whether she was forced or manipulated into a particular state of affairs. These legitimate complications aside, it is helpful to think of an independent agent as self-determining and an agent subjugated to the will of another as other-determined.

With a cursory sense in hand of what it means for an agent to be subject, in non-consensual fashion, to the will or dominion of another, the foundation is in place to ask: what rights are necessary to protect an agent from being subject, in non-consensual fashion, to the will or dominion of others?

Two broad categories of rights stand out as necessary (perhaps also sufficient, although that is less clear) in order to adequately protect an agent's moral status as independent. These are, rights that (1) protect an agent's *control of her self (body, mind, and labor)* and (2) rights that protect an agent's *access to, or benefit from, natural resources*. An agent cannot be independent, in any substantial sense, if others are at liberty to interfere or manipulate, at least in non-trivial ways, against her body, mind, or labor or if others are at liberty to prevent her from accessing, or benefiting from, a share of natural resources that allows her to determine the course of her life.

The categories of rights described above are broad in scope and the specific content of rights that could fill each category that allow for the moral status of agents as independent can vary widely. There is, for instance, stark disagreement among political philosophers as to whether the rights that an agent has with respect to her body, mind, and labor imply that she is at moral liberty to agree to terms of voluntary slavery or commit suicide. Similar disagreement surrounds whether an agent who has rights over her body, mind, and labor can nonetheless have a Samaritan duty to aid those in need of rescue.[18]

Note that the proposed broad categories of rights are not intrinsically morally valuable. They are, instead, instrumentally valuable in that they protect against threats to an agent's moral status as independent. If the rights described above fail to protect an agent from threats to her moral status as independent, then they would not have an important role in the proposed Lockean-minded theory of justice and should be questioned. Furthermore, if additional rights are needed to protect an agent's moral status as independent, then such rights should be incorporated into the proposed theory of justice. Rights are morally valuable because (and only because) they protect something of moral worth—an agent's equal and independent moral status. I shall now turn toward examining how a left-libertarian theory of justice is well suited to address both categories of rights that are needed to adequately protect an agent's equal and independent moral status.

The best way to approach left-libertarianism is by first considering libertarianism generally. This is because left-libertarianism is a variant of, and not a divergence from, traditional accounts of libertarianism. The substantive difference between right- and left-libertarianism, which will be considered at greater length toward the end of the chapter, is *limited* to how each view addresses the moral conditions governing the appropriation of natural resources from the commons. (This difference would in all likelihood expand to the moral conditions governing the use of natural resources in the commons but at present has not done so due to lack of attention to this issue from libertarians and other political philosophers.) Aside from this one, albeit important, difference, no substantive disagreement generally separates right- and left-libertarianism.

Although the substantive difference between right- and left-libertarianism can be put rather simply, there are often non-trivial differences with the way that libertarians of any stripe approach the rights (moral protections) of agents. Often these disagreements foreshadow more fundamental differences among libertarians concerning topics as broad as liberty and equality. Given the vast diversity of thought among libertarian thinkers, it is difficult to find a common kernel of thought that binds libertarians together in the same unique intellectual tradition. It is not enough, for instance, to simply conclude that what binds libertarians in the same intellectual tradition is that libertarian thought is deeply concerned with the liberty of agents. While it is true that libertarian thought is deeply concerned with the liberty of agents, this thought will not serve to distinguish libertarianism from classical liberalism, a view that is also deeply concerned with the liberty of agents. Despite the diversity of thought among libertarians, one promising way to approach libertarianism that renders the view interestingly unique from alternative accounts of justice is that libertarianism maintains that agents possess, at least very stringent, rights of *full self-ownership*.

This is different than saying that libertarianism is grounded in or based on self-ownership. Self-ownership demarcates a set of moral protections afforded agents; it does not in itself provide a grounding or basis for libertarian thought. The libertarian approach to justice endorsed here, for instance, is based upon an agent's moral status as equal and independent. Jan Narveson, alternatively, develops a libertarian theory based upon an account of contractarianism.[19] There is considerable disagreement among libertarians about what libertarianism is based upon or grounded in, but despite this disagreement all (or virtually all, as I am not aware of any exceptions) libertarians endorse the self-ownership of agents, in one form or another.

Two cautions are in order before delving into a discussion of self-ownership. First, the intellectual development of the *idea* of self-ownership can be traced back at least to Locke, but the *language* of self-ownership central to many contemporary discussions of libertarianism is only a few decades old. We will not nor should expect, for instance, to find Herbert Spencer, Henry George, or Max Stirner using the phrase self-ownership, although these thinkers clearly had the idea of self-ownership or something very close to it in mind when they wrote about the liberty and moral sovereignty of agents.[20]

Further, the degree to which contemporary thinkers writing about libertarian approaches to justice invoke the language of self-ownership varies widely. Some thinkers invoke the language of self-ownership frequently in their writings about libertarianism, while other libertarians and their critics write about ideas associated with self-ownership without much, or any, reference to the phrase at all.[21] Robert Nozick, for instance, only mentions self-ownership by name once in his groundbreaking libertarian treatise, *Anarchy, State, and Utopia*.[22] The use of the phrase "self-ownership" should not be of much concern to the arguments here; instead the proper focus should be geared toward the *idea* of self-ownership.

Henry George put the idea of self-ownership succinctly in the late nineteenth century when he wrote, "As a man belongs to himself, so his labor when put in concrete form belongs to him."[23] George's thoughts build on the Lockean tradition that holds that the moral entitlement to the product of one's labor follows from the notion that a person belongs to himself. Locke makes this position clear when he suggests that, "... every man has a property in his own person: this nobody has a right to but himself. The labour of his body and the work of his hands, we may properly say, are his."[24]

G. A. Cohen, with a more recent and rigorous treatment, describes self-ownership as the idea that:

> Each person is the morally rightful owner of himself. He possesses over himself, as a matter of moral right, all of those rights that a slaveholder has over a complete chattel slave as a matter of legal right, and he is entitled, morally speaking, to dispose over himself in the way such a slaveholder is entitled, morally speaking, to dispose over his slave.[25]

No agent, initially at least, has any moral claim to the self (typically understood as the body, mind, and labor) of another agent. An agent, and no one else, owns her self. Peter Vallentyne, taking a lead from Cohen, links libertarianism and self-ownership in the following way:

> Libertarianism (both right and left) holds that agents are, initially at least (e.g. prior to engaging in any commitment or unjust actions), full self-owners, and that any violation of full self-ownership is unjust. The core idea of full self-ownership is that agents own themselves in just the same way that they can fully own inanimate objects.[26]

The idea that an agent owns her *self* will sound odd or misplaced to many. Ownership applies to a car, house, or stock certificate and not, so the thought might go, to an agent's self. There are many reasons that could explain this reaction. One likely reason for this apprehension is that the notion of ownership is often understood in some sort of economic fashion frequently associated with a commodity, and many are uneasy with thinking about the self in this way. This is understandable. The self, after all, is not morally like a pound of coffee or a barrel of oil. Ownership, however, can be understood and demystified, in simple terms, as meaning merely a "bundle of rights."[27]

When an agent has ownership of some thing, whether it is a grove of pristine redwoods trees, a car, or her right index finger, this simply means that she has *some set of claims*, or in the very least liberties, in respect to the thing. This set of rights can vary greatly ranging from being very minimal up to and including a full set of rights in respect to a thing in question. A self-owner, then, has a bundle of rights (moral protections that take the form of claims against others) in respect to her self, where the self is understood as an agent's body, mind, and labor. When self-ownership is understood in this broad fashion, just about anyone who endorses the idea that agents have rights of any sort is also willing to endorse the view that agents have *some* bundle of rights with respect to their selves.

Vallentyne maintains above that the endorsement of *full* self-ownership is a necessary and sufficient condition of a libertarian view. Full self-ownership holds that an agent initially has a full set of rights (maximally consistent set of claims against others and liberties) in respect to her self. But what would possessing full ownership over some object of property (in this case the self) amount to? Rights of full ownership would encompass the broad categories of the right to possess, the right to use, the right to the capital, the right to manage, and the right to the income of the object of property.[28] An agent who possesses full self-ownership has *all* of the rights referenced above in respect to her self. In what follows, I grant that libertarianism entails that agents are full self-owners—that is to say, have full ownership rights in respect to their selves. An important caveat, however, to this endorsement of full self-ownership that often goes overlooked or underappreciated is that the endorsement of full self-ownership is a separate matter from questions concerning the stringency of rights. Thus, while full self-ownership is endorsed here, these rights, consistent with the earlier discussion of the stringency of rights, will be treated as very stringent constraints against others as opposed to absolute constraints.

Michael Otsuka, in his libertarian effort to reconcile self-ownership and equality, endorses a conception of self-ownership that according to him, "stops short of full self-ownership."[29] Otsuka defines the libertarian right(s) of self-ownership as the following two rights:

1. A very stringent right of control over and use of one's mind and body that bars others from intentionally using one as a means by forcing one to sacrifice life, limb, or labour, where such force operates by means of incursions or threats of incursions upon one's mind and body (including assault and battery and forcible arrest, detention, and imprisonment).
2. A very stringent right to all of the income that one can gain from one's mind and body (including one's labour) either or one' s own or through unregulated and untaxed voluntary exchanges with other individuals.[30]

Otsuka's definition of self-ownership is a promising way to describe the rights that an agent has in respect to her self that protects her against threats by others to her equal and independent moral status.

Additionally, Otsuka's definition of self-ownership nicely captures the Kantian prohibition of using another merely as a means. Eric Mack also stresses this Kantian idea when he describes, taking a lead from Berlin's "Two Conception of Liberty," that one implication of self-ownership is that, "No man is a means to any other man's ends—although each is a means (is morally available to himself as a means) to his own ends."[31] Agents, Kant famously argued, are ends in themselves and should not be treated merely as a means. I take it that this prohibition on treating agents merely as a means would generally apply to "benevolently" inspired means such as maximizing social utility or thwarting the will of another so that a paternalistic end may be sought. Given that I do not see any important area in which Otsuka's definition of self-ownership can be improved, I will adopt his definition, with one important addendum discussed in the next chapter, going forward.

Otsuka suggests that his definition of self-ownership "falls short of full self-ownership." But is he right? The two self-ownership rights that Otsuka explicitly embraces are not clearly missing any elements from the notion of full ownership. At the very least, the content that Otsuka assigns to the rights of self-ownership is not inconsistent with full self-ownership. Further, Otsuka never points out any specific ownership right that his account of self-ownership omits. What seems instead to prompt Otsuka to suggest that his account of self-ownership is "less than full" is the caveat that the endorsed rights are *very stringent*, presumably as opposed to being absolute.

The stringency of a right, however, is distinct from the content of the right, where content is understood as the specific moral claims or liberties that are protected by the right. An agent could possess both full ownership over her self and have some, part, or all, of the rights associated with her full self-ownership afford her less than absolute moral protection. She could even have one of her self-ownership rights protect her in an absolute sense and other self-ownership rights protect her in a lesser fashion. Often times the endorsement, usually advanced by a libertarian, of full self-ownership is trivialized by critics because such a right or bundle of rights is said to be "too strong." But such a critique fails to capture the distinction between the content of self-ownership rights and the stringency of these rights. It is simply misguided to reject full self-ownership on the grounds that it offers agents absolute or otherwise too much moral protection—full self-ownership in itself has no such implication.

Despite Otsuka's suggestion to the contrary, his definition of self-ownership could very well describe full self-ownership but with a set of rights that afford very stringent as opposed to absolute moral protections. It is possible that Otsuka's definition of self-ownership might not describe full self-ownership, although I suspect it does with one addendum to be discussed in the next chapter. If this is the case, it will not be because the rights he offers are very stringent as opposed to absolute; instead, it will be because there is an ownership right completely absent from the bundle of rights that constitute his conception of self-ownership.

Self-ownership is a morally compelling idea because it offers a set of rights that protect the moral status of agents as equal and independent.[32] *All* agents, in equal fashion, possess equal ownership rights (moral protections) over their selves. All agents, as such, are equally morally barred from taking as their own, without permission, the arms, kidneys, labor, or any other aspect of another agent's self. Self-ownership, when paired with the highly persuasive thesis that all agents possess equal moral rights, affords *every* agent a moral sphere of protection to live the life of her choosing with the self that she has. The moral protections afforded by self-ownership, likewise, bar all agents from living the life they wish to live by non-consensually using the self of another. No agent, that is, may live the life that she desires by making non-consensual use of another's self.

In addition to fostering equality in the sense described above, self-ownership protects the moral status of agents as independent—recall from earlier that the independent moral status of agents follows from the equal moral status of agents. The core idea, recall, behind an agent's moral status as independent is that she is free from the non-consensual subjugation or dominion of others. Self-ownership offers an agent clear moral protections that prevent her non-consensual subjugation or dominion by others. An agent who has stringent rights of ownership over her self can take steps, such as voicing dissent or simply not offering consent, to morally prevent others from treating her self *as if* it belongs to them to do with as they please. The moral authority to tell another "hands off, this is my self, not yours" is necessary to the moral status of an agent as independent. If an agent lacks the moral authority to decide who can use her self and who cannot, then she is not independent in any genuine sense.

Consider the alternatives to an agent possessing very stringent private ownership rights in respect to, for instance, her left arm. In any alternative scenario it would not be *her* left arm at all. If the arm were commonly owned it would *belong, in some shared sense, to everyone*. It would be, similar to the way that I have endorsed thinking about natural resources, subject to some equal claim by all agents. If the arm were collectively owned, then it would *belong to the community* to be used, in some fashion, to best serve the interests of the community. A community might decide these interests are best served by "allowing" agents to have something that approximates self-ownership, or the community might decide that the left arms attached to certain bodies should be used in lucrative arm wrestling contests to add to the wealth of the community whether or not the agent to whom to arm is attached consents to such use. If the arm were jointly-owned then it would *belong to some designated set of agents*. The arm, under these circumstances, would belong presumably to the body of the agent to whom it was attached (although under such a scheme it need not) *as well as* some set of other agents who would have a joint-ownership claim to the arm, similar to the way in which a building complex might be jointly-owned by a set of business owners. None of these alternatives to an agent being the (private) self-owner of her arm affords her adequate moral protection against the non-consensual subjugation or domination of others.

As self-owners, the only moral justification for using non-consensual force against another agent is in response to the unjust (rights violating force understood as aggression) by that agent. As Jan Narveson succinctly puts the point, "A libertarian morality, then, holds that force may only be used to counter force."[33] Murray Rothbard seconds this thought by arguing that:

> The libertarian creed rests upon one central axiom: that no man or group of men may aggress against the person or property of anyone else. This may be called the "non-aggression axiom." Aggression is defined as the initiation of the use or threat of physical violence against the person or property of anyone else.[34]

Libertarians generally strongly endorse the notion that agents should be allowed to *live the life they opt to lead so long as they do not violate the rights of others*. This idea is not new to libertarian-minded thinkers. In the late nineteenth century, for instance, Herbert Spencer sets out a principle of equal freedom that nicely captures this core libertarian idea by noting that, "every man has freedom to do all that he wills, provided that he infringes not on the freedom of any other man."[35]

The "libertarian creed" can be understood as the outcry to ***not use force against me unless I am violating the rights of another; otherwise, leave me alone to lead the life that I desire to live.*** Virtually no agent desires to live a life that another has forced upon her. It would be rare to meet an agent who was not, at least, sympathetic to the libertarian creed, even if she ultimately rejected libertarianism for other reasons. Even agents that bother others do not want to be bothered themselves. The challenge for those that find strong intuitive appeal with the libertarian creed but reject libertarianism is to offer a plausible account in which the libertarian creed is endorsed but very stringent rights of full self-ownership are rejected. It might be that this challenge can be met, but if so it cannot easily be met.

Libertarianism endorses the idea that agents are independent moral individuals, each with their own discrete moral existence to foster and live. An agent's life is her own moral canvas on which she should be afforded an opportunity to draw and design the life she wishes to live. The space on this canvas may of course be voluntarily shared with others—just about any agent with a normal psychology wants to share her canvas (self) with others given the importance of interpersonal relationships. Under no circumstances, however, does an agent have the moral liberty to usurp another's canvas and begin painting the life she desires another to live.

One of many great tragedies of slavery in the Antebellum South was the view that slaves were like children and could not be expected to live a meaningful life on their own terms. Thus, so the false view went, a slave needed a master who would look after her and write on the slave's moral canvas since the slave was incapable of this task herself.[36] Many who endorsed slavery as a moral institution, including many slave owners, felt the intellectual need to publicly endorse the above paternalistically inspired assumption—whether they actually believed such an endorsement is another matter. Supporters of slavery sought a way to dehumanize the slave and, as such, argue that the normal rules of respecting a person's ability to live a life of her choosing did not apply in the case of a slave since the slave was treated as a child incapable of authoring her own life.

It is no coincidence that the same method of reasoning has been used to oppress women for millennia. Women are emotional, not rational, so the false dehumanizing idea proceeds, and, as such, they need a "rational agent" (read as a man), usually in the form of father or husband, to help them direct their lives. How much of this oppression was motivated by genuine paternalistic concern and how much was motivated by selfishness, power, and greed and then presented in the cloak of paternalism is a question I will leave to historians, sociologists, and social psychologists, although I deeply suspect a great deal was little more than a power grab as opposed to genuine paternalistic concern.

Both in the justification of slavery and the oppression of women, agents who actively subjugated these groups often felt the intellectual need to justify the violation of the libertarian creed with an appeal to paternalism. It was the flaw or underdevelopment of the other, so it was argued, that allowed for what would *normally* be an unjust assault on the independent status of another to be legitimized (of course not morally legitimized but culturally or legally legitimized). It was a direct assault on the moral equity of agents that allowed for a refusal to recognize the independent moral status of agents, that is, for a violation of the libertarian creed to be made acceptable. What this suggests is that the libertarian creed has such strong intuitive force that even those who violate the creed will opt to invoke ridiculous empirical claims about who counts (or fully counts) as an agent and who does not rather than to deny that agents ought to be able to live the rights-respecting life of their choice and design.

Paternalism is viewed by many today as an outgrowth of the modern "nanny state," as an annoyance pertaining to things like seatbelt laws, motorcycle helmet laws, and the restriction of toys in fast food children's meals. The history of invoking paternalistic reasoning, however, is much darker and more dehumanizing than preventing a toy from accompanying a side of fries. It is not an exaggeration to say that aside from "might makes right" reasoning and action, there has been no greater contributor to the oppression of agents than paternalistic reasoning and action. The libertarian creed rejects paternalism and in so doing confirms the moral worth and dignity of every agent by recognizing the moral authority of all agents to live a life of their own design so long as they do not violate the rights of others.

Unfortunately the libertarian creed is often mistaken as demonstrating (or even encouraging) an uncaring or crass sentiment for the plight of others. This simply is not the case for at least three reasons. First, the recognition that all agents have their own lives to lead and that there should a very strong presumption against interfering with an agent's ability to lead the life she wishes to pursue can be viewed as a deep respect for all others rather than the demonstration of an uncaring sentiment. No doubt it is difficult to respect the moral status of agents as independent, especially those we care deeply about, when we suspect they are making foolish or ill-advised choices. It is an understanding temptation at times to direct the course of another's life—to direct the life of another as if it were your own. But libertarianism fights against this temptation in favor of allowing others to direct their lives as they wish so long as they do not prevent others from doing the same. It is no easy task—it can be absolutely heart-breaking—to watch another adult you care deeply about misdirect her own life, but ultimately it is *their life* to misdirect.

Second, libertarianism does not discourage acting charitably toward others. In fact, most libertarian commentators would encourage people to be charitable toward others. Jan Narveson goes so far as to say, "People who aren't ready to help others when it is comparatively easy to do so are people who deserve to be avoided when they themselves turn to others in time of need."[37] What libertarians, including Narveson, generally reject is the use of force to take the *legitimate* holdings of an agent so that they may be expropriated to another. Recall, however, from the discussion of illegitimately produced artifacts in the previous chapter that there could well be less (much less) legitimate holding in artifacts than is typically presumed by many libertarians. Additionally, as will be made clearer as we move along, legitimate private property holdings in natural resources will be subject to some fairly significant egalitarian conditions that have been almost completely ignored throughout history.

Force, it should be kept in mind, cannot be used to make an agent charitable or have regard for others; all force does is take things from one agent and direct them toward another. No one is charitable because they *give* at point of gun or tax order—the tax order is, after all, merely a "nice way" to say give to the state or the gun will be drawn. What happens in such cases of "forced charity" is simply that goods are *expropriated* from an agent to be gifted to another, and it is this taking of legitimately held goods that the libertarian is, and anyone ought to be, weary of.

Lastly, so long as self-ownership rights are not absolute there is moral room in exceptional circumstances to use in a non-consensual fashion, in at least some ways, the self or legitimate holdings of another. Imagine that one strand of Sally's loose hair will completely cure Jim of an extremely painful and fatal disease. Jim contacts Sally and tries to strike a deal for one loose strand of her hair, but Sally will not bargain. She is proud of the fact that she never helps others in need. Jim then follows Sally to a baseball game and on an elevator takes a loose strand of hair from her jacket without her knowledge or permission. (If one is skeptical that a loose strand of an agent's hair on her jacket is a component of her self, then imagine that Jim plucked the strand from Sally's head, but when this occurred she assumed that a mosquito had bit her.) If self-ownership rights are absolute, then Jim has acted unjustly by violating a right that Sally has against him not to use or take an aspect of her self without her permission. But self-ownership rights are very stringent as opposed to absolute, and as such, cases can exist in which, such as the one above, the self of an agent may permissibly be used without her permission. Sometimes this distinction is put in terms of *violating* versus *infringing* a right. Judith Jarvis Thomson, for instance, suggests:

> Suppose that someone has a right that such and such not be the case. I shall say that we infringe a right of his if and only if we bring about that it is the case. I shall say that we violate a right of his if and only if *both* we bring about that it is the case *and* we act wrongly in doing so.[38]

But what makes Jim's taking of Sally's strand of hair a reasoned exception to the presumption of self-ownership protecting an agent against being used by another rather than a convenient *ad hoc* exception? The best reply here is to appeal to the moral status of an agent as independent. Self-ownership rights are valuable, in an instrumental fashion, because they offer an agent moral protections that help secure and foster her independent moral status and not because they are intrinsically valuable. Jim's actions do not in any significant fashion lessen or threaten to lessen Sally's independent moral status. Sally is only in a trivial way subjugated to Jim's will. His actions do not prevent her, in any substantial way, from living the life that she wishes to live. Jim's actions do not serve to subjugate or exhibit dominion over Sally. The same, of course, cannot be said if Jim were to take, for instance, Sally's kidney, eye, or arm, control her decision-making abilities with psychological manipulation, or enslave her against her will, no matter how much these things would help his life prospects.

The same general argument applies to the second right of self-ownership, drawn earlier from Otsuka's definition of self-ownership, involving an agent's right to the income that she can derive from her self. Typically this involves income derived from her labor but could also include income from the sale or lease of her body, e.g., selling plasma or other bodily property. If the government (or anyone for that matter) were to confiscate .1 percent of all income to ensure that others do not starve to death, then such a taking does not pose any serious challenge to an agent's ability to live the life of her choosing or, in Lockean terms, to retain and enjoy her independent moral status. There is no good reason to think that an agent must retain *every bit* of the income derived from her self or labor in order to substantially enjoy her independent moral status and live the life that she wishes to live with the self that she has. To treat rights (of self-ownership or otherwise) as offering absolutely unbendable moral protection, as the cases above expose, is to engage in a type of rights fetishism, and fails to appreciate that rights are instrumentally morally valuable because of what it is that they protect.

A general rough rule might be that rights of self-ownership do not protect an agent's self from non-consensual use by another when (1) the use does not pose any significant threat to an agent's moral status as independent and when (2) the use plays a necessary role in significantly allowing for or fostering another agent(s) independent moral status. Such a rule would protect an agent against *all* incursions of self-ownership that pose a significant threat to her independent moral status regardless of what could be gained by others from the incursion as well as limit any incursions against self-ownership to those that significantly support the independent moral status of other agent(s).

An agent must plausibly be a self-owner as a safeguard against others from interfering with her moral status as independent. But rights in respect to the self are not sufficient to adequately protect an agent's independent moral status. An agent, in addition to being a self-owner, must also have rights that protect, in some way, her access to, or benefit from, natural resources. Both types of rights are needed if an agent is to, in any genuine sense, live a life of her own design and choice. Self-ownership cannot carry the full weight of the libertarian creed. It should come as no surprise that some of the weight of the creed should be carried by the ability of an agent to access, or benefit from, natural resources. It makes little sense for a libertarian, or anyone for that matter, to emphasize rights in respect to the self without also stressing rights in respect to the very things (natural resources) that allow for the operation, enjoyment, and integrity of the self.

Left-libertarianism is a variant of libertarianism that gives emphasis to the egalitarian implications that result from the rights that *all* agents have in respect to natural resources. Peter Vallenyne, Hillel Steiner, and Michael Otsuka describe left-libertarianism as follows:

> Over the past few decades there has been increasing interest in left-libertarianism which holds that agents fully own themselves and that natural resources (land, minerals, air, etc.) belong to everyone in some egalitarian sense. Left-Libertarianism agrees with the more familiar right-libertarianism about self-ownership, but radically disagrees with it about the power the acquire ownership of natural resources. Merely being the first to claim, discover, or mix labor with an unappropriated natural resource does not—left-libertarians insist—generate a full property right in that natural resource.[39]

Left-libertarianism, like all variants of libertarianism, maintains that agents are self-owners. Unlike right-libertarianism, however, left-libertarianism draws significant egalitarian implications from the equal initial claim that agents have in respect to natural resources. Left-libertarianism maintains, in particular, that appropriators of natural resources from the commons owe non-trivial duties to others. Typically this duty is understood in terms of

Locke's proviso that an appropriator must "leave enough and as good" for others.

The basic idea behind the "left" in left-libertarianism is that if an agent appropriates for herself a natural resource that was once part of the shared common stock, then she owes others with whom the thing was once shared some non-trivial duty. This core left-libertarian commitment, I shall argue in chapter 5, ought to be extended to the use of natural resources within the commons. Nothing aside from how to treat the duties owed by those who appropriate natural resources from the commons serves to generally intellectually separate right- and left-libertarianism. Right-libertarians generally hold that appropriators of natural resources owe nothing or very little to others in virtue of their appropriation, while left-libertarians hold that the appropriation of natural resources from the commons triggers substantial duties owed to others. If not for differences among libertarians involving the moral conditions governing the appropriation of natural resources from the commons, there would be no interesting distinction between "right" and "left" libertarianism.

The moral conditions governing the *use* of natural resources within the commons is not an issue that generally divides right- and left-libertarians. The reason for this is not because of considered agreement between right- and left-libertarians on this point—it is doubtful that there would be agreement between right- and left-libertarians about this issue. Instead, the reason consists in general neglect. Libertarian thinkers (and political philosophers generally) have been relatively silent about the moral conditions governing the use of natural resources within the commons. Political philosophers have generally side-stepped, as Locke did in his *Second Treatise*, the moral considerations governing the use of natural resources within the commons and instead set their moral sights toward the appropriation of these resources.

The term "left-libertarianism" is only a few decades old, but the essential elements of the idea can be traced back centuries to thinkers as diverse as Grotius, Locke, Pufendorf, Jefferson, Spencer, and George. Despite a rich history of left-libertarian thought, the idea is not yet a widespread view. Left-libertarian perspectives have, however, gained recent traction.[40] Libertarianism is typically associated with right-libertarian views that have been popularized by thinkers such as Nozick, Rothbard, and Narveson. These views put much less emphasis, or reject outright, the idea that natural resources initially belong to everyone. Left-libertarianism strives to reconcile a dual commitment to both the self-ownership of agents and the egalitarian implications that follow from the claim that natural resources initially belong to everyone. Left-libertarianism rejects, for instance, the notion that agents have the unfettered moral power to privately acquire (appropriate) natural resources from the commons (and owe no duties to others) solely because they were first to claim, discover, or mix their labor with the desired resource. Some right-libertarians, such as Nozick, also reject this idea and argue that appropriators of natural resources from the commons owe others (albeit fairly weak) duties.

Although Vallentyne, Steiner, and Otsuka ultimately offer competing proposals concerning the moral conditions governing the appropriation of natural resources from the commons, they share the view consistent with the view of most left-libertarians that *it is possible* to outline a set of moral conditions that govern the appropriation of natural resources from the commons. This left-libertarian commitment points to an important difference between left-libertarianism and Marxism; Left-libertarianism generally maintains that private property holdings *can be* morally grounded, while a Marxist perspective generally treats all private property as inherently morally dubious. This distinction, however, is not absolute. Nothing in principle, for instance, bars a left-libertarian from endorsing the claim that the private appropriation of natural resources that initial belong to everyone will always be unjust.

There is no definitive marker associated with the extent of duties had by an appropriator of natural resources from the commons that places a libertarian squarely within a "right" or "left" designation, although libertarians rarely have much trouble identifying themselves on either side of the divide. It is an open question just how stringent a libertarian must think the duties of an appropriator are before they are "properly" labeled as a left-libertarian. The main concern here is not with carving out conceptual space so that the labels of right- and left-libertarianism can be properly affixed like name tags to the shirts of various libertarian-minded thinkers. Instead, the concern is with defending a distinctively libertarian theory of justice that offers a plausible and compelling account of the rights that protect the moral status of agents as equal and independent.

For reasons already outlined, some of the rights needed to protect the equal and independent moral status of agents will concern access to or benefit from natural resources. No one can seriously entertain the idea that even if the ninety-nine men trapped on George's fictional island, described earlier in the chapter, were full self-owners that they are independent in any genuine fashion. Self-ownership is not sufficient to protect an agent's independent moral status. In such a case, full self-ownership seems akin to a right held by a starving agent with nothing to eat that no one take his empty plate. Surely a theory of justice, be it libertarian or otherwise, can do better than this, and if it cannot then so much the worse for a theory of justice that fails to recognize rights had by all in respect to natural resources. A thoroughgoing libertarian theory of justice, by whatever label it is assigned, ignores at its own peril the clear relationship between the ability of an agent to direct her own life free from the dominion of others and her access to, or benefit from, natural resources and the artifacts ultimately derived from these resources.

NOTES

1. Peter Vallentyne, "Distributive Justice," in *Companion to Contemporary Political Philosophy*, eds. Robert Goodin, Philip Pettit, Thomas Pogge (Cambridge: Blackwell Publishers, 2007): 548-549.

2. Nozick, *Anarchy, State, and Utopia*, 57.

3. See Wesley N. Hohfeld, *Fundamental Legal Conceptions*, ed. W.W. Cook (New Haven, Yale University Press, 1919).

4. For simplicity I am treating these "existing normative situations" as first-order normative situations and powers as second-order alterations to these first-order conditions. Powers, however, need not be second-order alterations. An agent, for instance, could have a third-order moral power to alter a second-order normative situation, a power to alter a power.

5. For discussions of the correlativity of moral rights and moral duties see David Lyons, "The Correlativity of Rights and Duties," *Nous* 4 (1970): 45-55; Hillel Steiner, *An Essay on Rights*, 61-62; Thomas Magnell, "The Correlativity of Rights and Duties," *The Journal of Value Inquiry* 45 (2011): 1-12.

6. Steiner, *An Essay on Rights*, 61*fn*9.

7. Admittedly, permission-giving can be treated as an interest-protecting concern. For instance, permission-giving might be a key feature of an agent's interests.

8. Grotius, *The Rights of War and Peace*, 92.

9. Nozick, *Anarchy State and Utopia*, 30.

10. Locke, *Second Treatise*, §6.

11. It might be that agents can *come to have* differential rights due either to the voluntary alienation of rights or by forfeiting rights through rights-violating actions. Both of these suggestions are plausible, yet complex and controversial. It could be, for instance, that an agent's rights are contingent upon her not voluntarily alienating herself from the right(s) and not taking action (violating the rights of others) to forfeit her right(s). If this is the case, then the same set of rights remains the same for everyone indefinitely; it will just be that some agents, through voluntary action, have taken action that enables others to exercise certain moral powers in respect to them that they otherwise would not be able to do. Punishment, for instance, is often viewed (and it was viewed by Locke) as a natural right to be exercised by anyone to curtail, "violations to the law of nature" (Locke, §7-14). Punishment, however, can also be viewed as a Hohfeldian power (as opposed to right) to be justly exercised against those who have performed certain actions.

12. Locke, *Second Treatise*, §22.

13. Ibid., §95.

14. Steven King, *Misery* (New York: Signet, 1987).

15. There is ample evidence (see W.R. Wells, "Ability to Resist Artificially Induced Dissociation," *Journal of Abnormal Social Psychology* 35 (1940): 261-272-12; W.R. Wells, "Experiments in the Hypnotic Production of Crime," *Journal of Psychology* 11 (1941): 63-102; J.G. Watkins, "Antisocial Compulsions Induced Under Hypnotic Trance," *Journal of Abnormal Social Psychology* 42 (1947): 256-259) that in, at least some cases, an agent who is subject to hypnosis can be persuaded to do what she otherwise would not have done absent the psychological manipulation. If this evidence is right it suggest that hypnosis does not merely serve to lower the inhibitions of agents but can actually serve to direct the behavior of agents. This evidence speaks against the commonly referenced suggestion that agents under hypnosis cannot be persuaded to do things that they otherwise would not have done.

16. Eric Mack, "The Natural Right of Property," 77.

17. Henry George, *Progress and Poverty*, 346.

18. For an excellent discussions of samaritanism see Richard Arneson, "Property Rights in Persons," *Social Philosophy and Policy* 9 (1992): 201-230; Christopher Wellman, "Liberalism, Samaritanism, and Political Legitimacy," *Philosophy and Public Affairs* 25 (1996): 211-237.

19. Jan Narveson, *The Libertarian Idea* (Philadelphia: Temple University Press, 1988).

20. See Herbert Spencer, *Social Statics*; Henry George, *Progress and Poverty*; Max Stirner, *The Ego and Its Own*, ed. David Leopold (Cambridge, Cambridge University Press, 1907).

21. For examples of thinkers that frequently use the language of self-ownership see Murray Rothbard, *For a New Liberty: The Libertarian Manifesto* (New York: Libertarian Review Foundation, 1978); G.A. Cohen, "Self-Ownership, World-Ownership, and Equality"; Hillel Steiner, *An Essay on Rights*; Peter Vallentyne, "Left-Libertarianism: A—Primer"; Michael Otsuka, *Libertarianism Without Inequality*.

22. Robert Nozick, *Anarchy, State, and Utopia*, 172.

23. Henry George, *Progress and Poverty*, 334.

24. Locke, *Second Treatise*, 27.

25. Cohen, *Self-Ownership, World-Ownership and Equality*, 97.

26. Vallentyne, "Left-Libertarianism: A—Primer", 2.

27. Frederic Pryor, *Property and Industrial Organization in Communist and Capitalistic Nations* (Bloomington: Indiana University Press, 1973) 2.

28. See A.M. Honoré, "Ownership," in *Oxford Essays in Jurisprudence*, ed. A.G. Guest (London, Oxford University Press, 1961): 107-147.

29. Otsuka, *Libertarianism Without Inequality*, 15.

30. Ibid.

31. Mack, "The Natural Right of Property," 61.

32. For a Hegelian, as opposed to Lockean, defense of (partial) self-ownership *see* John Christman, *The Myth of Property*, 147-160.

33. Jan Narveson, "The Anarchists Case," in *For and Against the State*, eds. John T. Sanders and Jan Narveson (Lanham, MD: Rowman and Littlefield, 1996): 200.

34. Rothbard, *For a New Liberty*, 23.

35. Spencer, *Social Statics*, 103.

36. For an excellent treatment of slavery in the antebellum South and the lengths to which paternalism was used to morally justify the practice see Lacy K. Ford, *Deliver Us From Evil: The Slavery Question in the Old South* (New York: Oxford University Press, 2009).

37. Jan Narveson, *Moral Matters* (Ontario: Broadview, 1999) 156.

38. Judith Jarvis Thompson, "Some Ruminations on Rights," in *Rights, Restitution, and Risk*, ed. William Parent (Cambridge, Harvard University Press, 1986): 51.

39. Peter Vallentyne, Hillel Steiner, Michael Otsuka, "Why Left-Libertarianism is not Incoherent, Indeterminate, or Irrelevant: A Reply to Fried," *Philosophy and Public Affairs* 33 (2005): 201.

40. Reasons for the recent traction of left-libertarianism can be owed to Hillel Steiner's (1994, 229-282) development of a Georgist account of left-libertarianism, see *An Essay on Rights*, 229-282 and Michael Otsuka's recent book-length defense of a left-libertarian theory of justice see *Libertarianism Without Inequality*. In addition Hillel Steiner and Peter Vallentyne have edited two full-length anthologies of left-libertarian writings. See Peter Vallentyne and Hillel Steiner, *The Origins of Left-Libertarianism: An Anthology of Historical Writings* (Hampshire: Palgrave, 2000); Peter Vallentyne and Hillel Steiner, *Left-Libertarianism and its Critics: The Contemporary Debate* (Hampshire: Palgrave, 2000).

Chapter Four

Property Rights and Access to the Self

My goal in this chapter is to further assess the role of property rights in respect to natural resources and the self within the constraints of the Lockean left-libertarian theory of justice outlined in the previous chapter. I shall begin by highlighting the broad and far-ranging nature of property rights. Next, I will address a distinction, made explicit by John Christman, between control-ownership and income-ownership. This distinction will help establish a core or foundational conception of private ownership. I will argue that a central feature of private ownership must include a right against others from impeding access to the privately owned object of property. The implications following from the "right of access" are then applied to self-ownership. I argue, on this note, that a "right of access" to the self (a core element of self-ownership) places restrictions on the way that others can use or appropriate natural resources.

The property rights that constitute an ownership claim, as mentioned briefly in the previous chapter, are very broad in scope. An agent has a property right in respect to an object, to some degree, if she has a liberty to use the object in certain ways—that is, others do not have a claim against her using the object in certain ways—or a right (claim against others) that others not use the object in certain ways. An agent might, for instance, have a property right that only allows her to stand on some designated spot of land for a few moments, or alternatively, an agent could have *full ownership* over a spot of land. John Christman, taking a lead from Honoré, describes "full liberal property rights" as:

> (1) *the right to possess* (the right of exclusive physical control that the nature of the thing admits, coupled with a claim right to non-interference); (2) *the right to use* (a claim right to exclusive use of a thing implying a general duty on the part of all others not to use the thing without the owner's permission);

> (3) *the right to the capital* (the power to make valid dispositions of the thing owned as well as the power to transfer title—this element can be separated into the rights of alienation, consumption, and modification); (4) *the right to manage* (a cluster of powers to contract with others concerning control over various uses of the thing); and (5) *the right to the income* (the right to increased benefit from the ownership, where this benefit is derived from others' goods given in trade; this right ranges over the increased income or material accrued from a holding by virtue of the productive use of that holding, including, most centrally, trades).[1]

The set of property rights in respect to a thing can range from the most modest liberty to use the thing in some very limited fashion up to and including the full complement of rights described above in respect to the thing and any set of rights in between. As a caution, keep in mind that full is not to be conflated with absolute protection against others. An agent may have a full set of property rights that do not (in full or part) afford absolute protections against others, and likewise she could have less than full property rights in respect to some thing that absolutely protects her against others to the extent allowed by her rights.

The full private owner of a car has the full complement of property rights noted above by Christman. An agent who leases a car for a three-year term from a car dealer has many, but not all, of the rights noted above. The agent who rents a car for a short amount of time from a rental agency still has a number or property rights listed above but likely less than the agent who leases the car. An agent who borrows her neighbor's car with permission from her neighbor to use the car *only* for the purpose of driving someone to the hospital has very minimal property rights in respect to the car. In each of these cases, an agent has property right(s) in respect to the car, even though the bundles of rights in respect to the car differ widely.

Some political philosophers—such as Hillel Steiner—have gone so far as to argue that *all* rights are property rights. Steiner, for instance, notes:

> the traditional Lockean view that all rights are essentially property rights far from being merely a piece of bourgeois ideology, actually embodies an important conceptual truth.[2]

Steiner reasons that *all* rights are property rights because if all rights constitute claims that agents use, or not use, their bodies in certain ways, then all rights turn out to be a type of property (use) right that an agent has in the bodies of others.[3] If an agent, for instance, has a right that others not punch her in the face, then this right correlates with the duty of others not to use their fists in a certain way. Steiner's argument that all rights are property rights is plausible and underscores the pervasive role that property rights have in a libertarian theory of justice or, for that matter, any theory of justice based upon the duties that agents owe to one another. His argument also serves as a further caution against the proliferation of rights generally. This is because rights generally correlate with duties that place restrictions on the ways that agents are at liberty to use their bodies. All rights, if Steiner is correct, mark out restrictions on the bodily autonomy of agents. Viewed in this light, the rights that an agent has in respect to natural resources (or any external object) will always be conceptually linked with the duties of others not to use their body or others aspects of their self in various ways.

The breadth of property rights makes them amenable to a wide range of applications. Property rights, for instance, can be applied to both the *use* of commonly held things such as natural resources within the commons as well as more traditional exclusionary private ownership rights. A city resident, for example, has a weak property right in respect to a city park bench. The park bench, in some shared fashion, belongs to everyone in the city, including her. The resident has a right, for instance, that others not bar her (without good reason) from sitting on the bench for at least some amount of time. All city residents have certain property rights in respect to the bench, even though no resident privately own, the bench.

An example of a very minimal set of property rights that include only the right to limited use would be the rights of *squatters*.[4] Squatters, typically, occupy a dwelling that has been effectively abandoned or neglected by its private owner and, in certain legal jurisdictions, are afforded very minimal property rights to use, in some limited fashion, the property that they occupy.[5] In fact the legal doctrine of adverse possession allows a trespasser or squatter under some circumstances to displace the private property rights of another.[6] Property rights, as the rights of squatters demonstrates can be very robust or rather weak and this in turn allows for a broad treatment of what having property rights in some thing amounts to.

The "occupy movement" that quickly spread across the United States and parts of Europe during 2012 reinvigorated a good deal of attention to the issue of what (property) rights agents ought to have with respect to public places. It seems fairly uncontroversial that an agent's right(s) to use a public or common space must be limited in some significant ways so that everyone may be afforded some equal chance or opportunity to enjoy and benefit from the public space. No one, for instance, should be allowed to put a fence around her favorite part of a public park and keep others out. Others have a claim against the deployment of such exclusionary tactics.

But the precise limitations that should be placed on agents to use public or common areas are controversial. This controversy is to be expected given the sparse attention generally afforded to the rights that agents have to use shared common spaces. One beneficial result or spillover effect of offering a systematic examination of the moral conditions governing the use of natural resources within the commons is that this analysis will likely provide helpful moral guidance in respect to the use of designated public spaces such as parks and roadways.

After having considered the far-reaching and broad nature of property rights, our focus can be directed toward establishing the core elements of *private ownership*. This will help set the stage to examine the moral conditions that govern the *appropriation* of natural resources from the commons. When an agent exercises a moral power and appropriates a natural resources from the commons, she comes to *privately own* the resource that she has appropriated. Appropriation is generally reserved to mean "original acquisition" from the commons, although coming to own a "common artifact" (discussed in chapter 2) should be treated as morally equivalent with the appropriation of a natural resource from the commons. Initially, all natural resources were privately unowned and belonged to everyone in some shared common fashion; hence the private ownership of all natural resources has an origin that is, in principle, historically traceable to an appropriation. In addition, recall from the second chapter that it is impossible to offer a comprehensive moral account of private property in natural resources or artifacts derived from natural resources without addressing the appropriation of natural resources. All roads to the contemporary private ownership of natural resources and artifacts must run through the historical intersection of appropriation.

Appropriation is a normative concept. To appropriate a natural resource is to exercise a moral power and come to privately own the resource. For this reason it is, strictly speaking, superfluous and mistaken to make reference to "just appropriation," although it is an easy slip to make because all appropriation is by its definition just. The tyrant, for example, who unjustly takes land that belongs to everyone has engaged in an unjust taking or expropriation of the land, but she has not appropriated the land because she has not exercised a moral power or come to a have a bundle of moral rights (ownership) in respect to the land.

In order to adequately assess the moral conditions that govern the appropriation of natural resources from the commons—a topic that will get full attention in chapter 6—it is important to first establish the rights that an agent must have in respect to natural resources in order to privately own the resource. It is too quick to assume that private ownership must include the entire bundle of rights needed for full ownership. An agent can privately own a natural resource even if she does not fully own the resource. Sally, for instance, can privately own a plot of land even if she lacks the right to bequest the plot after she dies. No doubt she would have greater (more full) ownership if she also had the right to bequest the land, but her lack of a right to bequest the land does not mean that she fails to be the private owner of the land in a meaningful sense.

John Christman offers a helpful distinction between *control-ownership* and *income-ownership* that can be used to establish which rights are needed in order for an agent to be the private owner of some thing.[7] The central idea of control-ownership, Christman explains is that, "the owner maintains primary say over what is to be done with the thing insofar as this capacity affects only the owner herself."[8] Alternatively, the central idea of income-ownership is "the right to transfer and the right to retain goods received in trade (income)."[9] A control-owner of a thing has rights to "use, possess, manage, modify, alienate, and destroy" the thing, while an income-owner of a thing has rights to the capital, or to the income derived from a thing.[10] A control-owner (lacking income-ownership) of a house, for instance, would have the right to paint the walls of the house pink or decide who is allowed to use the house but not a right to the income gained through the rental of the house. An income-owner (lacking control-ownership) of the house, by contrast, would have a right to the income gained through renting the house but lack the right to paint the walls.

Christman convincingly argues that control-ownership is more central to the autonomy of agents than income-ownership because:

> Income rights are essentially tied to the distribution of goods. And more crucially, they cannot be said to be a manifestation of individual's liberty or autonomy, since income is a product of things over which an agent can claim no independent sovergnity.[11]

An agent's ability to gain income or economic benefit through trade or agreement is contingent upon the preferences of others, while the ability of an agent to possess, use, modify, alienate, or destroy her property is not contingent upon the preferences or will of others. The economic value of a piece of property, for instance, is likely contingent on the willingness of someone to insure the property against catastrophic disaster. Accordingly, the rights of control-ownership track much better with the moral status of agents as independent. This is not to suggest that income rights play no role in respect to an agent's independent status: it is just that their role is often contingent upon economic, social, and political systems or structures and, as such, play a more tenuous role than that of control rights.

The Academy Awards helps to illustrate how the core element of private ownership is found in control rights as opposed to income rights. Concerned with the prospect of the award being sold, in 1950 the Academy began making Oscar winners sign an agreement saying that they would never sell the award to anyone except the Academy for the nominal price of one dollar. Presumably, winners of the award still retain the right to give the award away to another agent, although some restrictions on this giving might exist to prevent sale of the award from the gifted party. Oscar winners have no right to transfer the award through sale, with the one exception noted above. Nonetheless the holder of an Oscar is still plausibly the private owner of the award even though she has no right to sell the award. A private ownership claim to some thing is not negated because an agent's income right(s) to the thing are severely curtailed or in some cases altogether absent.

This example is not cherry-picked to yield the right answer against income rights being a core element of private ownership. To see this, replace the prohibition against selling the award with other prohibitions in respect to income rights over the award. Would it matter, for instance, if the Academy had barred a winner from renting the award to others or if they had barred her from charging agents an admission fee to view the award? No doubt such restrictions would serve to make the ownership rights the winner has over the award less than full, but none of them seriously challenge the idea that the winner of the Oscar still privately owns the award.

If the Academy, alternatively, had placed severe restrictions on the control rights of the award, then the recipient of the award would not clearly be the private owner of the award. Imagine that before being given physical possession of the award an Oscar winner had to agree that she would never take the award out of a pre-approved trophy case without the written permission of the Academy. Or imagine that the Academy retained the right to let others use the award as it sees fit. In these cases, the idea that the winner privately owns the award is much less clear. It seems in these cases as if the winner of the award is more a caretaker or chaperone for the award rather than its private owner.

This chaperone status is true for the Stanley Cup that is awarded each year to the National Hockey League team that wins the Stanley Cup Finals. The winning team has more rights over the cup than the losing team. The winning team gets to use the cup as a giant champagne decanter; the losing team does not. The trophy is, however, passed down year after year to the team that wins the Stanley Cup Finals. As such, the team that possesses the trophy during its yearlong reign as champions is plausibly not the private owner of the award. This is because the team that possesses the award must hand it over to the next team to win the Finals. The team (or team's owner) is a caretaker for, and not private owner of, the award. Contrast this with the Vince Lombardi Trophy that is awarded each year to the National Football League team that wins the Super Bowl. A new trophy is made every year and awarded to the winning team's owner to do with as he pleases. In this case, the owner of the football team is the private owner of the award.

Private ownership is not co-extensive with (full) control-ownership because it does not include the right to destroy. This is because there are a good number of cases in which an agent can rightfully be said to be the private owner of a thing yet lack the liberty to destroy the thing. Pets and classic artwork come to mind here. There is a genuine sense in which an agent is the private owner of a prized pet poodle yet is not at liberty to destroy the dog given its nature as a sentient being. This case is complex because the duty not to destroy would presumably be owed to the poodle. But this is controversial because if the poodle is not an agent, then it is not clear that duties can be owed to it, and if the poodle is an agent (to which duties can be owed), then it is not clear that it can be privately owned.

The case of classic artwork might stake out more clear territory in which an agent can be the private owner of some thing yet lack a moral liberty to destroy the thing. Classic artwork often holds such special historical, cultural, and sometimes religious significance such that the private owner of such a thing might not have a liberty to destroy it. Others, that is, could have a claim against such destruction. One might use the example of classic artwork and the plausible prohibition against destroying it to suggest the inability of anyone to be the private owner of classic artwork. This example could turn out to spur a clash of intuitions about what rights are required for private ownership, but it seems that bidders at auctions would still bid very high amounts for what they would still, in the vast majority of cases, properly label as private ownership of classic artwork, even absent a right to destroy the art. The frequently very high bids for classic art would likely not decrease by much (maybe not at all) if the prospective "owners" understood that they lacked a right to destroy the art that they obtain at auction. These art collectors would, I maintain, be correct to say that they privately own a piece of art even while granting the stipulation that they are not at liberty to destroy it.

The core of private ownership includes the *liberty right to the unilateral (without needing the permission of anyone) use of the object of property* and the *claim right that others receive permission from the private owner before they are permitted to use the object of property*. These rights covering the use of an object encompass *rights to possess and modify the object of property*. Additionally, a private owner has a *liberty right to alienate her rights in respect to her object of property*—no one, that is, has a claim right against the private owner of a thing from alienating her rights over the thing. If an agent cannot alienate her rights in respect to some thing because another has a claim against this alienating action, then there is an important sense in which she lacks the requisite control over her relationship to the thing to be its private owner.

When I say that the above rights make up the core of private ownership, I have in mind that these rights are necessary and sufficient for a minimal conception of private ownership. A more robust conception of private ownership including, for instance, various income rights or a right to destroy will include more rights than the core rights of private ownership. There is a wide gulf between a minimal conception of private ownership and full private ownership. An agent who has minimal private ownership rights in respect to a thing has a much less than full bundle of rights in respect to the thing.

Nonetheless, establishing the core set of rights that are needed for a minimal conception of private ownership is important because it serves to make clear what rights must be in place before an agent can be said to appropriate (come to privately own) a natural resource from the commons. This is important given the room for confusion or equivocation that could result from the multiple sets of rights that could be assigned to describe what having private ownership of some thing amounts to. In future references to private ownership or appropriation, unless stated otherwise, I shall be referring to the core or minimal conception of private ownership described above.

One important feature of the bundle of rights that constitute private ownership is that they can, for the most part, be described as use rights. They are rights, with the exception of the right to alienate, that allow the private owner to use her property in a unilateral fashion and bar others from using her property without her permission. Philosophers (and others) have said strikingly little about what it means to *use* a physical object such as a natural resource. The running assumption is typically that use is meant to imply some sort of physical impingement. This lack of attention is problematic given the critical role that use plays within the bundle of rights that constitute private ownership.

Use, unlike appropriation, is a descriptive as opposed to a normative concept. When an agent uses a physical object, this describes some type of relationship between the agent and the object; it is not suggestive in itself of any normative implications. The primary feature of use going forward will be, in line with the standard view, that of physical impingement. Physical impingement is meant to cover cases in which an agent uses her body to directly physically interact with some thing or when an agent sends a physical signal that physically interacts with some thing. If an agent shines a laser into the eye of another and blinds her, then she has used the eye of another by sending a physical signal that physically impinges on another. The idea that an agent uses some physical thing when she physically impinges on the thing will serve as a sufficient condition of use and, going forward, will serve as our default definition of use. For those especially interested in the concept of use as applied to physical objects such as natural resources, see the appendix where I venture an outlined account of the necessary and sufficient conditions of use as applied to physical objects.

The use (physical impingement) of a thing is often obvious. When an agent kicks in her neighbor's door, she uses the door. She also uses the door if she launches a boulder from a giant catapult that knocks over the door. Further, an agent's "intent to use" a thing does not seem to be necessary to ascertain whether she actually uses the thing. An agent who kicks in her neighbor's door while sleepwalking still uses the door. But some instances of use are trickier than the simple cases noted above. The farming of genetically modified crops represents one of these tricky cases. The concern by many is that cross-pollination between genetically modified plants and non-modified plants can occur when winds blow pollen from a genetically modified plant onto the property of another. Stephen Marsh, an organic farmer in Western Australia, claims this is exactly what happened to his crop. Marsh alleges in a lawsuit that his organic farm lost its organic status after genetically altered canola seed from a neighboring farm blew onto his land and contaminated his crop.[12]

Whatever the legal finding in Marsh's case, the evidence is fairly clear that cross-pollination (contamination) between genetically modified plants and non-modified plants is at least possible, although the scientific evidence regarding the extent of "escaped" genetically modified plants is mixed and controversial. According to Lindsey Konkel, roughly 80 percent of canola, for instance, that grows *wild* along North Dakota's roadways is now genetically modified, whereas a few generations ago none of these plants would have been genetically modified.[13] The likely culprits of this change are cross-pollination from wind and genetically modified seed spilling from trucks.[14]

The interesting question here is whether farmers of genetically modified crops engage in a non-consensual use of another's private property and, as such, engage in a potential rights violation when seed or pollen from their land "escapes" and mingles with the property of another. The answer is plausibly yes; a non-consensual use of another's property has, in such a case, taken place. There is a significant time delay between the planting of genetically modified seed and the physical impingement of another property that makes the case murky, but this temporal delay does not suggest that use is absent.

One might object here and say, "an act of God (the wind) caused the pollen to be spread, and as such no use of another's property took place," but this is a very weak objection. Notice that the same can be said about the laws of physics that maintain the trajectory of a bullet as it leaves a gun aimed toward the head of another or any other easily predictable natural phenomena—such as the near certainty that winds will blow pollen around.[15] An agent's private ownership claim right that others not use her property without her permission places a duty on others not to take actions that can be reasonably foreseen to physically impede on another's property.

This duty on the part of agents not to use—where sending a physical signal counts as a use—the private property of another also explains why boarding a plane with a contagious disease such as tuberculosis violates the rights of others. Unless an agent can hold her breath for the entire duration of the trip, her act of breathing enables a disease she carries to escape and physically impede the body (self) of other(s). The self-ownership rights of agents morally protect them against such non-consensual uses of their bodies.

Pollution, notice, often works in much the same way as genetically modified pollen or bodily germs. The nature of most pollution is such that it very easily *escapes* and impinges on the property of others; air and water pollution are notorious for doing this. If chemicals from an industrial factory or a deep well that enables hydraulic fracturing escape and contaminate the private property of another, then the operators of the factory or well have used another's private property without permission and, as such, have violated a duty owed to the private owner of the property.

There is one additional (and final) right that ought to be included in the bundle of rights required for a minimal conception of private ownership. This is the claim right that a private owner of a thing has against others *not to impede her access to that thing*. Others, that is, do not have a liberty to block or impede an agent from accessing that which she privately owns.

The justification for including a *right of access* to the bundle of core private ownership rights is that if such a right were absent from the bundle, then the owner of the thing would plausibly *lack the requisite control* over the thing to be its private owner. There is little moral difference between someone taking a thing that you privately own (and thereby preventing your use or control of the thing) and this same agent blocking or preventing you from accessing a thing that you privately own (and thereby preventing your use or control of the thing). It should not make much, or any, difference to you if someone takes your car and sells it for scrap without your permission or if someone builds an impenetrable wall around your car without your permission. In both cases, you cannot use or derive any benefit from what you own. If private ownership rights protect an owner against the unauthorized use of her private property, then for similar reasons they also ought to protect her against others impeding her access to what she owns.

Say that Larry privately owns a lake and the ten feet of land surrounding the shore of the lake that he uses to swim and fish. Tim privately owns all the land for some distance encircling the land that Larry owns around his lake with the exception of a small public trail that cuts through Tim's land and gives Larry access to his land and lake. Imagine three circles. A small circle representing Larry's lake, another small circle around this lake representing Larry's land, and then a large circle around this that represents Tim's land with a public trail cutting through Tim's land that leads to Larry's land and lake. Larry has accessed his land and lake by using the public access trail for decades, and there is no other feasible way to access these things. The public, broke and heavily in debt, decides to sell the access trail to Tim. Assume that this transfer gives Tim private ownership of the once public trail. Tim then opts to block Larry's access to his land and lake because he does not want other agents "trespassing on his land," and he cites his claim right that others not use his property without his permission as justification for preventing Larry's use of his land.

The example illustrates a tension within the bundle of rights that make up private ownership. With the inclusion of a "right of access" to the bundle of private ownership rights, the full set of rights that make up the core (minimal conception) of private ownership are:

1. The claim right of a private owner that others receive her permission before they are permitted to use a thing that she privately owns.
2. The liberty right of a private owner to the unilateral use of a thing that she privately owns.
3. The claim right of a private owner that others not impede her access to a thing that she privately owns.
4. The liberty right of a private owner to alienate (relinquish) any of the above three rights in respect to a thing that she privately owns.

The tension is between the first and third rights in the bundle. The first right affords a private owner say over who can use a thing that she privately owns. This right to exclude others can, as the case of Larry and Tim illustrates, conflict with an agent's right against others from impeding access to her property. Something has to give, but what?[16]

It is the right of exclusion that generally must yield to, or be trumped by, the right of access. The reason for this is because the ability of an agent to use and control a thing *at all* depends upon her being able to access the thing. This is not true regarding the ability to exclude. If an agent is shut out from accessing a thing that she privately owns, then her use and control of the thing is heavily (maybe even absolutely) curtailed. Alternatively, if an agent lacks the right to exclude others from a thing that she privately owns so that they, within limits, may access what they privately own, then, in many cases, she will still possess a substantial degree of control in respect to what she privately owns. As such, the burden placed on the private owner of a thing is generally much greater if the right to exclusion is allowed to trump the right to access rather than vice versa.

In many legal jurisdictions, this tension is resolved with an established "right of way" or easement principle that allows agents to access property that they privately own by using the private property of others that they otherwise would not have the legal right to use. In many rural areas of the United States, for example, it is not uncommon for one resident to own a private road that provides many agents access to their private residences. Typically the non-owners of the road have certain rights to access their private residence (property) by using the road without needing the permission of the agent who owns the road. The private owner of the road, however, can exclude anyone who is not accessing her private property or a guest of such an agent, while those who merely reside along the road lack such a right in respect to the road.

The right of access should be limited in three ways so that it is does not create too heavy a burden for those whose private property could be unilaterally used by another. The first limitation is that a right of access only allows an agent to unilaterally use the private property of another if such use is the only feasible way to gain access. A right of access should not be employed merely as a way to create a "convenient shortcut" for someone looking to access her property in the quickest possible fashion. If Larry has another feasible option to access his lake that does not require him to use Tim's property, then he should use it and heed Larry's "no trespassing" request.

The second provision is that the unilateral use of another's private property should be minimally intrusive—that is to say, the alteration or modification of another's property should be kept to a minimum to allow for extant uses. To say that Larry should have a liberty to the unilateral use of Tim's property so that he may access his lake should not be read to imply an unlimited liberty to use Tim's private property *in any way* that allows him to access his lake. It is impermissible, for instance, for Larry to drive a monster truck through Tim's property and destroy or significantly degrade Tim's property on the way to his lake.[17]

The third provision is that an agent who uses the property of another to access a thing that she privately owns is responsible for compensating the full cost of any loss resulting from such use. Any loss created by an agent who uses the property of another to gain access to her property ought to be borne out by the agent doing the accessing. In many cases, it is likely that such "compensation of use" will amount to little or nothing, but the provision is important to include as a way to protect the private owner of a thing against loss brought about by another exercising her right of access.

Thus far a right of access has been treated as a core component of private ownership, but the idea can also be extended to common or public ownership. Recall the absurdity of an agent who encloses her favorite area in a public park as a method to exclude others. Part of the reason that such exclusionary tactics are rightly treated as absurd is because everyone has a liberty right to access things that are part of the commons or things that are shared in common and, as such, plausibly possesses some type of claim right against others from impeding access to the commons. In the next chapter, the idea that agents have a right against others restricting their access to natural resources within the commons will be explored at greater length.

Given that a right of access is a core component of private ownership, it stands to reason that the right ought to be included among the rights of self-ownership.[18] The rights of self-ownership would then be, building from the conception of self-ownership offered by Otsuka and explored in the last chapter, as follows:

1. A very stringent right of control over and use of one's mind and body that bars others from intentionally using one as a means by forcing one to sacrifice life, limb, or labor, where such force operates by means of incursions or threats of incursions upon one's mind and body (including assault and battery and forcible arrest, detention, and imprisonment).
2. A very stringent right to access one's body and mind that bars others from non-consensually impeding one from accessing her body and mind.
3. A very stringent right to all of the income that one can gain from one's mind and body (including one's labor) either on one's own or through unregulated and untaxed voluntary exchanges with other individuals.

As a general guide, we can say that an agent impedes another from accessing her mind and body when she prevents another from controlling her mind and body, as she would have absent the impeding action. The addition of (2), as will be illustrated shortly, helps to shore up the moral protections that an agent has against others from interfering with the control of her self that are not adequately protected under (1) and (3).

The rationale for the inclusion of a claim right that an agent holds against others not to impede access to her self is the same as the rationale offered as to why an agent has such a right in respect to natural resources or artifacts that she privately owns. If others are at liberty to impede an agent from accessing her self, then she lacks the requisite control over her self to be a self-owner. This is important because, as highlighted in the previous chapter, the alternatives to an agent privately owning her self do not offer her adequate moral protections against others. If others have a liberty to impede an agent from accessing her self, then they are at liberty to exercise a type of non-consensual dominion or power over the will of another that is on the same moral par with forcible assault or imprisonment. An agent's ability to live the life of her choosing with the self that she has is placed in serious peril if others are at liberty to block or impede her access to her self.

The idea of an agent impeding another from accessing her self is more peculiar than an agent impeding another from accessing a spot of land or a car. To see how the right of access can be applied to the self, consider that some agents have detachable prosthetic body parts.[19] In the not too distant future, the use of advanced detachable prosthetic body parts might become commonplace rather than limited to medical treatment. Such prosthetic devices could foreseeably "cross-over" from being treatments to becoming normal and even expected ways in which agents advance their capacities. In what follows, assume that the prosthetic body parts of agents are made with advanced modern technologies that allow, for instance, the motor skills necessary for an agent to pick up a grape without smashing it or to pick up a raisin and be able to eat it.[20] These advanced prosthetic body parts are not fantasy; they have been around and successfully affixed to and used by United States soldiers that have lost limbs in combat since at least 2009.

The case of advanced prosthetic technology represents a clear way in which the bodily aspect of an agent's self can be in numerous discontinuous separate locations at the same time. Maggie, for instance, could have a prosthetic arm that she detaches before going to sleep. It is nearly impossible for Maggie to sleep while the arm is attached to the rest of her body, so she takes it off before going to bed and places it at the top of a closet ten feet from her bed. The arm, plausibly, is a part of Maggie's self whether it stays affixed to the rest of her body or whether it sits ten feet from her as she sleeps. If an agent were designed such that she had to detach her brain every evening before bed and place it on a charging station ten feet from where she slept, then parts of her self would be in two places: a brain in a charging station and the rest of her bodily self in a bed. There is no principled reason why an agent's physical self must be contiguous.

This line of reasoning can be challenged on two fronts. The first challenge suggests that prosthetic body parts are not parts of the self and, as such, have no place in an argument about self-ownership. The second challenge suggests that as soon as the prosthetic is detached (or perhaps detached and moved some distance beyond the proximate or immediate control of the agent) it fails to be part of the agent's self.

The first challenge is weak. There is no plausible reason to give moral privilege or priority to including *only* carbon-based fleshy body parts as constituting part of the self while excluding synthetic prosthetic body parts from the same classification. The intuition held by some to the contrary likely results from the relative rarity of prosthetic body parts. If receiving a prosthetic body part were a normal or expected part of life, then the idea that prosthetics were not really part of the self would likely be rejected, as it should.

As a matter of course, if all agents had their carbon-based fleshy left arm replaced when they were six years old with a prosthetic arm, then it would be very unlikely to take seriously the position that the prosthetic arm *is not really* a part of the self while their carbon-based fleshy right arm on the other side of the body that functions effectively in the same way *really is* part of the self. Imagine that space aliens abduct all six-year-old agents and have their left arms removed for experimentation, but the aliens are benevolent and do not want to harm others so they replace the arm with a *very* realistic synthetic prosthetic arm—so realistic, in fact, that human medical technology is far too primitive to figure out that the switch has occurred. The child is then sent back to Earth with no recollection of the switch, and no human agent can figure out that the switch has occurred. In such a case there is no serious doubt that the prosthetic left arm of an agent is part of her self.

The second challenge suggesting that the prosthetic is part of the self when attached to the rest of the body but not when detached is more formidable. The idea could be that an agent lacks the *requisite control* over a *detached* arm placed in a closet for it to properly count as part of her self. There are, however, two problems with this line of thought. The first is that there are many instances in which an agent lacks control over parts of her self as normally constituted but yet such parts are still part of her self. A drunken agent might not be able to immediately control her arms, but her arms are still part of her self. By the same token, an agent in surgery (or even asleep) might be unable to immediately control her arms, but again her arms are still part of her self. An agent who places her arm in the closet could have the same immediate control over her arm as an inebriated agent or an agent who is placed under anesthesia, but in all these cases the arm is still part of the agent's self.[21] One could always bite the bullet here and say that the arm of a sleeping agent, drunken agent, or an agent placed under anesthesia is not, under such conditions, part of her self, but that does not seem like a palatable option and would make the self a highly transitory notion.

The second problem with the argument from control is that it is not difficult to imagine a detached prosthetic body part that an agent controls in the same way that she controls a normally attached body part. The normal way of controlling a body part is by directing the part with a signal from the brain, but it is easy enough to imagine how wireless technology could make it possible for an agent to remotely control a detached part of her body in the same way. An agent can now, in fact, *wirelessly* move a cursor on a computer screen by using only her brain. With such technologies currently available, it will not be long until an agent can control a body part that is detached from her body in the same way as she would control the body part as if it were attached to her. A radio signal from an agent's brain, for example, could be sent to her detached arm directing the arm to go to the fridge and grab a soda. With advancements in neuroscience, an agent could even, in the very near future, experience the sensation of opening the fridge door with her detached arm as most of her body sits on the couch twenty feet from the fridge. There is no principled reason that can be offered to explain why an agent must have less control over a detachable body part than she has over a permanently affixed body part.

Granting that part of an agent's self (body) can be detachable, it is not difficult to see how an agent's access to her self (or a part thereof) could be impeded by another. It could happen in the same way that an agent's access to a natural resource or artifact is impeded, by enclosing the space around the detached part of the self. Maggie, for instance, could remove her arm at work and place it next to her desk so that she can use her break to take a nap in the conference room. When Maggie returns to her desk, she discovers that her co-worker Mark has built an impenetrable wall around her arm without ever physically impinging on the arm.

Mark has plausibly violated Maggie's self-ownership and not simply her private ownership rights that she has to an artifact such as a car or television set. Mark, notice, did not violate Maggie's self-ownership rights by using her body because he did not use her body. Mark used the space around Maggie's arm, but he did not use her arm. As such, Maggie's self-ownership right that others not use her body without her permission will not apply to what Mark has done. Mark, instead, has violated Maggie's self-ownership because he acted in a way that impeded her from accessing her arm. If Maggie's moral status affords her self-ownership rights that protect her against Mark's non-consensual use of her arm and against him from confiscating the income that she earns with her arm, then so too ought this status afford her rights against him from impeding her access to her arm.

Now I want to go a step further and explore what (if any) moral implications the right that self-owners have against others from impeding access to their selves has concerning the use or appropriation of natural resources. Many libertarians, both left and right, contend that self-ownership does not, *in itself*, imply anything about the use or appropriation of natural resources. Peter Vallentyne, on this score, says that:

> Full self-ownership on its own does not guarantee that agents have any effective freedom or any entitlement to their products. For agents, such as ourselves, who need to use natural resources (space to stand in, air to breathe, etc.) to exist at all, it all depends on how natural resources are owned. For if natural resources are *fully* ("maximally") owned by others, justice does not allow one to do anything without their permission (to use their resources). And without their permission one's products may be owned by others (since they may be the result of one's theft or trespass). So nothing of substance follows here from full self-ownership alone.[22]

Vallentyne's point is that the rights an agent has in respect to her self if not combined with rights in respect to natural resources do not guarantee her any effective freedom or any entitlement over artifacts that she produces from natural resources. As the thought goes, self-ownership, in itself, doesn't do much for an agent unless it is combined with rights in respect to natural resources. The idea is that even if we grant an agent full and absolutely protected self-ownership, she could still lack any effective freedom if she enters a world (as was the case of Newcomer in the first chapter) that is already completely privately owned by others. If self-ownership rights do not include a right to access the self, then Vallentyne's point stands. But if self-ownership rights include a right to access the self, then self-ownership itself will plausibly have moral implications concerning the use and appropriation of natural resources.

When a nurse becomes fed up with an extremely cantankerous patient and smothers him with a pillow, then she clearly violates his self-ownership. Now, instead, imagine that an evil genius builds a machine that changes the chemical composition of breathable air outside of an agent's body so that, within a mile radius of the activated machine, it is no longer breathable. The machine can be placed virtually anywhere, and with the click of a remote, the machine will instantly change the chemical composition of normally breathable air into a gas that agents can no longer breathe. Anyone within a mile radius of the activated machine will asphyxiate and die.

Would activating the asphyxiation-machine violate the self-ownership of someone near the machine? The answer, under traditional accounts of self-ownership is, at best, unclear. Activating the asphyxiation-machine, notice, does not use (physically impinge against) an agent without her permission. The machine only changes the chemical composition of a natural resource outside of an agent's body. I maintain, nonetheless, that activating the machine would violate the self-ownership of anyone near the machine. This is because activating the machine would violate the claim right of a self-owner against others not to (by way of using natural resource or any other means) impede her from accessing her self. This claim right implies the liberty of an agent to use natural resources in a fashion that allows her to access her self. The self is not merely a corporeal body. It is a living, conscious entity. Impeding an agent from accessing that which allows for the life and conscious action of her self *is* a way of blocking access to her self. If the above reasoning is correct, then self-ownership in itself has non-trivial implications concerning the use of natural resources and the effective freedom of agents.

Take the case of drinkable water or food as opposed to breathable air. If activating the asphyxiation-machine violates the self-ownership of others, then on the same moral grounds so too does blocking another access to drinkable water or food. An agent could, for instance, violate another agent's right of access to her self by hoarding all the food or drinkable water within a large area. An agent's liberty to use or otherwise take natural resources from the commons is limited by the right of access held by self-owning agents. This is not to say that an agent has a positive right to be fed by others—that is a separate matter and controversial within libertarian thought—instead, the position on the table is that an agent has a claim against others taking actions that prevent her from accessing her self.

The implications that stem from the self-ownership right against others from impeding access to the self place restrictions on the moral power of agents to appropriate natural resources from the commons. An agent does not have the moral power to appropriate in a fashion that impedes another agent from accessing her self. Recall Newcomer, who entered the world after others had appropriated all natural resources. This "total appropriation" of all natural resources is *prima facie* unjust as a violation of Newcomer's self-ownership because it impedes her ability to access her self. The same reasoning can be applied to Henry George's example in the previous chapter of a hundred men trapped on an island where *all* the land is privately owned by one man.

The moral implications that follow from the right to access the self are not reserved to agents with prosthetic body parts or the fantastic subjects of thought experiments. In an increasingly privatized world, a world with less and less common or public space, the homeless find themselves increasingly subject to restrictions on their ability to access their selves.[23] The parliament of Hungary in 2012, for instance, passed stringent anti-vagrancy laws that effectively criminalize homelessness. Those caught *sleeping* in public twice in a six-month period can be given a six-hundred-dollar ticket and can be jailed if the ticket is not paid. Hungary, it should be noted, does not have adequate shelter space to provide a place for all its homeless to sleep. The use of force against an agent who is sleeping, standing, or otherwise existing in the only public place that she can feasibly access to physically place her self is a violation of her self-ownership. Those with non-negligible amounts of private property that they can use to engage in activities necessary for the functioning of the self (such as sleeping) can easily forget that, for many agents, the world constantly appears as a giant "no trespassing sign" and that this lack of access to property outside the body clearly has ramifications concerning the ability of homeless agents to access their selves.

The basic idea that self-ownership itself has moral implications concerning the use and appropriation of natural resources goes through *even if* self-ownership does not include the right of an agent to access her self. Say that despite my best efforts in the last few pages, a supporter of self-ownership rejects the idea that self-ownership contains the right of an agent to access her self. This supporter of self-ownership endorses the two traditionally understood self-ownership rights (or something close to them) made explicit in the last chapter, but rejects the augmentation of self-ownership with a right to access the self.

Grant that self-ownership includes only the two rights made explicit in the third chapter and that the endorsement of the right to access the self in this chapter has been misguided or fallen short. This understanding, and any plausible understanding, of self-ownership ought to maintain that the nurse who smothers her patient with a pillow violates his self-ownership. This much is uncontroversial. *Activating the asphyxiation-machine* earlier described, whatever its status concerning a violation of self-ownership, is an action that *is morally equivalent with the nurse smothering her patient with a pillow.*[24] To see this moral equivalence, imagine that the nefarious nurse gained access to the asphyxiation-machine and fiddled with the settings such that it would render air unbreathable only within the space of a hospital room rather than the normal mile range. If the nurse activates the machine in the room of her disagreeable patient, then her action is no morally different than if she had smothered her patient with a pillow. Her actions, down to even the method of killing her patient by means of asphyxiation, are morally equivalent with one another.

If someone is committed to the view that it is morally wrong for the nurse to smother her patient because, for example, such an action violates the self-ownership of her patient, then they must also be committed to the view that the nurse's use of the asphyxiation-machine to kill her patient is also (equally) morally wrong. The only way to avoid this result is to find some feature that morally distinguishes the cases from each another, but this seems extremely unlikely. The nurse who kills her patient with the asphyxiation-machine did so by *using natural resources*; if the nurse had smothered her patient with a pillow, she would have killed her patient by *using a pillow and his body*. Thus, if someone is drawn to the view that the nurse acts wrongly by activating the machine and this follows as morally equivalent with the view that the nurse acted wrongly by smothering her patient with a pillow, then they ought to be committed to the view that the use of natural resources *can* have moral implications on par with the use of another's body. This is an important finding because it suggests that anyone who endorses self-ownership in a non-controversial case such as smothering an agent must also endorse the view that the use of natural resources can have moral implications on par with those of self-ownership, even if they reject the idea that self-ownership includes a right to access the self.

The above appeal to moral equivalency also suggests that self-ownership, even absent the right to access the self, implies restrictions on the moral power to appropriate. Just as the nefarious nurse is not at liberty to smother her patient with a pillow, she likewise (given the moral equivalency of the actions) lacks the moral power to appropriate all the breathable air in her patient's immediate vicinity and exclude him from using it. A commitment to self-ownership itself, either by appealing to the right to access the self or the moral equivalency maintained above, excludes as implausible the position that *no* moral conditions govern the use or appropriation of natural resources from the commons.

The important takeaway point from the discussion in the last section of this chapter is that self-ownership itself has moral implications concerning the use of natural resources within the commons, and the appropriation of these resources from the commons. An agent, for instance, is prohibited from using or appropriating natural resources in a fashion that impedes another from accessing her self or the moral equivalent of accessing her self. A commitment to self-ownership places restrictions on the acceptable range of answers that can be given to the questions: (1) what moral conditions govern the use of natural resources within the commons and (2) what moral conditions govern the appropriation of natural resources from the commons? The next chapter is devoted to this first question, while the chapter following it tackles the second question.

NOTES

1. Christman, *The Myth of Property*, 19.
2. Steiner, *An Essay on Rights*, 93.
3. The best candidate of a non-property right would be the right that a certain states of affairs obtain. I doubt that this is a good candidate, but it is probably the best possible candidate of a non-property right. For instance, an agent might have a right that it rain, or not rain, tomorrow. Such a right need not correspond with the way in that another agent use or not use her body. One could try to make the case that a farmer has the right that it rain because he deserves a good rain after the work he has put into the field. Such a right is not a property right. I thank Peter Vallentyne for bringing this example to my attention.
4. For an account of squatter's rights, particularly in England, *see* Peter Jones, "Private Property and Public Order: The Hippy Convoy and Criminal Trespass," *Journal of Law and Society* 13 (1986): 343-370.
5. Typically, in order to be afforded any protection of legally recognized property rights, a squatter must establish that she has permanently lived at a residence for some long period of time, sometimes many years.
6. For am excellent discussion of adverse possession see Carol Rose, *Property and Persuasion*, 14-16.
7. Christman draws the distinction between income-ownership and control-ownership in part by appealing to the distinction made by P.J. Proudhon between "the right to increase" and "possession."
8. Christman, *The Myth of Property*, 128.
9. Ibid., 130
10. Ibid., 128.
11. Ibid., 135-36.
12. For a news account of the story, see www.abc.net.au/news/2011-01-13/organic-farmer-to-sue-over-gm-contamination/1904328
13. Lindsey Konkel, "The Great Escape: Gene-Altered Crops Grow Wild," *Environmental Health Services* (January 27, 2012) www.environmentalhealthnews.org/ehs/news/2012/gm-crops-escape-and-grow-wild
14. Ibid.
15. Some farmers establish physical barriers around genetically modified crops as an attempt to prevent the unwanted "drift" of genetically modified materials.
16. One might view this tension in ownership rights as some evidence for the claim that full private ownership over natural resources or full self-ownership are conceptually impossible. But, harkening back to a discussion in chapter 3, this would be a mistake that depends upon confusing the content of a right with the stringency of a right. The tension that exists between a right of access property and a right to exclude others will, at most, only show that absolutely stringent conceptions of full ownership or full self-ownership are problematic.
17. The issues surrounding the extent to which an agent may unilaterally use the property of another in order to access her property are complex. Michael Hartsock, for instance, has asked whether it would be permissible for a farmer to drive a combine over another's property if it were the only feasible way to access her privately owned land that had the extant or planned use of farming. The case is difficult because the combine could have the potential to seriously damage the property of another. My general approach to the combine case is to say that such unilateral use of another's property is permissible so long as it allows access to an extant use and the agent doing the accessing fully compensates the owner of property used as an access route.
18. Eric Mack, "The Self-Ownership Proviso: A New and Improved Lockean Proviso," *Social Philosophy and Policy* 12 (1995): 186-218, offers a similar suggestion. Mack maintains

in the above-referenced work that self-ownership affords agents what he deems "world interactive powers." These world interactive powers, which Mack argues follow from self-ownership, offer agents moral protections against others from interfering with their ability to exercise effective self-ownership and interact with the world. My suggestion here, instead, is that the formal rights of self-ownership include the claim right against others not to impede access to the self in whatever form that takes.

19. For a thought-provoking discussion of prosthetic body parts and self-ownership, see Samuel Wheeler, "Natural Property Rights as Body Rights," *Nous* 16 (1980): 171-193.

20. This language of being able to pick up and eat a grape or raisin without smashing it is taken from Dean Kamen's 2007 TED talk. Kamen was directly responsible for developing the actual advanced prosthetic technology discussed here. His talk can be found at www.ted.com/talks/dean_kamen_previews_a_new_prosthetic_arm.html.

21. Of course, there are cases in which an agent no longer has the requisite control over a detachable body part, and as such the prosthetic body part that was once part of her self no longer is. For instance, if an agent sells a prosthetic body part to another person and has no connection with the part for a number of years or even a number of days, then the body part that was once part of her self plausibly fails to be so after the sale. I thank Peter Vallentyne for bringing this example to my attention.

22. Vallentyne, "Left-Libertarianism: A—Primer," 5.

23. For an excellent discussion of the relationship between homelessness and property rights see Jeremy Waldron, "Homelessness and the Issue of Freedom," *U.C.L.A Law Review* 39 (1991): 295-324.

24. Note here that the example of the asphyxiation machine does not tread on the debate concerning the controversial suggestion that killing and letting die are morally equivalent. Both the use of the asphyxiation machine and smothering someone with a pillow are both clearly instances of killing. An important seminal work on the distinction between killing and letting die is James Rachels's, "Passive and Active Euthanasia" *New England Journal of Medicine* 292 (1975): 78-80.

Chapter Five

The Use of Natural Resources Within the Commons

In this chapter, I offer a Lockean left-libertarian account of the moral conditions that govern the use of natural resources within the commons. I begin this task by drawing an analogy between the commons and a public library. With a few modifications, the public library stands out as a promising way to model the commons and how they ought to be treated. Then I defend the idea that Locke's proviso on appropriation (the duty of appropriators of natural resources from the commons to leave others "enough and as good") ought to be applied to use of natural resources within the commons—that is, I defend the claim that users of natural resources within the commons have a duty to leave others "enough and as good." The same reasons for applying Locke's proviso to the appropriation of natural resources from the commons work equally well for thinking that the proviso ought to also encompass the use of natural resources within the commons. I then conclude the chapter with a formalized account of the Lockean Proviso that offers a clear interpretation of the idea that users of natural resources within the commons have a duty to leave others enough and as good.

The commons, as discussed earlier, are the set of all natural resources that belong to everyone in some shared fashion. All agents, that is, possess an initial equal moral claim in respect to natural resources. A full defense of this claim was made in the first chapter. But it is not obvious what moral conditions concerning the use of natural resources within the commons follow from this initial position of equality in respect to the commons. To begin the evaluation of what moral conditions govern the use of natural resources within the commons, we can look to a familiar, maybe unexpected, comparable case—the public library. Considering how a public library addresses its primary concern of how to share goods held in common (books) is not meant to definitvely settle the broader question of what moral conditions govern the use of natural resources within the commons. The hope, instead, is that such a comparison will serve as a familiar way to animate the idea of the commons and hint in the right direction of an answer to our broader question concerning the moral conditions governing the use of natural resources within the commons.

A public library establishes rules governing how agents may use books that belong to everyone in some shared common fashion. This is analogous, in many ways, to the task of establishing the moral conditions governing how agents may use natural resources that likewise belong to everyone in some shared common fashion. The basic question confronting the library administrators—what types of rules ought to govern the use of things that belong to everyone in some shared sense—is essentially the same question this chapter tries to address; the only difference is that library administrators are concerned with books and the concern of this chapter is with natural resources. Natural resources within the commons, with some modifications, can be thought of as analogous to books within a public library. These modifications to help draw a tighter analogy between natural resources and books will be made as needed, but to get going with the idea, imagine the commons as a library in which the library books represent natural resources.

Books and natural resources share a number of important features. Some books, just like some natural resources, will be more sought after or desirable (and more valuable) than others. An agent, or agents generally, might, for instance, find certain books to be more useful and applicable to meeting the needs of everyday life than others. In a geographical area where agents are homesteading, a book about how to set up basic plumbing is more likely to be sought after than a biography about an obscure poet. Timber, likewise, that can be used to construct a cabin will be more useful to a homesteader than wildflowers, although the wildflowers could be more useful than timber to an agent who has no need for timber and loves the smell of wildflowers.

Some books, aside from their practical utility, will simply be more enjoyable to read than others. Of course, whether a book is enjoyable is, in part, a subjective matter, but it is also no coincidence that certain authors sell millions of books tc a very diverse set of readers, suggesting that the feature of "being an enjoyable read" probably has an objective component as well. The same can be said about natural resources. Some natural resources will generally be more enjoyable for agents to use than others. For most agents, though of course not all, a vacation to an oceanfront spot is more enjoyable than a trip to the frozen tundra.

The overlapping preferences that agents have for books (assuming a limited supply) will likely mean that not everyone can use the books in the exact way that they would desire. The library might have two copies of *Oliver Twist*, but at any given time six agents (or more) could desire to use the book.

The book is a rivalrous good in that its use or consumption by one agent prevents another from also using or consuming the good at the same time.[1] An agent, likewise, cannot occupy a coveted spot of land under a shade tree on a hot day for as long as she pleases without potentially interfering with a similar desire on the part of other agent(s). An agent's use of a spot of land by standing on it excludes others from using the spot. In a strict sense, when use is taken to mean physical impingement, all instances of using a physical object such as natural resources will, in at least some limited fashion, prevent another from using or accessing the object.

In order to take seriously the idea that the books belong to everyone, some rules need to be established to govern how the books may be used. These rules ought to strive to ensure that all agents are able to share the benefits conferred by the books. These rules, however, should be constrained by the self-ownership of agents. Those who read at a slower rate than others do not have a claim-right against faster readers to read to them—this would violate the self-ownership of the faster readers. Slower readers, however, could have a claim-right against others that allow for longer check-out times of books or other measures that allow them to derive some sort of equal opportunity to benefit from the books that belong to everyone. If an agent cannot read at all, then she might still be able to benefit from the books that she shares with everyone by renting or selling others "her share of time" or "her access" to the books.

If agents are at liberty to use the books in any way that they desire—that is, agents lack any claim-rights in respect to how others use the books—then presumably the first agents to get to the books will likely hoard or monopolize the books that agents generally feel are more useful, enjoyable, or otherwise valuable. They could monopolize only the books about obscure poets, but I would not count on it. With no rules governing the use of the books, these agents could then hand the books they grabbed first over to their children, and their children could do the same and so forth, or they could share these most valuable books only among their circle of friends. This, of course, leaves others and their descendants who were not first to grab the books from the library shelf shut out from any benefit derived from the books that others have monopolized. If an actual library operated in this fashion, agents would rightfully be outraged. The moral problem here is that agents are being denied *any* benefit from books that belong to them no less than the agents doing the monopolizing who derive *all* the benefit from the books. The monopolization of the books disregards the initial equal moral claim that all agents have in respect to the books.

As a starting point, we can say that all agents have a liberty right to use the books in a fashion that does not deprive others of some (to be clarified) fair and equal opportunity to benefit from the books. That is to say, under at least certain moral conditions, no agent has a claim that another agent not use a book that everyone shares. We can quickly rule out the idea that the books are jointly-owned by everyone. In the case of joint-ownership all joint-owners would be private owners of the books, and consistent with the rights of private ownership discussed in chapter 4, would have a claim right against others from using the books without their permission. A single agent would have a right to exclude others, potentially all others, from using the books by simply denying others permission to use the books.

If the books are jointly-owned, then one cantankerous, or just plain mean, agent could simply continually deny others permission to use any of the books. Of course, others could then exercise their rights as a joint-owner and deny this cranky agent permission to use the books, and a tit-for-tat would likely ensue. The books could go dusty on the shelves and be wasted because one agent, or a very small minority of agents, decided to prevent others from using the books. This is an unacceptable result if the books do in fact belong to everyone in some shared sense. The joint-ownership of the books is an implausible way to think about the initial normative status of the books, because it confers an agent with the right to exclude others (potentially everyone) from *any* use of *all* the books for any reason.

The implausibility of thinking of natural resources as initially jointly-owned by everyone is even more stark. If natural resources were initially jointly-owned, then one agent could prevent everyone else from using any natural resources including breathable air, water, food, or any other natural resources required to subsist by simply denying others permission to use these resources which she jointly-owns. This absurd result renders the joint-ownership of natural resources wildly implausible.[2] Agents do not need the permission of others to use, in a fair and equal fashion, natural resources from the commons.

The potential for one agent to exclude others from (all) the books under a scheme of joint-ownership has the same negative ramifications as the empirical exclusion that results when the first to get to the books grabs them up and refuses to let others use them. In *both* cases, others are not able to use the books from which they are excluded. The only substantial difference is that in the case of joint-ownership the excluded agent, being a joint-owner herself, can fire a similar shot and prevent others from using the books as well, but preventing others from a meal does not fill one's belly, and an envious agent might be prepared to go hungry just so long as others were hungry as well.

As opposed to being jointly-owned, it is much more plausible to think of the books as commonly owned. Under a system of common ownership, all agents have a liberty to use books, within some limits of fair use, without needing the permission of anyone. No agent has a claim against another that she not use a book, within some limits of fair use. An agent, then, would not need to get the permission of others in order to take a book from a shelf of shared books and browse through it.

Libraries have devised some very reasonable ways to set rules (constraints) on the fair use of books. An agent, for instance, can check out a book and use it for some extended time, but she must return the book in the same condition that she took it within a designated due date so that others can gain access to and benefit from the book. If the agent fails to abide by these standards of fair use, then she must pay a fine that presumably helps with library expenses and adds new books to the collection. A library fine for an overdue or damaged book can be thought of as a way to compensate others for the unfair use of a book. This method of simply "taking turns" with a desired thing marks one way in which commonly owned things can be fairly shared. Libraries also often enforce a limit on the total number of books that an agent can borrow at any one time, usually some fairly high number such as fifty books. This prevents any agent from borrowing so many books that others are *generally deprived* of an opportunity to use the books that belong to everyone.

If no one wants to use a book that an agent has checked out, then she may renew or extend the due date for the book until another agent desires to use the book. There is no good reason that an agent should be barred from continuing to use or exclusively possess a book that another does not want to use. Of course, actual libraries often place some arbitrary limit on the number times that a book can be remotely renewed so that the library can verify that the book has not been lost or damaged. If an agent desires to use a book that another has checked out, then she can reserve the book and stake out her place in line to use the book once it is her turn.

There will be occasions when an agent uses a book in a way that destroys or seriously degrades the book and in so doing deprives others of an opportunity or affords others a reduced opportunity to use and benefit from the book. A book, for instance, could be burned in protest, or it could carelessly be left outside and destroyed by rain. When an agent destroys or seriously degrades a book that is commonly owned, she owes a duty to others who have the same moral stake in the book as she does to replace the book. When replacing the book is not a feasible option, the agent who destroyed or otherwise prevented others from benefitting from the book owes others a payment of some sort to offset the injury that she has caused them. The injury results from the taking of another's effective liberty to use something that belongs, in some shared fashion, to her. This idea is similar to what motivates pressure on logging companies to plant trees that "replace" the trees they have removed. I am skeptical that many re-foresting efforts actually offset the injury caused by the original de-forestation, but that is the idea at least.

A library might also have a "special collections" room where they keep books that are too valuable to lend out for ordinary use and check-out from the library. In some cases, agents might be restricted to using these books within the confines of the library, perhaps even in a room that is under surveillance. Some books might be completely off limits for agents to use at all (except those specially trained to handle or restore these very valuable books) so that they may be preserved for as long as possible. This is similar to the idea of restricting or completely curtailing the use of environmentally fragile areas or placing such restrictions on the use of lands that hold special cultural, religious, or historical significance.

The analogy between books and natural resources thus far has not dealt with the perishable (subject to spoiling) or consumable nature of certain natural resources. This is because books are not normally perishable or consumable goods, although a book is perishable in the sense that even with the most carefully use a book will eventually wither away and become unusable. A book can be shared many times between many different agents before it is destroyed or significantly degraded, and this allows a "check-out" taking-turns-style system to generally work quite well in the case of books.

But this check-out-style system of sharing will not work for many natural resources. This is because many natural resources are either perishable or have a value that is almost completely (sometimes completely) used up after one or just a few uses. Take an apple, for instance. It is both perishable and consumable. If no one uses an apple, then it spoils and goes to waste. It cannot sit on a shelf and wait to be used for an indefinitely long time like a book. The apple can be physically divided among agents to share before a meal, but when an agent eats (consumes) the apple or part of the apple, her use excludes everyone else from deriving benefit from the consumed part of the apple.

With some modifications, it is possible to imagine books that are perishable or consumable. All books are perishable as eventually they physically deteriorate, but to relate this better with many natural resources that perish very quickly we can imagine that books perish at a very quick rate. We could imagine, for instance, that the *only* paper available to construct books withers away after two months from the date the book is printed. The book is a perishable good that must be read (used) quickly or else it goes to waste.

To envision how a book could be consumable, imagine that the words of a book disappear once they are read. An agent "mentally consumes" a book as she reads through its pages. If two (or more) agents try to read the book by passing it around they quickly become frustrated because the book's words disappear as soon they are read, either aloud or silently, by anyone. The only workaround that has been discovered to this problem is for an agent(s) to read the book aloud within ear shot of others, but this method usually proves too cumbersome for all but the most exciting or useful books. The result of reading the book is analogous with eating an apple—the value of each is completely used up by the agent who consumes the good.

The nature of perishable or consumable books does not change their being commonly owned goods that belong to everyone. But these types of books, given their nature, cannot be adequately shared with a check-out-style method. It is impractical for everyone to be given some type of equal and fair chance to use these types of books with a rotation scheme of sharing. The only option to the exclusion of some from the book is the universal non-use of the book, clearly a bad option since universal non-use excludes *everyone*, as opposed to *some*, from the benefits of the book. The challenge of some being excluded from the book is not solved by maintaining that "if some agents cannot use the book then no agents can."

One promising way to address the challenge presented by perishable or consumable goods that belong to everyone is to say that agents have rights against others who use such goods in respect to *the value of* these goods, but that fair use, given the nature of the thing being used, does not demand that others leave some share of the physical good itself for future use(s) by others. An agent, for instance, could have a claim-right in respect to the mentally consumable book that another not use the book *unless* she pays others for the value that she has taken from the book that belongs to everyone. An agent (all agents) would still plausibly have a liberty right to use the mentally consumable book without needing the permission of anyone, provided that she make a payment to others to offset the value of the commonly owned book that she has taken with her use. The form that such payments might take is a complex question that will have to wait until later in this chapter.

Admittedly, there are a number of various ideas bouncing around from the analogy drawn between a public library and the commons concerning the moral conditions governing the use of commonly owned things that have yet to find a clear focus. One helpful way to solidify this focus is by appealing to the position coined as the *Lockean Proviso* by Robert Nozick and maintained by Locke, that *appropriators* of natural resources must "*leave enough and as good*" for others.[3] The Lockean Proviso has found widespread support among many contemporary libertarian-minded political philosophers on both the right and left. For example, Robert Nozick, a right-libertarian; Hillel Steiner, a Georgist left-libertarian; and Michael Otsuka, an equal opportunity for welfare left-libertarian all endorse and make central to their respective treatments of justice some version of the Lockean Proviso.[4]

Traditionally, the Lockean Proviso has only been thought of as a duty owed by those who appropriate natural resources from the commons—this is, after all, what Locke had in mind—and not treated as a way to think about the duty owed by those who use natural resources within the commons. Shortly it will become clear that the duty to "leave enough and as good" for others is not only owed by appropriators of natural resources from the commons but by users of natural resources within the commons as well. Before delving into that topic, it is worth taking stock in the idea that leaving others "enough and as good" nicely encapsulates and ties together nearly all (if not all) preliminary efforts to describe what an agent must do in order to fairly use a thing that is held in common.

Locke's proviso on appropriation represents a clear concern with the potentially harmful and inegalitarian implications of appropriation, a concern that we shall shortly see applies equally well to use. Locke, for example, writing about the moral conditions governing appropriation from the commons in which natural resources are *not scarce*, says, "Nor was this appropriation of any parcel of land by improving it any prejudice to any other man, since there was still enough and as good left, and more than the yet unprovided could use."[5] The clear implication for Locke is that if an agent engaged in an appropriation that did not leave others enough and as good, then others would be prejudiced by such an appropriation. It is in virtue of the fact that an appropriation leaves others enough and as good that it does not serve to prejudice others. Locke continues, again operating under an assumption in which natural resources in the commons are *not scarce*, by noting:

> So that, in effect, there was never the less left for others because of his enclosure for himself; for *he that leaves as much as another can make use of does as good as take nothing at all.* Nobody could think himself injured by the drinking of another man, though he took a good draught, who had the whole water of the same river left to quinch his thirst; and the case of land and water, where there is enough for both, is perfectly the same (emphasis mine).[6]

Notice that while Locke directs his proviso toward appropriation, the measure by which he suggests we ought to assess whether an appropriation injures or prejudices others is directed toward the extent to which others can *make use of what is left* after an appropriation is made.

Locke's thought is powerful because it points directly toward the conditions in which an agent could legitimately claim that another's appropriation of natural resources from the commons is morally objectionable. Such a claim, for Locke, is directly related with limiting the opportunity of others to *use what is left* in the commons after an appropriation is made. The drinking of water from a river does not clearly injure anyone since there is an "as *good*" abundant amount of water still *left* for everyone else *to use*. But, alternatively, if an agent were to siphon all the water from the river and deprive others of any opportunity to make use of the water, such an action would be morally objectionable because it would deprive others of "as good" an opportunity to make use of what was left in the commons. Locke's brief discussion of leaving others enough and as good offers the important insight that the appropriation of natural resources from the commons can prejudice or injure others by restricting their ability and opportunity to "make use of" the commons.

Locke's proviso on appropriation also coheres nicely with his insistence that agents have an equal and independent moral status. If agents are allowed to take natural resources from the commons with no regard for what they leave others, then the independent status of some agents is placed in serious jeopardy because of unequal taking from the commons. Henry George's astute example of one hundred men trapped on an island in which one of them privately owns all the land on the island nicely demonstrates that a lack of natural resources, brought about by a violation of the Lockean Proviso, can clearly serve to subjugate an agent to the dominion of another.

Consider that historically the lack of access to (natural) resources has also subjected agents to the political will or dominion of others at the ballot box. Prior to the mid- to late-nineteenth century, only private property owners could vote in most elections in the United States and most other places in the world that held elections. This is because voting was once done openly and not by secret ballot—this did not change in most parts of the United States until late in the nineteenth century. The fear was that landlords would pressure their tenants to vote in a certain way under threat of eviction or other retaliatory action. This fear was not unfounded as open voting does render an agent susceptible to retaliatory action. The issues surrounding the virtue of a secret ballot versus an open ballot or vice versa are complicated; my point here is that the deprivation of some to natural resources made them especially vulnerable to the intimidation of others (such as their landlord) during open voting and that this vulnerability was used as justification to deny those without private property (usually taken to mean land) the opportunity to vote.[7]

Despite the appeal of the Lockean Proviso, it has been criticized on the grounds that it is impossible or virtually impossible to fulfill. This criticism is developed from the idea that the duty to leave others enough and as good is owed to both extant agents as well as future generations of agents. Given that there is an indefinitely endless supply of future generations it is simply implausible to suggest that agents could ever leave enough and as good for others, without perhaps making tremendous sacrifices. The concern seems most pressing when we grant a finite amount of non-renewable natural resources and an infinite number of future generations.

The philosophical issues concerning future generations are complex, and it would be too much of a divergence to discuss them in depth. How could it be that duties are owed to an agent who does not yet exist? It is puzzling. But despite the puzzle I grant that agents can owe duties to those who do not yet exist. Simply avoiding the worry by denying that duties can be owed to agents who are yet to be born is not a very palatable option.

The threat to the Lockean Proviso brought about an acknowledgment of duties owed to future generations is not as much trouble as it might first appear. In place of offering a full-fledged account of how to align the Lockean Proviso with duties toward future generations, instead consider the following effective "patch" suggested by Alan Tomhave.[8] Grant that agents have a duty to leave enough and as good to the generation of agents directly following them. Also, grant that a generation spans roughly twenty years. Those who are sixty must leave enough and as good for those who are forty, those who are forty must leave enough and as good for those who are twenty, and those who are twenty must leave enough and as good for those who are very young. If the focus is geared toward leaving enough and as good for the generation that proceeds, then adherence to the Lockean Proviso leaves for future generations in a way that is not overly burdensome. Although this suggestion is only a patch and not a full-fledged solution, it offers good reason to suggest that a concern with duties toward future generations does not spell doom for the Lockean Proviso. In fact, it is difficult to see how the Lockean Proviso, or something close to it, would not play a major role in a robust account of the duties that are owed to future generations.

The application of the Lockean Proviso to cover *only* the appropriation of natural resources from the commons and exclude the proviso from the use of unappropriated natural resources fails to appreciate that the same reasons to think that an appropriation can prejudice or injury, others—and in so doing threaten their moral status as equal and independent—can apply equally well to the use of a natural resource. To see this, consider that an appropriation *only* has the potential to harm others (in the ways Locke and others are right to be concerned with) because, among other moral rights, it affords an appropriator a moral claim (right) against others from *using* a natural resource without the appropriator's permission. But actually it is *always* an empirical use of (or the actual exclusion of others from using) natural resources, and never strictly speaking an appropriation *per se*, that injures or harms other(s). As such, the moral concerns surrounding appropriation are *really* at core, for the most part, concerns about the implications that appropriation has toward how agents empirically use and exclude others from using. Once this is acknowledged, it is not difficult to see that an agent may use an unappropriated natural resource and harm another in every bit the same (or even worse) ways *than if* she had appropriated the resource.

Further, given that appropriation is the exercise of a moral power by *coming to* privately own a natural resource that *initially belonged to everyone*, it is imperative to first uncover the moral conditions that govern how agents may use natural resources before uncovering what conditions govern any alternation (such as appropriation) to this initial status. This is because the moral conditions that govern the way agents may use unappropriated natural resources may well set limits or otherwise impact the moral conditions governing how unappropriated resources may become appropriated. In this way, the moral conditions governing the way in which agents may use unappropriated resources has a primacy or priority over the moral conditions governing the appropriation of natural resources. The Lockean Proviso, luckily, serves as a helpful guide to begin the process of ascertaining the moral conditions that govern the use of unappropriated natural resources.

I shall now proceed to consider a number of cases that motivate the plausibility of extending Locke's proviso on appropriation to the use of natural resources within the commons. The cases are meant to demonstrate that those who *use* natural resources within the commons have a duty to leave others enough and as good.

As a cautionary note, agents in the cases to be described might also be accused of violating the self-ownership rights of others, especially if self-ownership is taken to include the right of an agent against others from impeding her from accessing her self. Thus a shrewd observer might ask: why worry with cases that try to show the Lockean Proviso ought to apply to the use of natural resources within the commons when the morally problematic use of natural resources can be dealt with by appealing to self-ownership?

This is a fair question, and a number of replies are due. First, it could be that the impermissibility of some (or all) of the actions given in the cases to follow are overdetermined. That is to say that the actions depicting the use of unappropriated natural resources are unjust for two reasons—because they violate self-ownership and because they fail to leave others enough and as good. This would be an important finding even if it is the case that self-ownership rights can be invoked to show the impermissibility of some (or even all) of the action(s) in the forthcoming cases. Second, the cases to be presented are admittedly somewhat sensational to leave little doubt that the Lockean Proviso should be applied to the use of natural resources within the commons. It would not be difficult to develop less sensational cases where no plausible conception of self-ownership could possibly apply, yet the Lockean Proviso would still very plausibly govern the use of natural resources within the commons.

Third, the conception of self-ownership that I defended in the previous chapter (inclusive of the right to access the self) is controversial and could be rejected in favor of a different conception of self-ownership, or the right to access the self might be endorsed but given a different account than what was proposed. If so, then someone who defends a version of self-ownership (say, without the right to access the self) likely will not think that some or all of the forthcoming cases describe violations of self-ownership at all. Lastly and perhaps most importantly, a reader of this work might be sympathetic with the idea of the Lockean Proviso but reject self-ownership outright. This reader, skeptical of self-ownership, is invited to read the below cases as instances that speak to the plausibility of applying the Lockean Proviso to the use of unappropriated natural resources within the commons without concern for any potential role of self-ownership. The application of the Lockean

Proviso to the use of unappropriated natural resource does not depend upon the endorsement of any thesis about self-ownership.

Now, onward to cases that demonstrate the Lockean Proviso ought to apply to the use of unappropriated natural resources. In all the cases below, assume that agents are acting within the commons and that unless otherwise specified no natural resources have been appropriated.

DESTRUCTIVE USE

Consider the case of Toxic Jack and Sarah. Both agents share, within conditions of common use, a life-sustaining spring of fresh water. Toxic Jack decides, for the fun of it, to empty toxic sludge into the spring and thereby ruin the water source that is necessary to sustain both his and Sarah's lives. It is plausible that Toxic Jack transgresses a duty he owes to Sarah when he *uses* the spring they share, within conditions of common use, in this destructive fashion. Sarah, plausibly, has a claim against Toxic Jack, that he not use the spring in this destructive fashion. If this suggestion is correct, then agents have claims against others from *using* unappropriated natural resources in, at least certain, destructive ways.

Here it is worth noting that *consuming* natural resources is a type of destructive use. When, for example, Sarah consumes an apple by eating it, she engages in a type of destructive use. She engages in an action that destroys the apple. The consumption of natural resources can be as morally problematic as other types of destructive use. After all, it doesn't matter to others if Sarah destroys a natural resource by consuming it or by destroying it in some other fashion—in either event, the natural resource has been used in a fashion that deprives others from gaining (any) benefit or value from the resource. Of course, the scope of destructive use matters here. If Toxic Jack destroys an entire apple tree by poisoning it, he has harmed others much more than if he had simply consumed one apple.[9] Toxic Jack, however, has not clearly harmed others more by destroying an apple by polluting it rather than simply consuming the apple by eating it.

DEGRADING USE

Closely related to destructive use is *degrading use*. When an agent engages in the degrading use of an unappropriated natural resource, she uses in a fashion that reduces the value of the resource without destroying it even partially. Imagine, for example, that Toxic Jack doesn't destroy the spring but instead pollutes the spring with a chemical that ensures Sarah will become seriously ill whenever she drinks from the spring. Toxic Jack's polluting use, while not sufficient to destroy the spring, degrades the value of the spring. We should still, I maintain, rightly suspect that Toxic Jack violates a duty he owes to Sarah by dumping this less-than-lethal chemical into the spring. Acts of morally problematic use need not destroy, or remove *all* value from, a natural resource in order to invoke concerns of justice.

OVERUSE

Aside from concerns of destructive use and degrading use, considerations of *overuse* also give us good reason to suspect that users of unappropriated natural resources have a duty to adhere to the Lockean Proviso. The overuse of a natural resource generally occurs when an agent disproportionately uses, to the exclusion of others, the resource in question. Consider a scenario with Paranoid Bill and Mark. Both must touch an energy stone (a natural resource) once a day for ten seconds in order to survive. Paranoid Bill is first to grab the stone, but he refuses to share the stone with Mark for any length of time. Being stronger than Mark, Paranoid Bill holds on to the stone because he is paranoid and thinks that Mark will run off with the stone, and Mark perishes as he is unable to touch the stone. This case provides us with good reason to suspect that Paranoid Bill does not have the right to use the energy stone in any monopolistic fashion he pleases. This is because Mark, plausibly, has a claim against Paranoid Bill from overusing the stone that they share within the commons. Of course, the issue of what counts as overuse is complex, but it seems clear that there is some relevant sense in which an agent can overuse an unappropriated natural resource.

RESTRICTIVE USE

In addition to concerns of destructive use, degrading use, and overuse, cases of *restrictive use* also lend good reason to suspect that users of unappropriated natural resources have a duty to abide by the Lockean Proviso. Restrictive use generally occurs when an agent takes an action that prevents or blocks others from using either a particular natural resource or a broader set of such resources. There are at least two different types of restrictive use, *general access-restricting use* and *specific access-restricting use*. I shall consider each of these types of restrictive use in turn.

To illustrate general access-restricting use, consider a scenario, borrowed from Eric Mack,[10] with Wally Wall Builder and Jon. Wally Wall Builder enjoys, as a hobby, building impenetrable walls around others without their knowledge or permission. While Jon is in a sound sleep, Wally Wall Builder builds, without touching Jon, a forty-foot-tall six-foot-by-six-foot wall around him. Jon awakes to find that he is trapped with no possible way to escape from the walled structure. Wally's wall-building (an instance of his using natural resources) is morally problematic because his use of unappropriated natural resources *restricts* Jon's ability to *generally use* unappropriated natural resources which they share within conditions of common use. Wally's particular use of natural resources imposes a physical bar against Jon from enjoying the benefit and value of natural resources generally. He violates a duty owed to Jon to use unappropriated natural resources in a way that leaves Jon enough and as good. This is why, among perhaps other moral reasons, Jon has a legitimate moral claim against Wally that he not use unappropriated natural resources in this particular wall-building fashion.

Consider a revision to the access-restricting use case involving Wally Wall Builder and Jon. Earlier it was stipulated that *all* natural resources in this case were unappropriated and, as such, held in conditions of common use. Let us relax this assumption and suppose that Wally Wall Builder has appropriated the natural resources that he uses to build the wall around Jon. Wally has appropriated the naturally occurring bricks, clay to seal the bricks, and any other natural resources needed to build the wall around Jon. (Here one could argue that such an appropriation would be impossible because in such a case Wally would fail to meet the moral conditions of appropriation such as abiding by the Lockean Proviso, but for the sake of argument let us put this worry aside.) Assume no other natural resources in the world have been appropriated by anyone except these wall-building materials. What should be said then? Here, spelling out the exact content of the moral duties involved is important. If the duty under consideration is the duty that Wally leave others (Jon) enough and as good when he uses *unappropriated* natural resources, then Wally is not violating *this duty* by building the wall with his appropriated resources. Wally has, in this case, *appropriated* the wall-building material and, as such, cannot be said to be using *unappropriated* natural resources in a way that fails to leave Jon enough and as good because he is not using any unappropriated natural resources to build the wall.

Recall from earlier that no one has any greater initial moral claim to unappropriated natural resources than anyone else. The blocking or restriction of access to unappropriated natural resources, as is made clear in both the original Wally case and the revised Wally case, can be done by means of using either unappropriated or appropriated natural resources. Wally violated a plausible duty owed to Jon by blocking his fair and equal access to unappropriated natural resources regardless of whether or not Wally privately owns the instruments he uses to block Jon's access. This situation is comparable with conflicts over beach access rights along coastal areas. In many instances, agents are not able to legally own beachfront along the Pacific Coast in the United States. Legal ownership rights normally begin at some distance, typically somewhere between twenty-five to one hundred feet, from the water. The actual beachfront is often legally (and plausibly morally) an unappropriated natural resource for all to use and enjoy in some shared fashion. But often agents who purchase land with direct access to the beachfront make attempts to restrict the access of others to beachfront land that is adjacent to their private property. Such attempts are efforts to block others from using unappropriated natural resources by means of an appropriated natural resource. Issues of blocking access are complicated, particularly when we bring in right-of-way considerations. Does, for instance, a person have an obligation to allow another to cross into her property in order to gain access to unappropriated natural resources? Legitimate concerns of right-of-way aside, there is a relevant sense in which a plausible violation of moral duty has occurred by blocking the access of an agent to use unappropriated natural resources that belong just as much to her as they do anyone else. This violation of duty does not depend on whether the blocking was done by means of an appropriated (privately owned) or unappropriated resource.

To illustrate specific access-restricting use, consider a case involving Hiding Helen and Bob. Hiding Helen doesn't build impenetrable walls around Bob; instead she hides, in a very effective fashion, the most valuable natural resources from him. When Bob goes to sleep, Hiding Helen uses the very valuable natural resources, and before Bob awakes she hides the resources before he has a chance to use them. The natural resources that Helen hides are non-renewable resources, and she rightly fears that if she shares the resources with Bob, then the value of the resources will be depleted more quickly and, as such, she will be able to enjoy less benefit from the resources she hides.

Some might suspect that specific access-restricting use is a less serious concern than general access-restricting use, but this is not necessarily the case. Hiding Helen could, for example, restrict Bob's use of a particular unappropriated natural resource by hiding an energy stone which he needs to touch once a day in order to survive or, in a more realistic case, a nutritionally rich food source. Helen is using in such a way that is designed to remove Bob's effective liberty to use unappropriated natural resources. More specifically, Helen is gaining an advantage by hiding natural resource *at Bob's expense. Helen's hiding actions create a loss for Bob that she directly benefits from.* The less that Bob uses the natural resources that Helen hides, the more that she gets to use them. Helen clearly gains from Bob's expense that she brought about. Neither Helen nor Bob, keep in mind, have any greater initial claim to unappropriated natural resources. When Helen uses unappropriated resources in a hiding fashion and in turn restricts Bob's access to these resources that he has the same initial moral claim to as Helen, she harms Bob in a fashion that he has a moral claim against.

The above examples illustrating cases of destructive use, degrading use, overuse, general access-restricting use, and specific access-restricting use of natural resources taken as a cumulative whole offer strong reason to think that users of unappropriated natural resources (no less than appropriators) ought to be bound by the Lockean Proviso. Agents, plausibly, have claims against others from *using*, in certain ways, unappropriated natural resources within conditions of common use. The examples given above represent cases in which an agent clearly morally prejudices or harms others by disregarding the initial equal claim that all agents have in respect to natural resources. An important common link between the cases of problematic use noted in the above examples is that they all, in different ways, represent violations of the Lockean Proviso as applied to use. One substantial way in which an agent who uses unappropriated natural resources can take seriously the initial equal claim that all agents have in respect to natural resources is to leave others enough and as good.

The morally problematic feature of appropriation that prompted Locke to suggest a proviso governing appropriation was the potential for an appropriator to injure or prejudice others by depriving them of the opportunity "to make use of" natural resources. But notice that this very *same* morally problematic feature of appropriation can be equally as problematic when we consider the *use* of unappropriated natural resources. Toxic Jack, Paranoid Bill, Wally Wall Builder, and Hiding Helen all, via their use, *removed* unappropriated natural resources. Their actions, like those of appropriators, deprived others from the opportunity "to make use of" and benefit from natural resources. It does not seem to matter, in respect to their duty to leave others enough and as good that they used, as opposed to appropriated, natural resources. To suggest that *only* appropriation can invoke a morally problematic removal of natural resources from the commons falls victim to drawing a morally arbitrary distinction between removal via appropriation and removal via use.

If this is correct, then it is the *removal,* in some sense, of unappropriated natural resources from conditions of common use, irrespective of whether this removal takes the form of an appropriation or a using, which places a moral demand on the *remover* to leave others enough and as good. Any *removal* of natural resources confers the *remover* with the duty to leave others enough and as good. It does not morally matter if the *removal* is done via an appropriation or a use of natural resources. An agent, for example, should not be able to morally evade her duty to leave others enough and as good by opting to *use*, as opposed to appropriate, unappropriated natural resources. The important moral classification should ultimately be that of *remover*, not appropriator or user. By extending the Lockean Proviso to cover cases of using unappropriated natural resources, substantial progress is made toward squarely focusing on the morally problematic feature of removing natural resources from conditions of common use. In fact, no examples come to mind in which an agent removes, in any interesting moral sense, an unappropriated natural resource without either using or appropriating the resource.

It would be quite odd to suggest that Toxic Jack owes a duty to leave Sarah enough and as good *only if* he appropriates the fresh water spring but owes her no such duty if he *merely* uses the spring in a destructive or degrading fashion. Toxic Jack's destructive use of the spring injures Sarah to at least the same degree as his appropriation of the spring. Sarah perishes either way, assuming that Toxic Jack does not grant her permission to use the spring in the case where he appropriates.

Consider again the case of Paranoid Bill and Mark. Let us imagine that Paranoid Bill decides that he would like to exercise a moral power and appropriate the energy stone that is necessary to sustain Mark's life. Anyone who endorses the Lockean Proviso would, rightly, demand that Paranoid Bill leave Mark enough and as good. If the price of this leaving is more than he is willing or able to leave, then he is barred from appropriating the energy stone. He simply cannot *remove* the energy stone from the commons unless he leaves Mark enough and as good. Quite clearly, Paranoid Bill's removal of the energy stone by means of his *overuse* is every bit as injurious to Mark than would have been his *appropriation* of the energy stone. The duty to leave others enough and as good which Paranoid Bill owes Mark is not contingent *on his means* of removing natural resources from the commons. How it is that Paranoid Bill goes about removing natural resources, by means of appropriation or use, is of no moral consequence to the duty he owes to leave Mark enough and as good.

This same reasoning works, I maintain, equally well when we consider cases of either general access-restricting use or specific access-restricting use. Wally Wall Builder (in the original and revised version) and Hiding Helen each removed natural resources from conditions of common use in a fashion that failed to leave Jon and Bob, respectively, enough and as good. Again, there is no good reason to maintain that leaving enough and as good for others is demanded by Wally Wall Builder and Hiding Helen *only if* they remove natural resources by means of appropriation. Wally and Helen acquire the moral duty to leave others enough and as good whenever they, regardless of the means they employ, remove unappropriated natural resources from the commons.

One apprehension with the idea of applying the Lockean Proviso to the use of unappropriated natural resources might be that the above examples or ones like them where it *seems* plausible to apply the proviso to use are actually *all* cases of appropriation and not use, but this thought misunderstands the nature of appropriation. The concern can be addressed by appealing to the nature of appropriation as *the exercise of a moral power*. The agents in the examples very plausibly engaged in immoral actions and, as such, cannot be said to have exercised a *moral* power. Toxic Jack, for instance, very likely exercised no moral power when he polluted the water that he shared with Sarah and, as such, cannot be said to have engaged in an appropriation at all. Toxic Jack used the shared water source, but he did not appropriate it.[11] In the next chapter, I will give specific attention to the conditions required for an agent to engage in an appropriation, but it seems implausible or at least a philosophical over-reaching to hold that *all* morally problematic cases of removing unappropriated natural resources involve an appropriation.

The suggestion that the morally problematic removal of unappropriated natural resources must always involve an appropriation seems like a desperate attempt to reserve (preserve) the Lockean Proviso to only cover cases of appropriation. There is simply no good reason to extend (contort) an understanding of the scope of appropriation to these over-stretched limits. Some, arguably many, morally problematic instances of removing unappropriated natural resources will involve use and not appropriation. As opposed to extending the conceptual bounds of appropriation to cover *all* cases of morally problematic removal, we have a more palatable solution: simply extend the Lockean Proviso to cover cases of using unappropriated natural resources.

Political philosophers have traditionally been silent about the moral conditions governing the use of unappropriated natural resources and instead focused their efforts upon analyzing the appropriation of such resources. What explains this general silence? Here, three explanations are in order.

First, as a matter of contingent fact, the use of unappropriated natural resources is often less likely than the appropriation of these resources, to remove in a (seriously) harmful fashion. To offer a simple case, the appropriation of a trail in the woods has the strong potential to disadvantage others given the exclusionary nature of appropriation, but using the trail by walking along it typically will not. By extrapolating on such cases, we can think of many instances in which using an unappropriated natural resource—for instance, when an agent uses a trail in a walking fashion—where a user's duty to leave others enough and as good is trivially, or nearly trivially, satisfied. This observation nonetheless doesn't challenge the plausibility of the claim that both appropriators and users of unappropriated natural resources have a duty to leave others enough and as good. The observation does, however, partially explain why the use of unappropriated natural resources has been, unfortunately, a generally neglected concern.

It is worth stressing the contingent nature of the empirical observation that appropriation is *typically* a more disadvantaging type of removal than use. There is no reason why the appropriation of natural resources has to be generally more disadvantaging to others than the use of unappropriated natural resources. An appropriator, for instance, could simply grant permission which the appropriator never revoked to others that they may use the appropriated natural resources to the degree "which was necessary to leave others enough and as good," while a user of natural resources could engage in destructive use that failed to leave others enough and as good. If this were the case, then the appropriation of natural resources wouldn't be morally problematic (or not obviously problematic), but the destructive use of such resources would be extremely morally problematic. After all, the appropriator has granted others permission, which she never revokes, to use her resources to whatever degree is necessary for her to leave them enough and as good while the destructive use of unappropriated natural resources is morally problematic because the user failed to leave others enough and as good.

Second, it appears that many political philosophers view the commons as a type of primitive condition that will simply go away once all natural resources are appropriated. If this is the case, we should cut to the chase and focus our efforts on analyzing appropriation as opposed to the use of unappropriated natural resources. There are two significant problems with this position. First, as discussed in the first chapter and earlier in this chapter, analyzing the appropriation of natural resources will be deficient and lacking until the moral conditions governing the use of unappropriated resources are uncovered.

The second problem with this position is that there might be large parts of our natural world that ought to remain privately unappropriated (or large parts of the natural world that agents decide are better left privately unappropriated). For instance, it might be a grave mistake to allow parts (or all) of the atmosphere to be subject to appropriation. The atmosphere is a natural resource that agents depend upon to survive, and its deep importance suggests that arguably no one should be able to appropriate—and hence acquire the moral right to exclude others from using—the atmosphere. Alternatively, it is plausible to hold that all agents should be allowed to use the atmosphere within rules governing common use and abide by the Lockean Proviso in respect to this use.

Earlier, the example of beachfront property was considered. Beachfront property is a valuable natural resource. While somewhat controversial, a consensus exempting such lands from appropriation has emerged in numerous legal jurisdictions. This is a consensus supported by the idea that certain natural resources ought to remain in the commons for all to use, enjoy, and benefit from. This, after all, was the intuitive consideration behind the idea of the national park or preserve system that many countries adopted during the twentieth century. There are, so the intuition goes, certain parts of nature that should continue to remain in the commons or be brought back to a state on normative par with the commons and hence not subject to appropriation.

But the examples of natural resources that plausibly ought not be subject to appropriation do not end at the beachfront or other beautiful places. Holy Lands of deep religious significance, for example, or other important cultural lands should arguably not be subject to appropriation. These lands should plausibly be governed by moral and legal rules of common use. Such places are treasures that hold deep meaning and substantively shape the identity of millions of agents. To bar a pilgrim access to Mecca or the relative of a dead soldier access to the battlegrounds of Normandy under the guise of private property and the appropriation of land suggest an error in the thought that *all* natural resources (land in such cases) ought to be subject to appropriation. Some land is just too important and deeply significant to allow any person or interest to appropriate and exclude whom they wish.

If we maintain that certain parts of nature should not be appropriated or be brought back to a state on normative par with the commons and, as such, be kept in some condition of common use, then clearly it would be a great help to offer moral guidance or rules for those using these parts of the world. The view that the Lockean Proviso should be applied to any agent using unappropriated natural resources is a good starting place for this guidance. I am quite drawn to the view that certain parts of the world should not be subject to appropriation, but my outline and limited defense of this position, for now, ends here. The view has already been given a much more vigorous defense by the modern environmental and conservation movements.

Third, many political philosophers have simply regarded the moral status of unappropriated natural resources as subject, both empirically and morally, to a tragedy of the commons. The tragedy of the commons, as discussed in chapter 1, is the result of a situation in which everyone has an incentive to overuse and deplete natural resources. This is because in the commons no one has private ownership in respect to natural resources, and as such, everyone is in a race to use up as much of these resources as they can before others use these resources to the point of extinction. The situation, as discussed earlier, leads to a depleting "race to the bottom," wherein everyone overuses unappropriated natural resources before others have a chance to do the same.

Applying the Lockean Proviso to the use of unappropriated natural resources serves as a promising way to address the tragedy of the commons. If agents, or collectives of agents, have a moral obligation to use unappropriated natural resources in a fashion that leaves enough and as good for others, then they are morally barred from participating in the overuse of natural resources that motivates the worries associated with the tragedy of the commons. If the overuse of resources in the commons presents a tragic situation, then it is a tragedy brought about by agents (acting individually or collectively) *disregarding* their moral duty to use unappropriated natural resources in a fashion that leaves others enough and as good. The tragedy of the commons is, at base, a moral problem.

Another similarly spirited attempt to address the tragedy of the commons is offered by David Schmidtz.[12] Schmidtz's position has since evolved; as such, what follows should be treated as his circa 1990 view. Schmidtz argued that those who appropriate natural resources are bound by a duty to future generations not to use their appropriated resources in certain destructive ways.[13] This is an intuitively powerful idea that I have no objection with. He also maintained, more importantly to our present discussion, that given the overuse of unappropriated natural resources in the commons brought about by the tragedy of the commons, the appropriation and care of natural resources for future generations is, in certain cases, not merely permissible but *obligatory* as a requirement of the Lockean Proviso. After discussing a scenario in which the commons are confronted with significant scarcity and the tragedy of the commons rears its ugly head, Schmidtz explains that, "this is why I have insisted that the Proviso not only permits original appropriation (which is a significant point in itself) but actually requires it."[14] That is, there will be cases when the fulfillment of the Lockean Proviso mandates that agents *appropriate* natural resources.

Schmidtz's method of addressing the tragedy of the commons is well-crafted and plausible, but I think the present proposal of extending the Lockean Proviso to cover the use of unappropriated natural resources offers certain important advantages absent from Schmidtz's fix. Imagine, for instance, that a group of agents (perhaps the whole world, but it need not be the whole world) has voluntarily opted to live in a Marxist-style commune. Presumably there are actual agents who have voluntarily opted to live within such conditions. Being Marxists, these agents detest the idea of appropriation and private property. They view the appropriation of natural resources as intrinsically immoral. (Considering these Marxists also helps to demonstrate why focusing attention exclusively toward the appropriation of previously unappropriated natural resources and thereby neglecting the use of these resources is lacking.) These Marxists, very plausibly, do not appropriate natural resources. To hold otherwise would be to endorse the view that an agent can appropriate even if she claims no private ownership and further *explicitly disavows* private ownership. Nonetheless, the Marxists (who have not appropriated natural resources) are still governed by moral rules, a good candidate being the Lockean Proviso, regarding their use of unappropriated natural resources. These Marxists, I maintain, need never engage in an appropriation of natural resources in order to abide by the Lockean Proviso.

The idea of extending the Lockean Proviso to cover cases of use applies well to our Marxists and their use of unappropriated natural resources while respecting their choice not to engage in appropriation, but Schmidtz's solution does not offer this same result. In order for Schmidtz's solution to be effectual, agents can be morally mandated to appropriate natural resources. These private-property-hating-Marxists have, under Schmidtz's proposal, a moral duty in at least some cases to appropriate natural resources. The ability of these Marxists to live a life of their choosing is threatened if there will be cases in which they are morally obligated to become private property owners and appropriate natural resources. This is one important aspect whereby Schmidtz's proposal loses some of its appeal. There is something morally suspect, because of its direct affront to the moral status of agents as independent and the ability of agents to live a life their choosing, to mandating that agents *must*, in order to satisfy the Lockean Proviso, appropriate natural resources. No agent has a duty to appropriate natural resources, in virtue of the Lockean Proviso or any other reason, because the act of appropriation is not owed to anyone. No one has a legitimate moral claim against another to appropriate. What plausibly is owed to others is the duty to leave enough and as good when unappropriated natural resource are removed (whether by use or appropriation) from conditions of common use.

What motivates Schmidtz to propose that agents can have a duty to appropriate is understandable; he wants agents to be under an obligation to conserve for future generations, so he suggests that one way to achieve this goal (via the Lockean Proviso) is to maintain that agents can have a moral duty to appropriate. But when we see that applying the Lockean Proviso to the use of unappropriated natural resources renders the same theoretical result that Schmidtz desires, there is no longer a compelling reason to mandate that agents appropriate natural resources. Schmidtz's address of the tragedy of the commons produces no more benefit than applying the Lockean Proviso to the use of unappropriated natural resources but inflicts the cost of reduced autonomy by, in some cases, requiring agents to appropriate.

At this point, the application of the Lockean Proviso to the use of unappropriated natural resources should hopefully be seen as a plausible, if not compelling, idea. In the last part of this chapter, I strive to offer a formalized account of what it means for a user of natural resources to leave others enough and as good. The Lockean Proviso serves as a promising general guide for the duty that users of natural resources owe to others, but it is a general guide that must be specified in order to make substantial progress.

The Lockean Proviso can be divided between "payment" and "no payment" accounts.[15] One way in which a user of unappropriated natural resources may satisfy the Lockean Proviso is by using only a share of natural resources that leaves others enough and as good. For example, we might imagine a world with one hundred qualitatively identical agents and one thousand equally valuable acres of land. In a very straightforward fashion we can say that an agent may use ten acres of land for herself, leaving everyone else ten acres to use. This is similar to the idea of agents being about to check out and use books from a library—as long as they leave others with enough books that constitute a share that is enough and as good. No payment to others is required of an agent who uses *only* ten acres because she takes no more than her "enough and as good share." This version of the Lockean Proviso, that we can call the No-Payment Lockean Proviso, maintains that an agent may use *only* her "enough and as good share" and no more. An implication of the No-Payment Proviso is that, in the example above, no agent is at liberty to use more than ten acres of land.

A No-Payment Lockean Proviso can be contrasted with a Payment Lockean Proviso. A Payment Lockean Proviso account maintains that an agent may, in principle, use natural resources as she pleases just so long as she makes a *payment* that is equivalent with her leaving enough and as good for others. Considering again the scenario of one hundred agents and one thousand acres of land. A Payment Lockean Proviso maintains that any of these agents are at liberty to use the land as they please, provided that they make a payment that constitutes leaving enough and as good for others.

A payment account of the Lockean Proviso is more plausible than a No-Payment account. First, consider that a Payment Lockean Proviso is much better suited to handle cases of perishable or consumable natural resources (as discussed previously in the chapter) in which dividing up "equal shares" of the resources is not feasible. But other reasons suggest that a Payment Lockean Proviso is generally preferable to a No-Payment Lockean Proviso. To illustrate why this is the case, consider a scenario in which everyone's initial "enough and as good share" is very slight, and as such, everyone lives a life barely worth living. If, however, one super-genius agent is allowed to use most of the natural resources, then he can manage the resources in ways which benefit everyone ten-fold as compared to a life where everyone is only allowed to use their allotted share of the world. A No-Payment Lockean Proviso maintains that this super-genius is not at liberty to unilaterally use a vast share of natural resources and in so doing greatly improve everyone's life. A Payment account, on the other hand, maintains that our super-genius can use whatever natural resources he desires so long as he makes a payment which leaves others enough and as good. Presumably if the super-genius improves the lives of *all others* by ten-fold as compared to what their life would have been like had the super-genius been restricted by a No-Payment Lockean Proviso, he will have made a payment which leaves others enough and as good. A payment account of the Lockean Proviso in this, and many similar cases, yields the right result that an agent may use unappropriated natural resources as she wishes so long as she makes a payment that leaves others enough and as good.

With a Payment account of the Lockean Proviso in mind, the central question becomes the following: exactly what type of payment must be made by an agent who uses unappropriated natural resources in order to satisfy the duty to leave others enough and as good?

Before offering what I think is the best reply to this question, a few cursory points are in order. First, there are likely a number of plausible replies that could be given to address what payment those who use unappropriated natural resources owe to others. I will review a few possibilities inspired by the thoughts of Henry George and argue for a best answer, but this is not meant to definitively settle the matter. Second, at this point we are in unchartered philosophical waters. As far as I am aware, there are no other existent systematic accounts outlining the way in which the Lockean Proviso ought to be applied to the *use* of unappropriated resources. This is a maiden voyage of sorts. But to offer some familiar and established thought (and to avoid sailing too far off into the abyss) I will be addressing the above question by utilizing some existent thought regarding the ways that appropriators of natural resources can satisfy their duty to leave others enough and as good. It turns out that with little difficulty a good number of well-developed accounts of how appropriators of natural resources may plausibly satisfy the duty to leave others enough and as good can be easily converted into accounts of how users of unappropriated natural resources can satisfy the Lockean Proviso. This should not be too surprising given that both the appropriation and use of natural resources are ways of removing.

One influential and plausible place to begin the task of uncovering the nature of the payment that a user of natural resources must make in order to leave others enough and as good is a consideration of the ideas of Henry George.[16] George argued that those who appropriate or otherwise privately own land and other natural resources are obligated to pay the full rent on the competitive value of the *private property rights* that they claim over natural resources. Competitive rent is the market clearing price of the rights, where that is the price at which there is no left supply and no unmet demand. An agent who appropriates a natural resource from the commons (by gaining the claim right against others not to use the resource without her permission) *removes* the moral liberty of others to unilaterally use the resource that existed within the commons and hence *owes a payment to others that covers the value of what they have taken from others*. Note, as discussed in chapter 2, George's suggestion here still allows agents to keep *all* the value that they add (via their labor or other means) to the natural resources that they appropriate.

The idea motivating George's proposed rent is simple, yet quite powerful. Those who remove the moral liberty of agents to unilaterally use natural resources from the commons through *appropriation* should not be able to reap the competitive value of *this removal*. The full competitive value of private ownership rights in respect to natural resources (most notably the claim right that others must receive the permission of the private owner before using the natural resource) instead belongs to everyone since all agents have an initial equal moral claim in respect to natural resources. *Agents may reap the competitive value of what they add through their labor or other contributions of their selves to natural resources, but they may not reap the competitive value of natural resources or rights in respect to natural resources that initially belong to everyone.* When an agent *appropriates* a natural resource and removes the moral liberty of others to use the resource and hence takes all the competitive value that can be gleaned from the rights of private ownership all for herself, she harms others by depriving them of any stake in the competitive value of the resource that initially belonged to everyone. *She takes for herself what belongs to everyone.* She engages in a global theft. It would be analogous to an agent simply removing a book from the public library and taking it as her own private property.

The appropriator, in such a case, takes all the benefit (measured in terms of competitive value) from a natural resource that initially belongs to everyone. This violates the rights of (all) others who have the same initial moral stake in the value of natural resources. Insisting that agents who appropriate natural resources pay others the full competitive value of the private ownership rights that they acquire (an acquisition that involves removing the moral liberty of others to use unappropriated natural resources) is an effective way of leaving others enough and as good.

Notice, however, that the same motive for insisting that appropriators pay the full competitive value of the private ownership rights that they acquire over natural resources can be extended with little difficulty to the removal of unappropriated natural resources through use as opposed to appropriation. Users of unappropriated natural resources generally remove the effective, as opposed to the durable moral, liberties of others. When, for instance, Hiding Helen hides natural resources from Bob that he and Helen share within the commons, she removes Bob's effective liberty to use the hidden resources. Hiding Helen's actions, however, do not remove any durable moral liberties that Bob might have to use the hidden resources. He is, after all, *morally* free to use the hidden resources—he just cannot effectively use them because of the way Helen has used them. What users of unappropriated natural resources potentially remove—and what they should pay for removing—are the effective moral liberties of others to use unappropriated natural resources.[17]

The same Georgist appeal to paying the competitive value for what is removed, and hence others deprived of, works equally well to account for the duty of users to leave others enough and as good. We can, in Georgist spirit, employ the idea of competitive value to explain how it is that users of unappropriated natural resources can pay the price of removing the effective liberty of others to use these resources. This is because just as private ownership rights over natural resources have a competitive value, so too does the effective liberty to use an unappropriated natural resource.

To demonstrate that the effective liberty to use an unappropriated natural resource can have a competitive value, consider that multiple agents would often be willing to pay for the effective liberty to use (in some designated fashion) an unappropriated natural resource. Here one might ask: why would an agent pay for the effective liberty to use an unappropriated natural resource when she already has the moral liberty to use unappropriated natural resources? The answer is that the general moral liberty that all agents have to unilaterally use unappropriated natural resources (at least under certain conditions) does not provide any assurance that they will be able to actually or effectively use these resources. Bill, after all, has the moral liberty to use the unappropriated natural resources that he does not know exist because of Helen's stealthy hiding, and he would presumably be willing to pay for the effective liberty to use these resources. Both Paranoid Bill and Mark, likewise, would likely be willing to pay presumably quite a bit for the effective liberty to use the energy stone for some specified ten-second period during the course of a day. Notice neither would be paying for rights of private ownership over the stone in such a scenario; instead, both would be willing to pay for the effective liberty to use the stone in some designated fashion during some designated time. What such cases demonstrate is that the effective liberty to use an unappropriated natural resource can, when more than one agent is interested in using the resource, have a competitive value. The notion of competitive value need not be solely reserved for private ownership rights over natural resources but can also naturally be extended to encompass the effective liberty to use an unappropriated natural resource.

A general Georgist account of the moral conditions governing the use of unappropriated natural resources can be specified as follows:

> Georgism (general model): You can use an unappropriated natural resource X if and only if you leave others the full competitive rent value of the effective liberty to use X (in the precise fashion that you use X).

The general Georgist duty of users described above is flexible enough to account for *any* way in which an agent might use an unappropriated natural resource. The account, for instance, can specify the duty owned by an agent who uses an unappropriated natural resource only very briefly and with little or no impact to others, or it can describe the duty owed by an agent who uses in a way that removes all the competitive value from a natural resource. It is also worth noting here that while in principle the view allows for *any* use of natural resources, in practice the competitive rent of certain uses of natural resources might be so high that they are effectively barred.

To see an applied case of how a general Georgist account could be applied to the use of natural resources, consider that in some Native American reservations located within the territorial borders of the United States there is a system of allowing non-members to access and use lands and waters within the reservation for a fee. These fees can be thought of as a type of rent. The collected fees are then shared in various ways with members of the tribe or nation that the land belongs to. The members of the Native American community share in the economic value generated from the natural resources that they commonly hold. This example of land and water use "for a fee" is instructive because it illustrates a system designed to collect fees or rent that is then given back to agents who hold a common stake in the used natural resources.

Competitive rent value clearly plays a central role in the general Georgist account of the moral conditions governing unappropriated natural resources offered above. But how ought the competitive value of the effective liberty to use an unappropriated natural resource be determined? There are many different ways in which competitive value might be determined.[18] One particularly promising way to determine competitive value is by utilizing the model of a hypothetical Vickrey auction. This model maintains that the parties to the hypothetical auction seal the highest bid that they are willing to pay for the item. In our case, the "item" is the effective liberty to use—in a precisely specified way—an unappropriated natural resource. The highest bidder then pays the second highest price for the auctioned item, which represents the item's competitive value.[19] A Vickrey auction encourages agents to bid their true preferences because they know they will either be outbid for the item or (if they are the highest bidder) pay a price less than the bid expressing their true preferences.

Assume, for example, that an auction has two agents bidding for the effective liberty to use a shade tree—specifically, the liberty to sit under the tree between 3 and 3:30 in the afternoon on some designated day. The first agent seals a bid of fifteen dollars for this effective liberty, and the second agent seals a bid of ten dollars for the same effective liberty. The competitive value of the effective liberty to use the shade tree by sitting under it between 3 and 3:30 is now set at ten dollars and would be awarded to the agent who bid fifteen dollars.

I should point out here that there are very complicated questions concerning the relation between a hypothetical auction model and real-world agents. For instance, how is the hypothetical auction, which determines competitive value, related to the actual world with real-world actors? Here, I maintain that the hypothetical auction to determine competitive value should be thought to *as closely as feasible* approximate real world conditions and agents. The agents bidding in the hypothetical Vickery auction, for instance, should be thought to be much like agents in the actual world. The hypothetical nature of the auction simply brings these agents together in an auction (which might not be possible in the actual world given distance and other pragmatic considerations) and addresses certain epistemic limitations of real-world agents.

One important and difficult challenge that confronts the Georgist who utilizes an auction model of any sort to determine competitive rent value is how to ensure that agents bidding within the auction have *fair bidding power*. If the bidding power of agents is unfair—say for instance, the king "just gets" ten times more bidding power than the pauper—then the competitive rent value established by the auction will be built upon a deficient moral foundation. In fact, it would be difficult to think of any auction in the actual world that, given historical injustice, established a competitive value for some thing that was not built upon a deficient moral foundation. Agents must possess fair bidding power in order for a Georgist account of the moral conditions governing the use of unappropriated natural resources to be plausibly grounded. What then establishes, in the proposed hypothetical Vickrey auction that sets the competitive rent value of the effective liberty to use unappropriated natural resources, fair bidding power?

Consider the following proposal. Imagine that initially, before any natural resources have been used or appropriated, all agents possess a list (likely a very long list) of *all the possible ways* in which unappropriated natural resources can be used. This list then *both* constitutes what is to be bid on and serves as a mechanism to establish fair bidding power. The items on the list (the highly specified effective liberties to use unappropriated natural resources) could be put up for bid and auctioned off one by one.

The list, in addition to serving as the auction catalogue, can also serve as a mechanism to establish fair bidding power. This is because aside from offering the items up for bid, the list also specifies the complete set of moral liberties that all agents have to use unappropriated natural resources. Agents could bid for the effective liberty to use an unappropriated natural resource with the moral liberties that they initially possess to use unappropriated natural resources. The units of value being bid with would then be various "moral liberties to use natural resources." Instead of bidding with some standard currency on an item such as dollars (the way auctions are usually imagined), an agent would be bidding with her moral liberties to use unappropriated natural resources in various ways. Agents would, in effect, be competing to gain effective liberties to use natural resources by bidding away their moral liberties to use natural resources. One virtue of this approach is that all agents would possess *equal* bidding power because everyone would be bidding with the same complete set of moral liberties to use unappropriated natural resources. This is because all agents initially possess the same set of moral liberties to use unappropriated natural resources. No agent would be able to bid with something (a moral liberty to use an unappropriated natural resource) that others could not bid with as well if they opted to do so.

To see how this proposal would work, imagine a very simple scenario (the actual world would clearly be vastly more complicated) where the only way in which agents can use natural resources is by sitting on various spots of land during one day. These are very short-lived agents, and there are very few natural resources. Say that the item up for bid is the effective liberty to use (by sitting on) a certain designated spot of land from eight to nine in the morning of a designated day. Two agents desire the effective liberty to do just this, so they bid with moral liberties they have to sit on other spots of land at various times. The agent who is willing to part with (bid) greater moral liberties to use natural resources wins the auction and pays the moral liberties bid by the second-highest bidder.

The payment that an agent who makes a winning bid to effectively use an unappropriated natural resource must leave for others is her moral liberty to use some set of natural resources (whatever set the second-highest bidder made for the effective liberty to use). Others, then, would have a moral claim against this winning agent from using the unappropriated resources that she used to bid with to gain the effective liberty to use, in a highly specified fashion, the unappropriated natural resource up for bid. As agents bid away their moral liberties to use unappropriated natural resources, other agents (all others) accordingly gain a greater moral stake in unappropriated natural resources.

It is even possible for a situation to arise in which all agents, or nearly all agents, bid away all rights to use a natural resource(s), and only one or a few agents remain with the moral liberty to use, in any fashion, a natural resource(s). An agent might even become the *de facto* private owner of a natural resource if all other agents bid away their moral liberties to use the natural resource. In such a case, the agent who has not bid away liberties to use the unappropriated natural resource would be the only agent left with the moral liberty to use the natural resource in question because everyone else has alienated their rights to use the resource by bidding them away in the proposed resource auction.

In addition to bidding for effective liberties to use unappropriated natural resources with moral liberties to use such resources, an agent could also bid with aspects of her self, such as a commitment of her bodily resources or labor. A self-owning agent is at liberty to alienate rights over her self in exchange for something that she desires such as the effective liberty to use unappropriated natural resources. An agent, for instance, could bid for the effective liberty to use unappropriated natural resources with some hourly commitment of labor or with her plasma, reproductive material, or other bodily resources. One might even be willing to bid one of her kidneys in order to gain the effective liberty to exclusively use a spot of beachfront land for a number of years. One concern with this suggestion of "bidding with aspects of the self" is that it is unfair because in all likelihood agents will have differential personal endowments to bid with. A normally functioning agent, for instance, will be able to bid a greater contribution of physical labor than an agent with a severe physical or mental disability.

One preliminary way to address this concern is to say that agents could bid with aspects of their selves under a Rawlsian style "veil of ignorance" in which they bid away specific blind *opportunities* to use their self (or bid away claims against others from unilaterally using their selves in various ways) rather than specific actual *outcomes* brought about by the self. An agent, under this suggestion, would bid with opportunities that they can reasonably expect to pay but may not end up paying given what her actual endowments turn out to be after the veil of ignorance is lifted. If an agent, for instance, bids to perform ten hours of manual labor, and it turns out that when the veil of ignorance is lifted she is a quadriplegic, then she could still win the auction of a highly specified effective liberty to use an unappropriated natural resources but would not be expected to make the labor payment that she bid with in good faith.

One complicating question is worth spelling out and addressing. When agents bid with sets of moral liberties to use unappropriated natural resources and aspects of the self, how ought the value of what is bid with (and hence the winning bid) be determined? It is not clear or obvious, for instance, whether the moral liberty to use a spot of land by sitting under a shade tree for two years and twenty hours of a specified labor commitment is any more or less valuable than the moral liberty to use a spot of land by sitting perched over the ocean for one year and thirty hours of a specified labor commitment. If a standard currency such as dollars were used to bid with, then this task of determining the comparative value of bids would not be a concern. If two agents are bidding with dollars for an item, and one bids fifteen dollars and the other bids ten dollars, then it is clear the bid of fifteen dollars has more value and hence is the winning bid. But there is no standard currency in the commons or at least no good reason to assume that there must be. As such, stipulating that agents bid with a standard currency such as dollars for the effective liberty to use unappropriated natural resources is a convenient fiction, but it is far less preferable to maintaining that agents bid with things that they do possess, i.e., moral liberties to use unappropriated natural resources and aspects of the self.

A number of strategies might be used to address the concern of how to determine the comparative value of bids made in the proposed natural resource auction. One strategy is to establish some objective rank ordering of various uses of unappropriated natural resources and aspects of the self. While this is possible, I am skeptical that any such objective ordering exists outside of perhaps extreme cases and even more skeptical that even granting some objective ordering, human agents would be able to determine such an ordering with any great degree of precision.

A more promising strategy to determine the comparative value of bids would involve the social construction of value. Imagine the following scenario to describe how the social construction of value might proceed. Before bidding on the effective liberty to use unappropriated natural resources takes place, all agents are given a comprehensive list of all possible uses of unappropriated natural resources as well as aspects of the self (specifying various types of labor and bodily resources). Agents would then express preferences as to the desirability of the items on the list. This expression of preference could be done by simply ranking items or by giving some subjective measure, say on a scale of desirability from 1 to 100. Notice that agents are not bidding at this point. They are instead simply expressing preferences about the desirability of the moral liberty to use unappropriated natural resources and aspects of the self—the very items that will be used to bid with. The cumulative preferences of all agents are then tabulated, and a new list is generated that discloses the socially constructed value of each item.

One point in favor of socially constructing the value of the effective liberties to use natural resources is to appeal to the idea that natural resources initially belong to everyone. If natural resources initially belong to everyone, then it stands to reason that the value of the effective liberty to use these resources should be determined or set in some way that takes the preferences of everyone into account. This market-based solution allows everyone's preferences to count equally as a way to determine the value of any particular bid in the proposed natural resources use auction. Although the issue is complicated, I reject the view that the effective liberties to use natural resources that initially belong to everyone have value detached from the rational preferences of the very agents that the resources belong to.

Agents then, after socially constructed values have been assigned to the effective liberties to use unappropriated natural resources and aspects of the self, engage in the proposed resource auction (again, all with the same bidding power) by bidding with the moral liberty to use unappropriated and aspects of the self that have been assigned a common value. Now when an agent bids away her moral liberty to use unappropriated natural resources and aspects of her self for the opportunity to gain the effective liberty to use unappropriated natural resources, she is bidding with items that have a codified value that can be compared on the same terms with bids from others. This way of socially constructing the value of the moral liberty to use unappropriated natural resource and aspects of the self creates a clear way to determine the value of what is bid with as well as setting the terms of who gains the effective liberty to use an item up for bid in the proposed resource auction.

There is a great deal more that can be said about the complex issue of fair bidding power in a Georgist auction. My hope is that the suggestion of bidding with the moral liberty to use unappropriated natural resources and aspects of the self under a Rawlsian veil of ignorance offers a plausible way to think about what form fair bidding power in a Georgist auction might take. The virtues of the above suggestion of bidding with moral liberties to use unappropriated resources and with blind opportunities to use the self is that agents possess equal bidding power without introducing any implausible assumptions. Agents, after all, do all have the same moral liberties to use unappropriated natural resources, and the suggestion that agents ought to be able to bid with blind opportunities to use the self, while more controversial than the idea that all agents have the same moral liberty to use unappropriated natural resources, is not implausible.

Aside from concerns with fair bidding power, it is worth noting that the competitive value of common resources will be *contingent* upon technology and the preferences of agents. If, for example, more agents prefer to use the beachfront rather than a barren desert, then it will, given supply and demand pressures, cost agents more to leave others enough and good when they use the beach than it will when they use the barren desert. This is the right result because the effective liberty to use a coveted spot on the beach is more likely to prejudice or injure others than the use of barren desert that no one is very much interested in using.

Moreover technological abilities could also influence the competitive value of the effective liberty to use unappropriated natural resources. The use of a remote desert island that can receive a satellite internet connection, for example, will be in higher demand, and hence have a higher competitive value, than a remote desert island that cannot receive a satellite connection. Given the strong potential for changing competitive rents over time (granting changing preferences owed to technological and other reasons) we should expect that the rent that one owes others by using unappropriated natural resources will not be static over time but will change as the competitive value for various types of effective liberties to use change.

The general Georgist account examined thus far is silent as to whom a user of unappropriated natural resources must pay the full competitive value of the effective liberty to use unappropriated natural resources; it merely demands that such a payment is due to others. Addressing the question of *to whom the rent is owed* will distinguish traditional Georgist accounts from Equal Opportunity Georgist accounts. Traditionally, Georgists have endorsed an *equal share model* in which rents are split in an equal fashion among all agents.[20] Other Georgists, such as, Vallentyne, endorse a distribution of Georgists rents that is "divided so as to promote effective equality for a good life."[21] These traditional Georgist accounts have been directed toward the *appropriation* of natural resources, but for our purposes the focus is redirected toward the use of unappropriated natural resources. Before assessing the merits of each position, it is important to take stock that each variant of Georgism holds that agents who use unappropriated natural resources fulfill the duty they owe to leave others enough and as good when they pay the competitive rent value on the effective liberty of their use. The views simply differ in respect to how the rent payment is shared.

A traditional Equal Share Georgist account applied to the use of unappropriated natural resources maintains that everyone has a right to their same share of an equal per capita distribution of the full competitive rent value on the effective liberty to use natural resources. The Equal Share Georgist account can be formalized as follows:

> Equal Share Georgism: You can use an unappropriated natural resource X if and only if you leave others their equal per capita share of the competitive rent value of the effective liberty to use X (in the precise fashion that you use X).

George was a proponent of the equal share model and maintained that agents could appropriate up to an *equal share* of natural resources without *effectively* owing others competitive rent. This is because George took the view, later defended by Hillel Steiner, that all agents have an initial right to an equal share of the competitive value of all natural resources. If an agent "over-appropriates" more than her equal share of the competitive value afforded by natural resources, only then would she effectively owe rent to others.

To illustrate how Equal Share Georgism would work in a comprehensive fashion, consider a world housing only Able and Unable, in which the *full* competitive rent value of the effective maximal liberty to use *all* unappropriated natural resources is 1000 units of competitive value. (Able is a normally functioning agent, and Unable is a quadriplegic.) This figure of 1000 units of value is the amount that would result if the maximal effective liberty to use the entire set of all unappropriated natural resources were bid on. Each agent, given these parameters, has a claim to be left 500 units of value, her per capita share of the competitive rent from the maximal effective liberty to use the entire set of unappropriated natural resources. The implication from this is that either Able or Unable may use unappropriated natural resources in unilateral fashion so long as they leave the other her per capita share of competitive rent value, in this case 500 units.

Able or Unable could fulfill this duty to the other by simply leaving the other effective liberties to use unappropriated natural resources that equal no less that 500 units. Or plausibly, if either Able or Disable "over-uses" natural resources that exceed 500 units of competitive value, then either could leave the other no less than 500 units of value that could include a contribution of labor or bodily resources. The key idea is that according to Equal Share Georgism an agent has a right against others to be left her equal per capita share of the competitive rent value of the effective liberty to use unappropriated natural resources.

One can object to Equal Share Georgism on the grounds that it can fail to capture the idea of leaving others enough and as good. The equal share model rendered the implication that either Able or Unable were at liberty to use unappropriated natural resources so long as she left the other 500 units of competitive value (the other's equal per capita share of the competitive rent value of the effective liberty to use unappropriated natural resources). But imagine that Able, consistent with the equal share view, uses natural resources in such a way that he removes 500 units of competitive value from the shared stock of unappropriated natural resources and leaves Unable the effective liberty to use unappropriated natural resources with a competitive value of 500 units. Able's use of the shared common stock of natural resources affords her a fantastic life, but Unable perishes with the 500 units she is left—since, say, she will perish unless she gets 600 units of value. The effective liberty to use unappropriated natural resources totaling 500 units of competitive value that Able leaves Unable is not enough to sustain Unable's life. Further (and importantly), the differences in the enjoyment of the units of value are not the fault of, or result of choices made by, either Able or Unable. It is not Unable's fault that the effective liberty to use natural resources totaling 500 units of competitive value are not enough to sustain her life, nor is it result of good choices that afford Able a fantastic life from her equal per capita share of the competitive value of natural resources.

The equal division of the competitive rent value of the effective liberty to use natural resources mandated by the equal share model is unfair to Unable because, through no fault of her own, her equal share affords her *much* less opportunity for a good life than Able's share affords him. The contrast here is stark. Able uses unappropriated natural resources that afford her a fantastic life and then leaves Unable her per capita share that does not allow Unable to subsist. Intuitions might differ here, but there is at least a strong case for the claim that Able has not left enough and as good for Unable when *what she leaves* Unable is not enough to sustain Unable's life and what she takes is enough to afford her a fantastic life. Equal Share Georgism endorses a distribution of competitive rent value that affords Able a wonderful life and Unable no life at all.

The salient question when assessing whether a user of unappropriated natural resources has satisfied her duty toward others should not be "how much, in terms of material amount, did the appropriator leave others," but instead ought to be "how does what is left by the appropriator impact the life prospects or opportunities of others?" The reason why the emphasis should be placed upon how a leaving impacts the *condition* of others as opposed to a specific material *amount* of resources left is because, at base, what we should care about is how the leaving *actually impacts* the lives of others. The emphasis should be on impacts to other agents and not with amounts of resources left *per se*. Michael Otsuka offers the following example to successfully motivate the idea that a concern with what is left should focus upon the welfare of agents rather than the amount of what is left:

> Suppose that the only worldly resource available for use by each of two individuals who are stranded on a desert island is an unowned large blanket that can be divided into portions of any size. If the blanket did not exist then both would freeze to death. One of these individuals is, through no fault of his, twice as large as the other. If the blanket is divided into equally large portions, then the smaller of the two will have enough to enjoy the luxury of being able to wrap the blanket around himself twice, whereas the larger of the two will suffer the (non-life-or-limb-threatening) discomfort of partial exposure to the

> cold because he will be able to cover only a portion of his body. The blanket could, however, be divided into unequal portions that enable each to cover his entire body once, thereby leaving them equally comfortable. (But neither is as comfortable, as he would have been if he had a greater share of the blanket.) Intuitively, it would be unfair for the smaller person to acquire half of the blanket rather than the lesser portion which would leave him as comfortable as the other.[22]

A compelling reason in favor of adopting an approach that favors paying much closer attention to the impacts on agents that result from what is left by an agent who uses unappropriated natural resources as opposed to the *amount* that is left is to ask: why, at core, would an agent use unappropriated natural resources in the first place? Ultimately, the reason(s) in normal cases, maybe in all cases, will have to do with the positive *impact* that such use provides the agent, e.g., increased autonomy, increased well-being, and so forth. It would be a gross disconnect if the duty had by users of unappropriated natural resources to leave others enough and as good focused on something other than the very thing (positive life impact) that motivated their use in the first place. The thought here is simply that when we assess what it means for a user of unappropriated resources to leave others enough and as good we should not stray far from the very reasons that motivate agents to use natural resources in the first place—positive impacts on life prospects.

A series of examples can help better illustrate why the focus of the Lockean Proviso ought to be geared toward how a leaving impacts others rather than with the amount or quality of what is left *per se.* Imagine, for simplicity, a world with two agents (Ann and Isabel) and three unappropriated natural resources—two spots of land that are qualitatively identical in every way and ivy that sits outside the entrance to one of these parcels. The ivy causes Isabel to have an extremely bad allergic reaction (it turns her into Itchy Isabel) but causes no such reaction for Ann. For Ann, the ivy is merely a very slight inconvenience that she hardly notices. There is no avoiding physical conduct with the ivy, nor can the ivy be destroyed or mitigated if one wishes to access the spot of land flanked by it. Wearing clothing, furthermore, does not seem to help Isabel avoid an allergic reaction from the ivy. Ann uses for herself (removes) the spot of land that is not near the ivy with the plan of planting a vegetable garden and leaves Isabel the spot of land that is flanked by the ivy for her to use in a similar fashion. The land is equally well suited to grow vegetables, and both agents would glean similar benefits from a vegetable garden.

I take it as fairly obvious that Ann's leaving fails to leave Itchy Isabel enough and as good—even though the land that she leaves Isabel is as equally well suited for the use of vegetable growing as the land that she removed in order to grow vegetables. It does not ultimately matter that the unappropriated natural resources that Ann leaves Itchy Isabel are as well suited for the use that she engages in with the unappropriated natural resources that she removes. What is important is that Itchy Isabel has less opportunity to make use of what Ann leaves her given that she is constantly driven to itch than the opportunities that Ann derives from what she removes.

Now modify the above example by eliminating the ivy, and imagine again that the spots of land in the world shared by Ann and Itchy Isabel are qualitatively identical to one another with the exception that the average temperature of one of the spots is one degree Fahrenheit warmer than the other. One spot with law-like regularity always has a daily high temperature of 74°F while the other has a daily high temperature of 73°F. The difference in temperature has no discernable impact on the productive use of the land itself. Itchy Isabel, however, has a rare genetic condition that causes her body to break out in excruciatingly painful hives whenever she perspires. Itchy Isabel can avoid perspiring so long as the temperature does not exceed 73°F, but as soon as the temperature hits 74°F she perspires and consequently breaks out with an awful case of hives. Ann, I maintain, fails to leave Itchy Isabel enough and as good when she uses (removes) the spot with the high temperature of 73°F and leaves Itchy Isabel the spot with a high temperature of 74°F. This is not because what Ann leaves is itself any worse than what she removed. Quite the contrary, both parcels of land are equally suited for productive uses such as gardening. Ann, instead, fails to leave Itchy Isabel enough and as good because what she leaves Isabel is clearly much worse *for her* than what Ann takes for *herself*.

For those not yet convinced that the Lockean Proviso ought to be squarely focused with how a leaving impacts the welfare of agents and not myopically focused on amounts or resources left *per se*, consider one last modification to the Itchy Isabel scenario. Keep the parameters of the scenario from above the same, except now imagine that when Isabel perspires her perspiration activates a chemical in the air and soil that releases a noxious gas which makes her violently ill for hours. This chemical reaction occurs anywhere in the world and makes only Isabel sick. As long as Isabel does not perspire she will not get sick, but once the temperature hits 74°F she cannot help but perspire and as such activate a chemical process that makes her fall ill.

Ann sets out to exclusively use the parcel of land that has the high temperature of 73°F and leaves Isabel the land to exclusively use with the high temperature of 74°F. Ann does this because she just has a "better feeling" about the land that has the slightly lower temperature. Both spots of land are physically indiscernible to Ann, and she does not know, nor could she discern given available technology or her empirical senses, the difference in temperature between the two spots of land. The parcels of land are equally suited for productive use and would afford the same life prospects to qualitatively identical agents. Once again, however, Ann fails to leave Isabel enough and as good because what she leaves affords Isabel a far worse life than the one she gleans by the natural resources that she removes.

With a focus on how what is left by those who use unappropriated natural resources impacts others rather than leaves some designated amount, a new variant of Georgism can be considered. For a direction toward this variant of Georgism that is sensitive to the impacts on agents had by what users of unappropriated natural resources leave others, we can look to the idea advanced by Peter Vallentyne that the competitive rent payment owed by those who remove from the commons should be divided so as to promote effective equality of opportunity for a good life. Here I will understand an *equal opportunity for a good life* to have no important differences with an *equal opportunity for welfare*. This is to say the greater an agent's opportunities for a good life, the greater her opportunities for welfare.

Equality is a goal worth promoting. As discussed earlier in chapter 3, the moral status of agents as independent is built upon the foundation of moral equality. But noting that equality is a goal worth promoting does not yet address the question: *equality of what* is worth promoting?[23] When considering an answer to the question equality of what, *initial opportunity for welfare* is among the plausible replies. There are, however, a number of different well-developed answers to the question: equality of what? For instance, a few of the contenders include: *equality of social primary goods,*[24] *equality of resources,*[25] *equality of well-being,*[26] and *equality of opportunity for welfare or well-being.*[27]

Offering a full, or even partial, comparative defense of an initial equality of opportunity for welfare view as the best answer to the question "equality of what" would carry us too far astray from the goals of this chapter, but here we can briefly cite two non-conclusive reasons that favor the plausibly of an equal initial opportunity for welfare account. First, such an account focuses on the *opportunities* that agents should be afforded and not actual outcomes. The account, as such, allows the free choices of agents to make a difference to the actual outcomes that befall them. A concern for equality that focuses on opportunity instead of outcome allows for agents that have made different free choices (such as the choice to gamble on a roulette wheel) to have very different outcomes. If an agent's free choices are to actually count in a way that impact her life outcomes, then considerations of equality ought to be focused on opportunities and not outcomes.

Second, to reiterate a recent point, the welfarist aspect of the account is sensitive to how a given distribution (or leaving in the case of the Lockean Proviso) *impacts* the welfare of others rather than focusing on splitting up resources in some equal share fashion. One attempt to avoid this problem, not to be extensively considered here but worth a mention, is to move to a model of equality of resources more generally, where this includes both external (worldly) and internal (personal) resources.[28] Although this is a controversial topic, I shall assume that equality of something related to welfare is the relevant conception of effective equality.

The view that initial equality of opportunity for welfare ought to be pursued can be built into a Georgist proviso on the use of unappropriated natural resources as follows:

> Initial Equal Opportunity for Welfare Georgism: You can use an unappropriated natural resource X if and only if you leave others their initial equal opportunity for welfare share of the competitive rent value of the effective liberty to use X (in the precise fashion that you use X).

The above proviso on the use of unappropriated natural resources demands, as have past Georgist accounts offered thus far, that users of unappropriated natural resources leave others the full competitive value of the effective liberty of their specified use. This new proviso on use, however, mandates that what is left must give others their initial equal opportunity for welfare share rather than a per capita equal share. The result is that in a world like ours where agents are often born with vastly different initial opportunities for welfare, some agents will be owed a greater share of the competitive rents paid by users of unappropriated natural resources than others. An agent born, for instance, with a severe genetic disability that affords her very little in the way of opportunities for welfare will be owed a greater share of the competitive rents paid by those who use unappropriated natural resources than an agent who is born with plentiful opportunities for welfare. A concern somewhat along these lines is likely what drives many developed countries to provide disability payments to those that are unable to productively labor. An agent who is not able to labor (at least through no fault of her own) should not suffer the pains of abject poverty because she is unable to sell her labor to others in an established market based economic system.

One similar idea to equalizing initial opportunities for welfare is that what ought to be equalized are brute luck inequalities. Brute luck is luck that happens to an agent that was not in her power to control. Being born with a genetic disability is a matter of *brute luck*, while placing money on a roulette wheel is a matter of *option luck*. Brute luck egalitarianism, unlike initial equal opportunity for welfare egalitarianism, maintains that effective equality ought to always be concerned with compensating for bad brute luck irrespective of whether it occurs initially or later in life. While brute luck views are plausible, Peter Vallentyne has argued that justice does not always demand compensation for bad brute luck after the initial conditions because, "the net result of the administrative costs, incentive effects, and all other relevant factors, may be that the initial opportunities for advantage are less valuable under the brute luck compensation scheme than without it."[29] These thoughts offer limited, but reasonable, support for an initial equal opportunity conception of effective equality that will often, though not necessarily always, compensate for brute luck rather than a pure brute luck model of equality.

A strong challenge to Initial Equal Opportunity for Welfare Georgism can be made by pressing the point that if initial equal opportunity for welfare is such an important goal, why restrict a proviso on use to only *promoting* the goal through the payment of competitive value? Why not, instead, devise a proviso that strives to *ensure* (through means that go beyond the paying of competitive rent) initial equal opportunity for welfare? To fully appreciate this challenge, we can look to an account offered by Michael Otsuka of a non-Georgist proviso on the appropriation of natural resources from the commons. Otsuka maintains that agents are owed a duty by those who appropriate to be left an enough and as good share that ensures they are afforded an equal opportunity for welfare.

Otsuka, a committed Lockean left-libertarian, thinks that those who remove natural resources (his focus is on appropriation) from the commons owe a duty to leave others enough and as good, in a fashion that brings about equality of opportunity for welfare. But Otsuka is not a Georgist (he actually never addresses Georgism in his discussions about acquiring unappropriated natural resources) and offers the following proviso on appropriation:

> Egalitarian Proviso: You may acquire previously unowned world resources if and only if you leave enough so that everyone else can acquire an equally advantageous share of unowned world resources.[30]

Otsuka's mention of "unowed world resources" is comparable to "unappropriated natural resources." Otsuka argues that shares are equally advantageous, "if they are such that each is able to attain the same level of welfare as anybody else given the combination of her worldly and personal resources."[31] According to Otsuka's interpretation of the Lockean Proviso, an appropriator leaves enough and as good for others if and only if she leaves others enough to acquire, at least, the same level of opportunity for welfare as the appropriator acquired from her removal of natural resources.

Otsuka specifically directs his egalitarian proviso to the appropriation of natural resources from the commons (although his language of "acquired" in the wording of his proviso suggests an openness to the idea of acquiring or removing natural resources in a way other than appropriation). With little difficulty, we can take Otsuka's egalitarian proviso on appropriation and covert it into a proviso governing the use of unappropriated natural resources. This conversion can take the following form:

> Pure Equal Initial Opportunity for Welfare Proviso: You may use an unappropriated natural resource if you leave enough so that everyone else can acquire an equally advantageous share (where this means everyone else is able—has

> the opportunity—to attain the same level of welfare given their combination of natural and personal resources).

For comparison, see again the Initial Equal Opportunity for Welfare Georgist proviso on use that has been proposed.

> Equal Initial Opportunity for Welfare Georgism Proviso: You can use an unappropriated natural resource X if and only if you leave others their initial equal opportunity for welfare share of the competitive rent value of the effective liberty to use X (in the precise fashion that you use X).

Before comparing the two views, one background point is in order. Part of Otsuka's broader theory of justice includes what he deems "robust self-ownership."[32] This includes the two formal rights of self-ownership that we saw in chapter 3 *and* the right to a subsistence share of natural resources. What this effectively means is that Otsuka thinks that the duty to leave others enough and as good (and abide by the egalitarian proviso that he offers) kicks-in or becomes activated only *after* an agent has appropriated a subsistence-share of natural resources. Otsuka offers this robustness condition of self-ownership because of his concern that abiding by his proposed egalitarian proviso might demand in rare cases that an agent become virtually enslaved (by being forced to contribute labor) in order to leave a share that affords others an equal opportunity for welfare. I will not discuss the merits of Otsuka's "robustness" condition on self-ownership here, but it is important to put the view on the table so that Otsuka's position on removing unappropriated natural resources can be contextualized in light of his broader understanding of self-ownership.

Before locating and assessing the differences between the Pure Initial Equal Opportunity for Welfare Proviso and the Initial Equal Opportunity for Welfare Georgism Proviso, it is worth first pointing out an important implication *shared* by both views. Notice that where the competitive rent of the effective liberty to use unappropriated natural resources is enough to *ensure* equality of initial opportunity for welfare the two views will not differ in outcome. When the competitive rent left by those who pay for the effective liberty to use unappropriated natural resources is enough to ensure, as opposed to merely promote, equality of initial opportunity for welfare, both views share the implication that a user of unappropriated nature resources must leave a share that affords others an initial equal opportunity for welfare.

In order to identify scenarios in which the two proposals yield different implications, we must consider cases in which the competitive rent of the effective liberty to use unappropriated natural resources is not enough to *ensure* equality of initial opportunity for welfare. In such cases, the Georgist proposal, given that it limits the duty of users to paying no more than the full competitive value of the effective liberties to use unappropriated natural resources, implies that a user's duty could fall short of leaving others enough to *ensure* an initial equal opportunity for welfare. But the same is not true of the Pure Initial Equal Opportunity for Welfare proviso. The Pure Initial Equal Opportunity for Welfare proviso maintains that a user of unappropriated natural resources has a general duty to leave enough to *ensure* equality of opportunity for welfare, and if the fulfillment of this duty means that a user must leave more than the full competitive value of the effective liberty to use unappropriated natural resources that she uses, then so be it.

The conflict, if we are to locate an area of disagreement with real consequence, is found in the question: could the user of unappropriated natural resources have a duty to leave others more than the full competitive value of the effective liberty of her use? The Pure Initial Equal Opportunity for Welfare Proviso renders a positive answer and Initial Equal Opportunity for Welfare Georgism Proviso renders a negative answer to this central question.

Here, a number of things can be said in support of the Georgist's negative reply. First, consider the feasibility point that typically an agent will not purchase a good (in our case the liberty to use an unappropriated natural resource) that is priced above its competitive value. They will "walk away" without using the unappropriated natural resource. Further, a respect for the independent moral status of agents should allow for this "walking away." If an agent does not use a natural resource, then under any plausible version of the Lockean Proviso she has no duty to leave others enough and as good because she has not removed anything from the shared commons. If the effective liberties to use unappropriated natural resources are priced above full competitive value, the prospective users will simply opt *not* to use the "over-priced" resources. The effective liberty to use an unappropriated natural resource simply will not be worth more than its full competitive value to a prospective user.

It would be a mistake to suspect that generally anything more than the full competitive rent would be paid by an agent considering whether the benefit of using an unappropriated natural resource is worth the duty that she owes to others as a result of such use. This point is not to be overlooked because unless users of unappropriated natural resources would leave (pay) more than full competitive value in order to use these resources, then the Pure Initial Equal Opportunity for Welfare proviso lacks any real strength to bring about equal initial opportunity for welfare not already had by the Equal Initial Opportunity for Welfare Georgism proviso. In other words, in order for the Pure Initial Equal Opportunity for Welfare Proviso to distinguish itself as a feasibly stronger egalitarian account than the proposed Georgist Proviso we must imagine cases in which prospective users *would* pay more than the full competitive value of the effective liberty to use unappropriated natural resources. These cases will be, at best, non-typical.[33]

But for the sake of argument, let us grant that there will be cases in which a prospective user of unappropriated natural resources would pay *more* than full competitive rent of their effective liberty to use. What should be said about such cases? First, we should note that in such cases users of unappropriated natural resources are subject to *monopoly pricing*. The payment for the effective liberty to use an unappropriated natural resources that a user must make is not its competitive value but instead is "whatever it takes" to bring about equal initial opportunity of welfare. Admittedly, the goal behind this monopoly pricing (to ensure equal initial opportunity for welfare) is much more noble than the typical image of monopoly pricing involving a capitalistic price gouger that preys on the desperation of agents for the sake of sheer selfish economic advantage. Still, something seems suspiciously immoral about monopoly pricing even when the intent of such pricing is to ensure equal initial opportunity for welfare.

Two concerns drive this suspicion about monopoly pricing. First, related to a recent concern, it is difficult to imagine anyone paying monopoly prices for something unless she was swindled into doing, operating under significant epistemic limitation, or just extremely desperate. Agents do not typically knowingly and voluntarily pay more than competitive value for things unless, perhaps, they need the good to subsist. We can envision a sleazy or rigged auction in which the owner of a object up for bid spreads false information about the item or even places plants to make false bids inducing interested agents to bid more than they would if they had full information. Second, it is plausibly unfair and exploitive to make an agent pay more than the competitive value for a thing she purchases *even if* this payment in excess of competitive value is used to help ensure equal initial opportunity for welfare. Again, this assumes that an agent would even be willing to knowingly and voluntarily pay more than competitive value to use an unappropriated natural resource.

The only occasion in which an agent would voluntarily and knowingly be willing to pay more than the competitive value for some good is likely if she needs the good to survive or live a minimally decent life, but charging someone more than the competitive rent value for some good that they need to survive or live a minimally decent life is presumably exploitive. We can go a step further here and say that the exploitation inherent in an agent being subject to pay more than the competitive value for some good that she needs to survive or live a minimally decent life has the strong potential to threaten her moral status as independent. One way for one agent to exercise a type of dominion over another is to subject them to monopoly pricing on goods that are necessarily for living a minimally decent life. (As noted earlier, Otsuka's addition of a robustness condition to self-ownership shows his sensitivity to this concern.) Placing the limit of the payment owed by those who use unappropriated natural resources at the competitive rent value of the effective liberty to use the resource in question affords agents an important protection against being subjected to the will or dominion of another.

This exhausts my positive defense of an Initial Equal Opportunity for Welfare Georgist Proviso on the use of unappropriated natural resources. The Lockean Proviso is not only for appropriation any more. My hope is that this chapter has offered a compelling case for the claim that those who remove (via their use) natural resources from the commons are bound by the Lockean Proviso and, as such, owe a duty to leave others enough and as good. And that one plausible way to interpret the Lockean Proviso is to say that those who remove from the shared common stock of natural resources, irrespective of how this removal takes place, should pay the full competitive value of their removal in a way that best promotes initial equal opportunity for welfare. I now proceed in the next chapter to discuss the appropriation of natural resources from the commons.

NOTES

1. The book is not an absolutely rivalrous good as it is possible for two or maybe even a few agents to read the book at the same time by standing very close to another and reading the pages simultaneously, but it is much closer to being a rivalrous good than not.
2. For further rejection of the idea that the world is initially jointly-owned see Anthony Fressola, "Liberty and Property: Reflections on the Right of Property in the State of Nature," *American Philosophical Quarterly* 81 (1981): 315-322.
3. For an account that denies the traditional account endorsed above that Locke invoked "leaving enough and as good" for others as a necessary condition of appropriation see Jeremy Waldron, "Enough and As Good for Others," *The Philosophical Quarterly* 117 (1979): 319-328.
4. For a defense of the Lockean Proviso by a non-libertarian, or at least non-committed libertarian, see Clark Wolf, "Contemporary Property Rights, Lockean Provisos, and the Interests of Future Generations," *Ethics* 105 (1995): 791-818.
5. Locke, *Second Treatise*, §33.
6. Ibid.
7. Those familiar with Robert's Rules of Order (and perhaps have been to a few too many organizational meetings) will recognize that secret ballot is not guaranteed under those procedures. In order for a secret ballot be part of the voting procedure a majority of the attendants at the meeting must vote openly for a secret ballot.
8. Alan Tomhave has given this idea considerable attention in his paper, *A Lockean Approach to the Fair Consideration of Future Generations*. Tomhave has presented this paper at both the 2005 meeting of the New Mexico West Texas Philosophical Association and the 2007 meeting of the Midwest Political Science Association.
9. I thank Alan Tomhave for bringing the important distinction between consuming an apple and destroying an entire apple tree to my attention.
10. See Mack, "The Self-Ownership Proviso."
11. Here one might say that Toxic Jack expropriated the shared water source when he dumped toxic chemicals into it. I do not have an objection with invoking the language of expropriation to describe what Toxic Jack did in respect to the water source because I take expropriation to simply mean unjustly use over some span of time.
12. Schmidtz, "When is Original Appropriation Required."
13. Ibid., 514.
14. Ibid., 510.

15. I thank Brian Kierland for bringing this distinction to my attention.

16. George, despite having been raised in poverty and receiving only a seventh-grade formal education, became one of the most recognized and celebrated American intellectuals of the nineteenth century. His most famous work, *Progress and Poverty* , sold millions of copies throughout the world and influenced the tax code in Australia, parts of Canada, the United States, and numerous other countries.

17. One could challenge whether this appeal to users removing the effective liberties of others is correct in cases of degrading and destructive use. In cases of overuse, general access-restricting use, and specific access-restricting use, the idea that a user has removed the effective liberty of others to use some, or a class of, natural resources seems clear, but the removal of an effective liberty to use is less clear in cases of destructive or degrading use. After all, it is true that Sarah can still use the spring that Toxic Jack has polluted. It is just that if she uses the spring she will die or get very sick. But her liberty to use "the spring" has not been removed. In such cases the appeal to a user removing an effective liberty can still make sense if the effective liberty being removed is carefully specified. For instance, what Toxic Jack removed would be a "clean spring suitable for healthy drinking" or the effective liberty of others to use a clean spring suitable for healthy drinking. When the effective liberty is properly specified, an appeal to the removal of effective liberties to use natural resources can be applied to all five types of morally problematic use.

18. Two different ways of assessing how competitive value should be determined popular in the economic literature are by utilizing an assumption of either perfectly competitive markets or various auction models. The more plausible strategy, I suggest, for assessing how competitive value ought to be determined is by employing some type of auction model. Employing an auction model allows us to ask what something (a natural resource) would fetch at an auction in the specific cases we are examining as opposed to relying on highly abstract constraints of "perfect markets."

19. A Vickrey auction has the advantage over a traditional auction (where the highest bidder pays their actual bid for the item) because it encourages agents to bid their true preferences. In a traditional auction an agent often has no good reason to bid the full value of what the item is worth to her. If having an item is worth exactly ten dollars to an agent, then that agent is indifferent to having the item or ten dollars and as such has no good reason to bid ten dollars. But if the agent knows that she will get the item at the second-highest price bid (or miss out on the item to a higher bid), then she has good reason to bid the full price she is willing to pay for the item.

20. See Henry George, *Progress and Poverty*; Hillel Steiner, *An Essay on Rights*; Nic Tideman, "Global Economic Justice," *Geophilos* 00 (2000): 134-146.

21. Peter Vallentyne and Nic Tideman, "Left-Libertarianism and Global Justice," in *Human Rights in Philosophy and Practice*, eds. Bruton Leiser and Tom Campbell (London: Ashgate, 2001) 451.

22. Otsuka, *Libertarianism Without Inequality*, 26.

23. Amartya Sen is to be credited with bringing the question of "equality of what" to the forefront of philosophical interest see his 'Equality of What' in *The Tanner Lecture on Human Values*, Vol. 1, (Cambridge: Cambridge University Press) 197-220.

24. See Rawls, *A Theory of Justice* (Cambridge, Harvard University Press, 1971).

25. See Steiner, *A Theory of Rights*; Ronald Dworkin, "What Is Equality: Part II Equality of Resources," *Philosophy and Public Affairs* 10 (1981): 185-245.

26. See Larry Temkin, *Inequality* (Oxford: Oxford University Press, 1993).

27. See Richard Arneson, "Equality and Equality of Opportunity for Welfare," *Philosophical Studies* 56 (1989): 77-93; G.A. Cohen, "On the Currency of Egalitarian Justice," *Ethics* 99 (1989): 906-44.

28. Ronald Dworkin, "Part II Equality of Resources" argues for an equality of resources model in which a hypothetical insurance scheme is used to compensate for unequal personal endowments. In addition Hillel Steiner's, *An Essay on Rights*, endorsement of a tax on genetic germ-line information that parents pay can be seen as a move to consider both the equalization of both external and internal resources.

29. Peter Vallentyne, "Brute Luck, Option Luck, and Equality of Opportunities," *Ethics* 112 (2002): 529.

30. Otsuka, *Libertarianism Without Inequality*, 24.

31. Ibid, 25.

32. Ibid, 15.

33. Additionally, if we grant that agents possess "robust self-ownership," as Otsuka endorses, and may acquire a subsistence share of natural resources before the demands of the Lockean Proviso are to be factored in, then the idea of any agent willingly *leaving more* than the competitive value of her removal of natural resources is strained even further under Otsuka's interpretation of the Lockean Proviso.

Chapter Six

The Appropriation of Natural Resources from the Commons

In the previous chapter, I defended a Lockean-style proviso on the use of unappropriated natural resources. In this chapter, I build upon the similar feature of use and appropriation within the commons—that they both *remove* natural resources, or their value, from the shared common stock of unappropriated natural resources—and extend the Initial Equal Opportunity for Welfare Georgist Proviso to cover the appropriation of natural resources from the commons.

When an agent uses a supply of drinking water by emptying toxic chemicals into it, she *removes the effective liberty* of others to use the water, possibly permanently, for drinking at least. All uses of natural resources involve, at least in a very minimal sense, some sort of removal. Any agent who physically impinges on a natural resource prevents, in at least some minimal fashion, others from doing the same. Alternatively, when an agent appropriates a supply of drinking water, she exercises a moral power and *removes the moral liberty* of others to use the water without her permission for drinking or other purposes. Both use and appropriation remove in a way that can serve to prejudice or injure others, but *what* is removed in both cases is different.

This suggests that the moral concerns associated with *removal* that spurred a proviso on the use of unappropriated natural resources can generally carry over to motive a similar proviso on appropriation. The difference is that when a proviso on appropriation is devised it must specifically be focused on the *removal of the moral liberty* that others enjoyed prior to the appropriation rather than (in the case of use) the *removal of the effective liberty* to use that others enjoyed prior to the scrutinized use. Before offering a formalized proviso governing the appropriation of natural resources from the commons (spoiler: this proviso will look a lot like the proviso governing the use of these resources within the commons), a question and some cursory points are in order.

Why address appropriation at all? Couldn't everything that needs to be said about the appropriation of natural resources from the commons be addressed in a thoroughgoing account of using unappropriated natural resources? Use is a very broad concept and could, for instance, cover cases in which an agent exclusively uses a natural resource on a permanent basis. With a few slight modifications, it seems plausible to think that appropriation, at least the core aspects of appropriation emphasized thus far, could for the most part be absorbed under some description(s) of use. But before any rush to drive a stake through the heart of appropriation is made a few points are in order.

First, there are cases in which an agent could appropriate a natural resource without ever using it. An agent could appropriate a large parcel of land that she simply wishes to exclude others from using, perhaps to afford her greater privacy over land that she is using. Agents can use a natural resource without appropriating it, but they can also appropriate a natural resource without using it.

Second, appropriation—even if it can often be thought of under a description of use—would constitute a type of use that deserves special attention whatever label we use to describe it. A type of use that allows an agent to permanently exclude others from using without her permission is important because, among other reasons, of the implications this has toward fostering an agent's ability to live the life of her choosing and, by the same token, preventing others from doing the same. The idea here is that while we might be able to often describe appropriation under the description of use, it is such an important type of use that it is deserving of separate attention and perhaps also a special label.

Lastly, talk of appropriation is probably not going anywhere anytime soon. No book or philosophical treatise is likely to change this, and that might be a good thing. Given that agents talk in terms of appropriation (even if they *could* often convert this into talk of use) and that talk of appropriation has important moral, social, and economic implications is a good enough reason to devote attention to appropriation as such.

Agents, for good reason, often want to be able to do more than use natural resources in non-permanent or non-exclusive ways; instead, they frequently want to become the private owner of a natural resource or an artifact that is derived from natural resources. In particular, agents frequently want a right against others from using (or blocking their access to) natural resources that they have (or desire to) make part of their plans and projects. As Richard Arneson puts the point:

> A salient fact bearing on the justifiability of appropriation is that people want to carry out projects that require secure possessions of land for extended periods of time. If A wishes to build and occupy a cabin, she needs assurances that the logs she chops on one day will lie where they fall until it is time to fashion them into cabin walls, and that once the cabin is completed, no one will occupy it without her consent. A's liberty to carry out such projects on a particular piece of land requires that B and all others not be at liberty to initiate their own projects on that piece of land which might interfere with A's project.[1]

Agents pursue plans and projects of their own and, as illustrated by Arneson's example, natural resources which agents incorporate into their personal and private plans and projects are often integral to pursuing autonomous aims and living lives of their choosing.

Consider that Bill plans to construct a log cabin and appropriate a small plot of land where he wishes to pursue a life of private seclusion and contemplation. He does not want anyone bothering him or using either the cabin he plans to build or land near the cabin. Bill simply does not want to share space with Sarah and Mark, the only other people in the world. He just wants to be left alone. There are plenty (thousands) of easily accessible logs that everyone can use to construct their own cabins, and both Sarah and Mark are capable of building their own cabins. Bill only wishes to appropriate the natural resources needed to construct a small cabin and the land needed to secure a small area around the cabin. Under any plausible version of the Lockean Proviso, Bill's leaving the rest of the world and its value to others who have the same capacities as he does satisfies his duty to leave others enough and as good.

Sarah, nonetheless, dissents to Bill's appropriation because she wants the three to share the entire world in perpetuity in a communal-like setting. She insists that Bill's plan to appropriate interferes with her plans and projects. Sarah is right that Bill's appropriation would interfere with her plans and projects. It would bar her from using a very small part of the world, and that is not the way that Sarah thinks a commune-style arrangement should work. Likewise, Sarah's plan to block all appropriation interferes with Bill's plans and projects. Does this tension create an unsolvable stalemate? No, at least not for most libertarians or Kantians. This is because Sarah's plans depend upon treating Bill merely as a means to live the life of her choosing, while Bill's plans do not treat Sarah in similar fashion.

Here, the objection might be made that the charge of "using another merely as a means" applies no less to Bill than it does to Sarah. Bill, so the thought might go, by appropriating is dictating the way that Sarah must live her life. But this objection is weaker than it first appears to be. To see this, note that Bill's desire to live a life of quiet seclusion is not contingent upon the actions or choices of others. He can bring his plans to fruition even in a world where he is all by himself, but the same is not true for Sarah. In order for her plan to be realized, she must live in a world with multiple agents who participate in a communal setting, as there are no communal settings of one. Others must take certain actions in order for Sarah to live the life of her choosing. Sarah's appropriation-blocking plan depends upon others acting as she desires them to act, while Bill's plan to appropriate does not. Bill is at liberty to unilaterally appropriate natural resources in the fashion described above, just so long as he leaves Sarah and Mark enough and as good.

Further, recall that agents do not need the permission of others to *use* (and thereby remove) unappropriated natural resources, at least when they meet certain moral conditions such as adherence to the Lockean Proviso. The moral precedent, as such, is already established for unilateral removal from the commons. Given this precedent, one has to point to some principled reason that distinguishes removal via use and removal via appropriation that would bar the unilateral appropriation of unappropriated natural resources but not the unilateral use of unappropriated natural resources. Given the moral similarities of both types of removal, I am skeptical that any principled reason(s) could be offered that would allow for the unilateral use of unappropriated natural resources but categorically disallow the unilateral appropriation of unappropriated natural resources. The important caveat lurking in the background is that this unilateral use or appropriation is subject to the Lockean Proviso.

Given the Lockean theoretical framework of this project, it would be a glaring oversight, given Locke's protracted defense of labor as a necessary condition of appropriation, to ignore the role that labor plays in the appropriation of natural resources.[2] To frame this discussion we can ask: is an agent's mixing her labor with an unappropriated natural resource either a necessary or sufficient condition of her exercising the moral power of appropriation?

Locke, rightly, rejected the idea that mixing one's labor with a natural resource is sufficient to appropriate the resource. This is because Locke held that in order to appropriate or at least retain rights of appropriation agents must, in addition to mixing their labor with the resource, leave others enough and as good *and* not allow what they appropriate to spoil or go to waste.[3] Locke goes so far as to say that an agent who takes more than his share by allowing what he gathers to spoil has "robbed others."[4] For Locke, the moral legitimacy of an appropriation goes beyond assessing whether an agent mixed her labor with a natural resource.

Robert Nozick provides a nice example to challenge the idea that labor mixing is sufficient to appropriate as he skeptically asks:

> If I own a can of tomato juice and spill it in the sea so that its molecules (made radioactive, so I can check this) mingle evenly throughout the sea, do I thereby come to own the sea, or have I foolishly dissipated my tomato soup?[5]

Nozick's example is informative because it demonstrates that mixing one's labor (if this is indeed what the soup-mixer does) with something *can be* a trivial and morally unimportant action. Pouring a can of soup into the sea seems as morally relevant in respect to appropriating the sea as doing jumping jacks in a boat traveling the sea.

There is ample reason to think that mixing one's labor with a natural resource is not sufficient to appropriate the resource. But is mixing one's labor with a natural resource necessary to appropriate the resource? Locke's answer is that labor mixing is necessary for appropriation. A significant challenge, however, can be brought against the idea that labor mixing is necessary for appropriation. This is because the endorsement of a labor mixing condition as necessary for appropriation would exclude agents with certain disabilities from appropriating natural resources. Imagine that Sarah is a quadriplegic who can alter nothing, or next to nothing, in the world. Sarah cannot effectively physically mix her labor with anything. Is Sarah's inability to mix her labor with anything a plausible bar to her being able to appropriate? I seriously doubt it. Say for the sake of argument that Sarah claims private ownership of a lake without displacing anyone or anyone's private ownership claim over the lake. No agent other than Sarah has observed the lake. Sarah, further, does whatever is required of her to leave others enough and as good. There might be some who would reject Sarah's appropriation of the lake under these conditions, but no one could plausibly suggest that *now* what prevents Sarah from appropriating the lake is that she fails to meet the necessary condition of mixing her labor with the lake. To maintain that agents *must* mix their labor with a natural resource in order to appropriate the resource is unfair to those who, through no fault of their own, cannot mix their labor with natural resources.

Given this criticism of the labor-mixing view, a defender of the view might adjust the view to suggest that mixing labor (when this is possible) with a natural resource is necessary for appropriation. We could imagine that Sarah could mix her labor with the lake but simply does not, for whatever reason, desire to mix her labor with the lake. She likes the lake just the way it is and wants to keep it pristine and untouched by anyone including her. Would anyone seriously maintain that it is Sarah's refusal to mix her labor with the lake that prevents her from exercising a moral power and gaining private ownership of the lake? I doubt such a position could be given any serious defense. Requiring that Sarah mix her labor with the lake before she is permitted to appropriate the lake is an unjustifiable restriction of her autonomous choice to "not alter or labor upon" her private property (or an object that will soon become private property). No one has a legitimate claim that Sarah must mix her labor with the lake before she is allowed to appropriate it .

Maintaining that labor is a necessary condition of appropriation is also an unacceptable hindrance to an agent's moral status as independent and her self-ownership, as it requires an agent to use her body (self) in certain ways before she is permitted to appropriate from the commons. Opting *not to labor* is every much an expression of an agent's moral status as independent and protected by her rights of self-ownership as opting *to labor*. That might sound like a "slackers creed," and it might be, but it is (also) an important aspect of an agent's moral status as independent that helps show the implausibility of suggesting that a labor-mixing condition is necessary to appropriate natural resources from the commons.

Perhaps a more plausible thought behind those who endorse labor-mixing as a necessary condition of appropriation is this: when agents improve natural resources, through their labor, then they have some claim to benefit from the improvement (added value) that their labor brought about. This view has found support amongst some notable contemporary political philosophers such as Baruch Broady and Hillel Steiner.[6] But notice that this view, however plausible, does not speak toward appropriation. Even if we grant the suggestion that an agent "owns her labor" and is, in some fashion, entitled to the value which she adds to an unappropriated natural resource through her laborious activity, this tells us nothing about how labor is connected, if it is at all, with appropriating such resources.[7] One can consistently hold the following two positions:

1. An agent mixing her labor with an unappropriated natural resource is not a necessary condition of appropriating the resource.
2. An agent is entitled to the improvement or value that she adds to unappropriated natural resources when she justly adds value to the resource.

It is, nonetheless, implausible to hold that "laborious *improvement*" is a necessary condition of appropriating natural resources from the commons. Imagine that a group of agents come to exist at the same time in a world that is a beautiful and pristine island paradise. As it turns out, *all* labor extended toward these natural resources would *reduce* the initial value of the natural resources on the island. If laborious *improvement* were necessary for appropriation, then this would imply that no one could appropriate anything on this island since no laborious improvement is possible. But, as considered earlier, appropriation typically allows an agent a greater degree of autonomy than arrangements not allowing for appropriation at all, and such a benefit should not be blocked merely because an agent happens to live in a place where natural resources cannot be improved via labor.

Now that mixing one's labor with a natural resource or laboriously improving a natural resource have been rejected as either sufficient or necessary for appropriation, we can consider whether *claiming* private ownership over an unappropriated natural resource is a necessary condition of appropriation. Appropriation, recall, is coming to privately own, where this ownership comes about by the *exercise* of a moral power to alter the initial normative situation of the commons. In order for an agent to appropriate she must, at least, take positive steps to exercise a moral power. An agent cannot appropriate in her sleep. Of course, an agent might have to fulfill other conditions before she appropriates such as leaving others enough and as good, but she must, at least, take positive steps to exercise a moral power.

It is plausible that claiming is one way, perhaps the only way, in which an agent may take a positive step to exercise the moral power of appropriation. This is not to suggest that merely claiming private ownership is sufficient to exercise the moral power of appropriation. Adhering, for instance, to the Lockean Proviso is necessary to exercise the moral power of appropriation. Additionally, it is not obvious what, if anything, besides claiming private ownership would count as exercising the moral power to appropriate. When an agent, for instance, is accused of exercising a moral power and appropriating a natural resource, an appropriate dismissal of this charge seems to be the denial of ever claiming such a power. Absent alternatives that would point to something other than claiming private ownership as a means to exercise the moral power of appropriation, I maintain that claiming is a necessary condition of appropriation.[8]

But what does it mean to claim ownership over something? This is a complex question that I will not give full attention to here; however, a few helpful observations can be made.[9] First, it seems that a claim of private ownership ought to have both a subjective and objective component. An agent who makes an ownership claim should understand the conceptual content of the claim. Uttering an ownership claim in a language that one does not understand, for example, does not count as claiming in the relevant sense, even if *others* fully understand the content of the ownership claim.

Further, a claim of private ownership should be more than an internal monologue with one's self. A claim of private ownership must outwardly expressed to the world that private ownership has been claimed. But what counts as an "outward expression to the world?" In some cases, a verbal declaration might satisfy this demand. In other cases, it might be plausible that building a fence and enclosing a piece of land will satisfy the demand of making an outward expression to the world. Or it might be that merely putting a door that shuts on a structure is enough to stake a claim of private ownership. Often times the contingencies of the world, and in particular social norms and customs, will mandate the proper objective conditions one must satisfy in order to stake a private ownership claim.

In a world with very few agents merely verbalizing a claim to everyone at the same time might suffice, but in a world with a substantial number of agents where such a verbalization is unlikely to reach everyone it might be that one must label or somehow mark the object which they are claiming private ownership over. This might be compared with an agent who posts a public announcement in a local newspaper announcing that she has found lost property and if no claims it, then she will take this to mean that the property has been abandoned and that after so long she will claim private ownership over the found item. In the case of an abandoned artifact, as discussed in chapter 2, I maintain that all agents have a type of equal claim over such artifacts and, as such, an agent who wishes to appropriate these artifacts must leave enough and as good for others.

Given that claiming is a necessary condition of appropriation, we can ask what, if any, moral advantage is had by being a *first-claimant* of private ownership in respect to an unappropriated natural resource. This question was not relevant in the case of use *per se* because everyone has a unilateral moral liberty to generally use unappropriated natural resources within the commons as long as they leave others enough and as good. But when an agent appropriates a natural resource from the commons she removes the unilateral moral liberty of others to use the appropriated natural resource. Does the status of being a first-claimant, as opposed to being a subsequent claimant, confer any greater moral advantage to appropriate? It is difficult to think of any reason why merely being first to get to an unappropriated natural resource should confer any moral advantage at all. But to find one such reason we can make an appeal to Pufendorf's astute observation that a first-user or claimant of a natural resource is morally different than subsequent claimants because this first-claimant, unlike her subsequent counterparts, did not *displace* the private ownership claims of others.

When an agent stakes first-claim as opposed to a later claim to an unappropriated natural resource, she is not making a claim which comes into conflict or displaces the private ownership claim of any other agent. When an agent claims private ownership of a natural resource she will often invest her time, labor, plans, and desires (her life) into the claimed natural resource. Subsequent claimers could then could displace, or attempt to displace, these investments made by the first claimer.[10] Because first-claimants are not engaging in a displacement of another's claim and subsequent claimers are, it is plausible to think that first-claimants have some, at least weak, moral advantage to appropriate not had by latecomers. I stress that the plausibility of assigning *some* moral importance to first claiming is, as we will soon assess, of significantly limited moral importance.

The takeaway of the above discussion is that mixing one's labor with or laboriously improving a natural resource is not a necessary condition of appropriation, but claiming is necessary for appropriation. An agent cannot come to privately own what she does not claim to own. Further, being the first to claim private ownership of a natural resource does hold some moral significance. With this background in place we are in a promising position to offer the moral conditions under which an agent may appropriate natural resources from the commons.

The same reasons for thinking that the Lockean Proviso applies to the use of unappropriated natural resources apply equally well to the appropriation of natural resources from the commons. These reasons, recall from the last chapter, revolved around the injury to others that can be brought about when a natural resource is removed from its initial shared condition. An appropriation *always* has the potential to injure others. This is because an agent who appropriates natural resources gains the claim right that others not use the appropriated resource without her permission, and this *always* removes the moral liberty of others to unilaterally use a resource that was removed from the commons *via* an appropriation.

The removal of a moral liberty as opposed to an effective liberty in the case of use will change the content, though not the character, of the duty owed to others by those who appropriate natural resources from the commons. The Equal Initial Opportunity for Welfare Georgist Proviso used to specify the duty owed by those who use unappropriated natural resources can also, with some modifications, be applied to describe the duty owed by those who appropriate natural resources in the following way:

> Equal Initial Opportunity for Welfare Georgism Proviso on Appropriation: You can appropriate a natural resource X if and only if you are the first to claim X and you leave others their equal initial opportunity for welfare share of the full competitive value of rights claimed over X.

Given the similar feature of *removal* from the shared common stock, the account of how an agent appropriates a natural resource will be very similar to how she justly uses an unappropriated natural resource, but some differences exist between the provisos on use and appropriation.

The proviso on appropriation makes explicit that it is the first agent to claim private ownership rights *and* pay the full competitive value of these rights that gains private ownership in an unappropriated natural resource. Merely being first to claim ownership rights, by itself, gains an agent nothing. In order to appropriate a natural resource, an agent must be the first to claim ownership rights in respect to the natural resource *and* pay the full competitive value of the rights that she claims in a fashion that best promotes equal initial opportunity for welfare.

The auction that sets the full competitive value of what an agent must pay in order to appropriate a natural resource can be structured exactly as it is to determine the full competitive value that an agent must pay in order to use an unappropriated natural resource within the commons. Further, as made explicit above, the full competitive value that is owed to others by appropriators must be paid so as to give others their initial equal opportunity for welfare share of the competitive value. The important difference between a use-auction and an appropriation-auction is *what* is being bid on. In an appropriation-auction, what is being bid on are moral rights of private ownership. This is different than a use-auction in which agents bid on the effective liberty to use natural resources.

In order to appropriate a natural resource, an agent must come to have, at minimum, the core private ownership rights discussed in chapter 4—including the right to exclude others from the resource and the right against others not to impede access to the resource. The rights claimed by an agent who appropriates a natural resource must minimally include these rights. The appropriation-auction, that is, must at minimum establish the full competitive value of these core private ownership rights in order to be auctioning appropriation.

The bidding power of agents could look different in an appropriation-auction than it does in a use-auction. Recall that in a use auction agents were bidding with their moral liberty to use unappropriated natural resources as well as blinded aspects of their selves. An appropriation-auction could incorporate both of these aspects of bidding power, but it could also include the ability to bid with the effective liberty to use unappropriated natural resources that had been previously acquired in a use-auction. If an agent previously gained an effective liberty to use an unappropriated natural resource through a use-auction, she could then add to her bidding power in an appropriation-auction by increasing her bid with her acquired effective liberty to use.

The proposed proviso on appropriation, additionally, is flexible enough to account for how an agent could appropriate a bundle of private ownership rights that goes beyond the core or minimal notion of private ownership. An agent could, for instance, in addition to the core set of private ownership rights, also claim the right to sell or otherwise transfer her property to another agent. This claimed income right would then go up for bid and, like other ownership rights, be assessed a full competitive value. An agent could, in principle, claim and pay the full competitive value of the *full* set of private ownership rights over a natural resource. The private ownership rights that an agent comes to have over a natural resource will depend upon her paying the full competitive value of the rights that she claims. As the private ownership rights claimed in respect to a natural resource increases, it stands to reason that the payment owed to others also increases accordingly. This is because each additional private property right gleaned by an appropriator brings with it an additional claim against another, where no such claim previously existed before the exercise of the moral power. The more rights had by a private owner, the more duties that others have in respect to the owner. This increase in injury to others, in the form of saddling others with additional duties, by an appropriator ought to be offset by leaving others enough and as good consistent with the ownership rights that are removed from the commons. The Initial Opportunity for Welfare Georgist Proviso on Appropriation offers a clear path by which this duty owed by those who appropriate can be met in a wide range of cases.

Before concluding my defense of an Initial Equal Opportunity for Welfare Georgist Proviso on the removal of unappropriated natural resources, I shall consider Murray Rothbard's challenge to Georgism. Rothbard stands out as a strong right-libertarian critic of Georgism, and his clear reasoning as well as his popular appeal makes his critique worth exploring. Rothbard, begins his challenge to Georgism by stating that:

> If every man owns his own person and therefore his own labor, and if by extension he owns whatever property he has "created" or gathered out of the previously unused, unowned, "state of nature," then what of the last great question: the right to control the earth *itself*.[11]

Our focus will squarely be upon what Rothbard deems the last great question: *the right to control the earth itself*. (Rothbard seems to suggest that agents do not have claims against the way that others treat or remove from the commons. For reasons defended throughout this work I have rigorously denied such a stance, but I will not return to this issue here.) Rothbard focuses on this question because he rightly maintains that labor itself cannot ground private property rights over natural resources. Labor can only ground claims to artifacts or the value added to natural resources.

Rothbard offers three alternatives concerning how private property rights in respect to the earth, e.g., natural resources, could be determined. Here he says:

> either the land belongs to the first user, the man who first brings it into production; *or* it belongs to a group of others; *or* it belongs to the world as a whole, with every individual owning a quotal part of every acre of land.[12]

The real competition is between the first and third alternatives. The second alternative is vague, and Rothbard does not afford it any extended consideration. Rothbard endorses the first alternative primarily because he criticizes the third (Georgist) alternative as an untenable option that would almost inevitably regress into some type of tyrannical political system. (I would not describe Georgism in the same way as Rothbard because his description suggests a system of initial joint-ownership over natural resources that I explored and rejected in chapter 5. Nonetheless, let us grant Rothbard's description of Georgism for the purpose of addressing his challenge.)

Rothbard most directly challenges Georgism by maintaining that:

> George's option for the last solution hardly solves the moral: if the land itself belongs to God or Nature, then why is it more moral for an acre in the world to be owned by the world as a whole, then to concede individual ownership? In practice again, it is obviously impossible for every person in the world to exercise effective ownership of his four-billionth portion (if the world population is, say, four billion) of every piece of the world's land surface. In practice, of course, a small oligarchy would do the controlling and owning, and not the world as a whole.[13]

The question that Rothbard offers to begin his line of reasoning misunderstands and confuses the Georgist position. Putting aside the role or relevance of God in a theory of private property, no one (Georgists included) seriously thinks that natural resources *belong* to nature. Natural resources are a part of nature, but they do not belong to nature. Things cannot belong to nature. To suggest otherwise is a category mistake. The Georgist, instead, should argue—the view that I defend in the first chapter—that natural resources initially belong to everyone. The suggestion that natural resources initially *belong* to nature or God only serves to help demonstrate the implausible or inapplicable position that one is driven to hold if she denies that initially natural resources belong to everyone. As discussed at length in chapter 1, the alternatives to the view that initially natural resources belong to everyone are strikingly bad—Rothbard's thoughts on the matter do not change this.

Rothbard's pragmatic rejection of Georgism is flawed for at least two reasons. First, it is not impossible for all agents to exercise effective ownership over some portion of the world to which they have some claim. An agent need not be in close physical proximity to a natural resource in order to exercise effective ownership in respect to it. Many private landowners, for instance, have never been within hundreds of miles of their private property but gain rental income from the land and as such maintain (income) rights of ownership. There is no theoretical bar against this same reasoning applying to ownership rights held by all agents in all natural resources. The rental value of the removal of unappropriated natural resources could be determined by an auction and the rental income gained from the auction could be divided among agents in the fashion suggested in the previous two chapters.

Second, Rothbard offers no compelling reason why his concern over an over-reaching and potentially tyrannical small oligarchy applies uniquely to a Georgist account and not to his preferred "first laborer" alternative. An abusive and tyrannical government will likely disregard any just system of private property, but this is not a charge that disproportionally undermines the Georgist position in favor of a "first laborer view." A corrupt oligarchy could just as easily abuse a system to establish the removal of natural resources based on "first laborer" as they could abuse a Georgist account. This seems especially true given the spotty and often disputed historical record that is ill equipped to determine, in the vast majority of cases, who was first to labor on an unappropriated natural resource.

The divine right model of private property that cast an immoral cloud over Europe for hundreds of years was based on a perversion of a "first laborer" theory of private property in unappropriated natural resources. The king, so the fairy tale went, was a direct descendant of Adam and, as such, inherited the earth from him. God gave Adam the world, and Adam, through his labor, was the *first* to bring the process of transforming natural resources into artifacts. The king, as the direct descendant of Adam, then claimed to be entitled to the fruits of the Earth. Of course, Rothbard would rightly reject the idea of divine right to unappropriated natural resources. The example shows, nonetheless, that the "first laborer" or "first possessor" approach favored by Rothbard—and many other right-libertarians—is no bar against corruption by a corrupt and power-hungry oligarchy. There is more than just a pang of irony when defenders of a "first laborer" account of removing unappropriated natural resources from the commons suggest that the Georgist position will inevitably lead to oppression, when historically the actual threat to agents has come from those who taut a first laborer account, *not* a Georgist account.

In the previous two chapters, I set out to offer the moral conditions that govern the use of natural resources within the commons as well as govern the appropriation of natural resources from the commons. The analysis of these conditions led to an endorsement of the Lockean Proviso that was interpreted in a Georgist fashion for both just use and appropriation. The duty of those who use unappropriated natural resources, consistent with a Georgist interpretation of the Lockean Proviso, is to leave others the full competitive value of their (highly specified) effective liberty to use in a fashion that best promotes equal initial opportunity for welfare. The duty of those who appropriate natural resources, again consistent with a Georgist interpretation of the Lockean Proviso, is to leave others the full competitive value of the private ownership rights that they claim in a fashion that best promotes equal initial opportunity for welfare. I now proceed in the final chapter to bridge the above theoretical findings with real-world practice that will prove to have significant implications concerning environmental degradation and global poverty.

NOTES

1. Richard Arneson, "Lockean Self-Ownership: Toward a Demolition," *Political Studies* 39 (1991): 40-41.
2. Locke, *Second Treatise*, §27-45.
3. Ibid. §31,38,46.
4. Ibid. §46.
5. Nozick, *Anarchy, State, and Utopia*, 173.

6. See Brauch Brody, "Redistribution without Egalitarianism"; Hillel Steiner, *An Essay on Rights*.

7. For a similar discussion see David Miller, *Market, State, and Community* (London: Oxford University Press, 1989) 55-56.

8. Brian Kierland has suggested that claiming is not necessary to appropriate and that alternatively, "using with the intention of exclusively using" could be sufficient to appropriate natural resources when others conditions such as leaving enough and as good for others are satisfied. Kierland has suggested the case of a slightly mentally impaired agent who builds and uses a log cabin with the intent of exclusively using this cabin but never claims ownership rights over the cabin because he lacks the mental ability or imagination to do so. If claiming is necessary for appropriation, then this agent cannot appropriate the cabin. Kierland takes this fascinating case to challenge the view that claiming ownership rights over a natural resource is necessary to appropriate. I am less convinced than Kierland that this case poses a compelling challenge to the idea that claiming is necessary for appropriation. The first thing to note about this case is that claiming can take many different forms. It might be that by taking certain actions in respect to his construction of the log cabin the builder has actually claimed ownership rights. If this agent, for example, really did intend to exclusively use the cabin, then he might have built a fence around the cabin or taken others steps to claim exclusive use (control private ownership) over the cabin. But let us say such actions didn't occur and, consistent with Kierland's example, the agent who has the intent of exclusively using the cabin never makes an "outward expression" of this intention to exclusively use the cabin he plans to exclusively use. If this is the case and no claiming at all has been made, then I am prepared to bite the bullet and maintain that the cabin user has not appropriated the cabin. Although, this result is probably not nearly as strong as it initially sounds since the agent who built the cabin could well have gained effective liberties to use the cabin which offer him moral protections against others using the cabin he constructed in various ways (even if he does not engage in an appropriation) by abiding by the earlier proposed Lockean Proviso directed toward the use of unappropriated natural resources.

9. For an excellent discussion of what is required in order to claim ownership or stake effective possession over some object see Carol Rose, *Property and Persuasion*, 11-23.

10. Not all acts of subsequent (displacing) private ownership claims are equally harmful. A subsequent claimer, for example, could claim a natural resource three second after the first claimer and before the first claimer made any investments of time, labor, plans, or desire in respect to the claimed resource. In such a case, admittedly, the morally troubling aspect of a "displacing claim" is either very minimal or non-existent.

11. Rothbard, *For A New Liberty*, 33.

12. Ibid., 34.

13. Ibid.

Chapter Seven

Global Poverty and Environmental Degradation

Thus far this work has been primarily focused toward developing and defending a Lockean left-libertarian theory of justice. The core idea of this proposed theory of justice maintains that equal and independent self-owning agents possess an equal initial claim to natural resources. This equal initial claim to natural resources was then used to motivate the idea that agents who remove natural resources from the commons either by means of use or appropriation have a duty to abide by the Lockean Proviso and, as such, leave others "enough and as good." This duty of removers was correlated with two claim rights. The first claim right of agents against users of unappropriated natural resources is to be left their equal initial opportunity for welfare share of the full competitive value of the effective liberties that users of unappropriated natural resources take from the commons. The second claim right of agents against appropriators of natural resources is to be left their equal initial opportunity for welfare share of the full competitive value of the private ownership rights that appropriators of natural resources take from the commons.

This final chapter moves away from defending the above theory of justice and instead concentrates on the implications that the proposed theory has toward global poverty and environmental degradation. Throughout, concerns surrounding the lack of material resources (poverty) and environmental degradation have been introduced and considered. But thus far these concerns have been considered as examples, both real and hypothetical, to bolster support for the developed Lockean left-libertarian theory of justice, and in particular what the proposed theory ought to say about the use and appropriation of natural resources within the commons. This concluding chapter seeks to cover new ground by discussing the implications that the proposed theory of justice has toward global poverty and the degradation of the environment that greatly, and often gravely, impact the lives of real agents. I will not, however, spend a good deal of time in this chapter offering empirical evidence to defend the claim that global poverty and environmental degradation are very serious problems. A mountain of empirical evidence already exists which chronicles the vast extent to which global poverty and environmental degradation pervade our world, and I have little to add on this score that has not already been said in a very persuasive fashion.[1]

Why focus on global poverty and environmental degradation? There are plenty of very good reasons to be particularly concerned with global poverty and the ruin of the environment that generally have nothing directly to do with Locke's political philosophy or libertarian thought. Such reasons, for instance, include the virtue of acting charitably toward those in desperate need or the general disutility created by pollution. In fact, it is difficult, if not impossible, to think of any plausible theory of justice that would have little or nothing to say about global poverty and environmental degradation. Libertarianism is no exception.

Global poverty and environmental degradation ought to be extremely salient concerns for *any* libertarian theory of justice or, for that matter, any liberal theory of justice in the Lockean tradition. This is because poverty, especially the abject poverty that confronts so many around the world, and the ruin of the earth serve as two of the most wide-ranging threats and existing impediments to the independent moral status of agents and with it the ability of agents to lead the rights-respecting lives of their own choice and design. Libertarians ought to be first in line, or at least racing to get to the head of the pack, to voice a concern over global poverty and the ruin of the environment.

It would be bizarre to take seriously the idea that *all* agents, in virtue of their moral status as equal and independent, should be able to live the rights-respecting life of their choosing with the selves they have without also having a good deal of concern with how poverty and environmental degradation bear on this ability. For a libertarian to ignore or be unconcerned with global poverty and environmental degradation would be to endorse a "toothless libertarianism" that could say the right things about the liberty of agents *in the abstract* but then refuse to adequately recognize and explore two of the gravest threats to the liberty of agents *in the real world*. Libertarians have traditionally shown a good deal of concern with how force and fraud, as rights violating actions, undermine the moral status of agents as independent. This concern is well founded, and libertarians have been right to show special attention to these worries. A thoroughgoing and complete libertarian theory of justice, however, ought to be no less concerned with the violation of rights that occurs when an agent is left so little of the commons by another that she is placed at risk of starvation than with the violation of her rights that occur when she is punched in the face.

The data surrounding the magnitude of global poverty is staggering. At least 870 million agents worldwide suffer from chronic undernourishment.[2] These agents, the poorest in the world, have been referred to Paul Colliver as the "bottom billion."[3] A mind-boggling five and half million children under the age of five die each year due to malnutrition, and millions more die of preventable disease.[4] In the short time since you have started to read this chapter, somewhere in the world roughly half a dozen children have died from lack of nutrition or some related cause. Thousands of children will die from malnutrition in the time it would take even a fast reader to read this book from cover to cover. If this does not serve to sound a very loud and troubling moral alarm, then I cannot imagine what statistic or description about the desperate plight of others would do so. It is difficult to imagine a graver threat to the independent moral status of agents than mass starvation.

The child who digs through a garbage dump in an economically underdeveloped county so that she may scavenge enough recyclable materials to fend off starvation *has the same initial moral claim to natural resources* as the child of an affluent parent in a developed country. Neither of these children has any greater moral claim to natural resources or the value of these resources. Of course, you could not ascertain this by comparing the actual plight of these children. There are many reasons, most of them grounded in historical injustice e.g., the mass colonization of the world and heavy debt burdens forced upon developing countries trying to escape the historical scars of colonization, that explain the monumental disparity between the opportunities for welfare had by the "bottom billion" and those had by the "top billion." Aside from instances of straightforward historical injustice in which natural resources were simply expropriated and taken from the commons with no regard for leaving others enough and as good, some of these reasons can be traced to the economic advantage had by those who are "early developers," governmental corruption, war and other conflict, and the lack of charitable giving by those with the means to do so. The reasons for the abject poverty of the "bottom billion" are numerous and often complex but can be summed up in simple terms: *for a multitude of reasons, the "bottom billion" have been denied their rightful claim to the value of natural resources.*

It is difficult to estimate the amount of competitive value that could be gleaned by requiring those who remove natural resources from the commons, or those who have greatly benefitted from such removal, to pay the full competitive value of either their removal or, in some fashion, for the removal that they have greatly benefitted from.[5] The amount of this competitive value, for lack of a better description, would be massive. This would still be true even if the full competitive value for removing natural resources began tomorrow and a type of "amnesty" was given for any past instances in which an agent removed from the commons, or benefitted from such removal, without satisfying the Lockean Proviso.

This mass amount of competitive value in all likelihood, if left to agents in a fashion that promoted equal initial opportunity for welfare, would put an end to the abject poverty that confronts the world's poorest agents. Thomas Pogge has proposed that a global resource dividend ought to be collected on the sale of natural resources, such as petroleum and precious metals that would then be used to help alleviate the poverty of the world's poorest agents.[6] Pogge, while not a libertarian, offers a clear way in which the moral claim that all agents have in respect to natural resources can find its way back to actual agents within the parameters of the existing global economic structure. What prevents this, of course, is primarily that agents, by and large, would rather not pay the "moral cost" of removing natural resources, and at present there is little political will within the international community, or most communities generally, to make removers pay such costs.

There is nothing infeasible or outlandish with the idea of building a global resource dividend into the cost of commodity trading or other exchanges of natural resources. A variation of this idea has been employed by the state of Alaska for the last three decades. The state of Alaska sets aside a portion of the money it receives from the sale of oil (or lease of lands for the purpose of removing oil and other natural resources) into a permanent fund that, among other things, pays an annual dividend to most state residents.[7] The state has been paying this annual dividend to state residents since 1982 and the amount of the payment ranges roughly between 500 and 2000 dollars per year.[8] The payment in 2012 was 878 dollars per resident.[9]

The "Alaska Model" has its flaws. The model, for instance, does not demand that removers of natural resources leave enough to adequately satisfy the Lockean Proviso, although in fairness the permanent fund that allows for the dividend payment is meant to leave payments for future generations of Alaskans, and this partly explains the relatively small leaving. The dividend payment, additionally, leaves agents a "per capita share" as opposed to an "equal initial opportunity for welfare share." Further, consistent with the idea that *all* natural resources initially belong to everyone, there is no compelling reason to think that political boundaries demarcate legitimate claims to natural resources or their value. But despite its flaws the Alaska Model is a promising and encouraging advancement because it demonstrates a framework and workable path toward how the Lockean Proviso might be incorporated as an enforceable duty of justice in actual practice.

Despite some notable partial exceptions such as the Alaska Model, at present next to nothing is done *to enforce* the right that all agents have against removers of natural resources to be left enough and as good. This lack of enforcement is a major contributing factor to the desperate poverty that plagues the world's poorest agents. Aside from reasons of greed, this lack of enforcement can in many ways be traced to the prevailing belief that alleviating global poverty ought to involve charitable giving but not enforceable justice. This thought suggests that not giving to others might represent a bad or vicious character, but it is not a something that the state, or anyone for that matter, ought to make an agent do.

This thought about charity needs to be carefully considered to discern its relevance in respect to removers of natural resources leaving others enough and as good. Charity involves giving an agent something that she has no moral claim to receive. Enforceable justice, alternatively, can involve leaving an agent something that she has a moral claim to be left. This is clear in the case of compensatory justice. An agent, for instance, who has been victimized by another has the right to be left some value compensating for her loss by the guilty party. Making the guilty party compensate her victim is clearly not an instance of charity but instead is a payment or leaving demanded by justice.

It is reasonable to think that whether an agent opts to give from *her personal stock* of privately owned goods to others who have no claim to what she is *giving* is a matter of charity and not enforceable justice. This description of charity, however, bears little relevance to the obligation of agents who remove (or have benefited significantly from such removal of) natural resources that initially belong to everyone. The difference between giving and leaving, in this context, is crucial. When an agent *gives* in a charitable sense, she transfers something that she has legitimate claim over to another who has no such legitimate claim to what is given. On the other hand, in the context of removing natural resources that initially belong to everyone, when an agent *leaves*, in accordance with her enforceable duty of justice, she does not take all for herself something that others have a legitimate claim to.

The image of desperately impoverished agents who lack access to basic necessities and even arguably access to their selves evokes in many of us who have such access a great degree of sympathy and concern. One practical way to make good on this concern and eradicate the poverty that prevents so many from living a decent life is to shift the focus, both in terms of language and action, from that of giving to that of leaving. Alaska does not give charity when it sends dividend checks to its residents. The state, instead, leaves (albeit an inadequate approximation of) what its residents are owed as a result of natural resources being removed from their state. When the language of leaving is invoked, this (unlike talk of giving) acknowledges and attempts to directly address that it is the taking of natural resources and their competitive value without leaving others enough and as good that greatly contributes to the desperate poverty of the "bottom billion." None of this is meant, however, to deny that charitable giving can make a lasting and profound impact to help alleviate global poverty.[10]

Aside from shifting the focus from giving to leaving, another important advancement in the fight against global poverty is to foster and support the idea that agents possess a *basic human right* against removers of natural resources to be left their equal initial opportunity for welfare share of the competitive value of such removal. I leave open what the precise content of basic human rights include except to say that they include rights in respect to self-ownership as well rights in respect to being left enough and as good. An agent's basic human right to be left enough and good by those who remove natural resources is grounded in the initial equal moral claim that all agents have in respect to natural resources. For an agent, or group of agents, to remove from the commons without leaving others their enough and as good share is an instance of theft on a global scale and plausibly constitutes a human rights violation by an often identifiable party.

The designation of basic human rights is important in this context, at least pragmatically, because it signals that the right is one held by all agents despite their national origins, ethnic background, religious affiliation, or other contingent features of their humanity. I would maintain that all moral rights work in this fashion as separate from an agent's political, social, cultural, and religious identity. The lines between moral and political rights, however, are often blurred in practice, and designating that agent being left her enough and as good share constitutes a basic human right signals that the right transcends her contingent identity.

There are a plethora of ways in which the duty of removers to leave others their enough and as good share could be discharged. But, by far, the most efficient and almost certainly most effective way for removers of natural resources to discharge this duty is to work through international non-governmental institutions or nation states. Allen Buchanan has suggested that all agents have a *limited* moral obligation (what he deems the *Natural Duty of Justice*) "to help ensure that all agents have access to institutions that protect their basic human rights."[11] Buchanan's suggestion of a Natural Duty of Justice is informative and helpful for our larger discussion because it is difficult to image how a remover of natural resources could leave *all* others enough and as good without acting through (and fostering where necessary) institutions that protect basic human rights.[12]

The pragmatic difficulties associated with removers of natural resources delivering the competitive value of their removal to others would likely demand that they work in some fashion within an international institutional framework or arrangement. But the role of the Natural Duty of Justice to the fulfillment of the Lockean Proviso goes beyond delivery concerns. This is because the protection of an agent's basic human rights is intimately related with her opportunity for welfare. Agents who lack access to institutions that protect their basic human rights will almost always suffer, in varying ways, from putrid opportunities for welfare. This claim needs to be qualified in light of what rights are included within the set of basic human rights as well as the extent and frequency to which these rights are violated, but the basic point carries through. Where we find agents who lack access to institutions that protect their basic human rights, we find agents who by and large have much less opportunity for welfare than their contemporaries who have access to institutions that protect basic human rights. Helping to ensure that agents have access to institutions that protect their basic human rights is a clear way to enhance their opportunities for welfare. If removers of natural resources have a duty to leave others their *competitive value equal initial opportunity for welfare share* as I have maintained, then this leaving would plausibly be done first and foremost *in ways that ensure agents have access to institutions that protect their basic human rights*. Giving priority to the Natural Duty of Justice viewed in this light serves as a means in our world to *begin* to meet the demands of the Lockean Proviso.

There might be exceptions to the idea that the fulfillment of the Lockean Proviso ought to be first directed toward the Natural Duty of Justice. Leaving in a fashion that saves another from immediate starvation, for example, would likely be demanded of a remover before leaving in a fashion that adhered to the Natural Duty of Justice. But aside from clear cases where others have an immediate need to be left a share that is necessary for their subsistence, a good rule of thumb is that the best place to begin the process of adhering to the Lockean Proviso can be found with the Natural Duty of Justice. Leaving others their competitive value equal initial opportunity for welfare share is not necessarily satisfied once the Natural Duty of Justice is exhausted. That is, the Lockean Proviso does not lose its force even if all agents one day gain access to institutions that protect their basic human rights. The Natural Duty of Justice is merely a plausible place to begin satisfying the Lockean Proviso.

Presently, within the international community concerns of global poverty are largely relegated to the realm of charity and not enforceable justice. This can be seen, for example, when considering the Universal Declaration of Human Rights (UDHR). The UDHR passed without any dissenting votes by the General Assembly of the United Nations in 1948 and was adopted at the time by the United States. Article twenty-five of the UDHR states that:

> Everyone has a right to a standard of living adequate for the health and well-being of himself and his family, including food, clothing, housing, and medical care and necessary social services, and the right to security in the event of unemployment, sickness, disability, widowhood, old age, or other lack of livelihood in circumstances beyond his control.[13]

The human rights made explicit in article twenty-five, however, are generally not treated by the United Nations or the international community at large as correlating with any enforceable duties. The UDHR is sometimes described as falling under the umbrella of international law, but this is a misnomer. Given the lack of will of the international community to enforce nearly all the articles in the UDHR, it is better deemed an "international suggestion" rather than an aspect of "international law." Matters of economic justice are, within the international community, nearly always treated as charity—that is, as a voluntary giving that ought to be encouraged and praised but not mandated in any enforceable fashion.

There is reason for guarded optimism, nonetheless, that international bodies (or at least large collections of nation-states) could hold matters of economic justice (including the fulfillment of the Lockean Proviso) to be concerns of enforceable justice rather than suggestions of charity. At present, the European Court of Human Rights (ECHR) is the best available model to see how this might be done. The ECHR is made up of forty-seven member states, all of which recognize the courts legal jurisdiction to make enforceable rulings in respect to the European Convention on Human Rights. A complaint about a human rights violation can be brought either by an individual agent or by a member state.

The ECHR, while not without flaws, has issued rulings against member states that have been accepted by the offending party and been instrumental in bringing about change that better protects the human rights of agents and, on occasion, provides compensation for the victims of human rights abuses.[14] Members found to be in violation of the European Convention of Human Rights by the ECHR frequently lodge appeals, heard by the ECHR, against the Court's decision. The willingness of a losing party to appeal, rather than merely refuse to acknowledge the legitimacy of the decision, suggest that the ECHR generally enjoys a good deal of recognition from its members. If an agent or nation does not recognize the authority of a court they, at least when they have the power to do so, do not lodge an appeal with the very same court that they do not recognize. The ECHR functions as an at least quasi-effective arbiter of enforceable justice in respect to human rights, in large part because the member states *recognize and accept* the authority and legitimacy of the Court.

The European Convention of Human Rights does, interestingly, mention property. A right in respect to property does not appear in the original 1950 convention agreement, but is covered under article 1 of the first protocol agreed to by member states in 1952. Article 1 of the first protocol states that:

> Every natural or legal person is entitled to the peaceful enjoyment of his possessions. No one shall be deprived of his possessions except in the public interest and subject to the conditions provided for by law and by the general principles of international law.[15]

The working assumption is almost certainly that "peaceful enjoyment of his possessions" refers to legitimately acquired *private* property. But with a little creative vision, this clause can be interpreted to encompass a common property right that all agents initially possess in respect to natural resources. When an agent, or groups of agents, remove from the commons without leaving others enough and as good they could be subject to the complaint that they interfered with the "peaceful enjoyment of others possessions" and hence are violators of basic human rights. This charge could be, consistent with the rules of the ECHR, brought either by an individual agent or by a member state. At present, there would likely be little sympathy from the ECHR shown to a claim of violation brought about by the failure of a remover of natural resources to leave others enough and as good. The possibility exists, however, that the apprehension to such a claim of violation might slowly wither away as the belief that natural resources initially belong to everyone blossoms, and agents begin to take more seriously the idea that removers who fail to abide by the Lockean Proviso violate the basic human rights of others.

One final cautionary note in respect to how the proposed Lockean left-libertarian theory of justice impacts global poverty and economic justice is in order. The elimination of global poverty—which, granting a few reasonable empirical assumptions, could be accomplished if the proposed Lockean left-libertarian theory of justice were implemented—does not imply that economic inequality, even vast inequality, would or should be eliminated. There would still be some agents with more, perhaps much more, than others under the proposed Lockean left-libertarianism theory of justice. This is for at least two reasons. First, agents have a right against removers of natural resources to be left an equal initial *opportunity* for welfare share, and it is highly likely that some agents will come to have less than others because they will squander their shares. Second, self-owning agents plausibly have a right to the value that they add, through their labor or other means, to natural resources which they justly remove from the commons. If we grant that agents will add disproportionate amounts of value to natural resources that they justly remove, then some agents will end up having more than others.

Thus far in this chapter, I have defended the view that the proposed Lockean left-libertarian theory of justice offers a path toward eliminating global poverty that is consistent with the self-ownership of agents. For the remainder of the chapter, I will defend the view that the proposed Lockean left-libertarian theory of justice is equally well suited to offer a path toward vastly curtailing the degradation of the environment. Before defending this position, however, one background consideration is in order.

Earlier, specifically in chapter 2, I expounded on the view that natural resources play a crucial role in the survival, autonomy, and well-being of agents. This was done, in part, with the use of examples that helped demonstrate how polluting actions and other misuses of the environment can gravely harm agents. Additionally, I advanced the claim that access to natural resources plays a crucial role in fostering the moral status of agents as equal and independent. It is fairly clear that rational agents normally have—or if they had relevant information, would normally have—a great deal of concern with the treatment of, and in particular removal of natural resources from, the environment. But I have not addressed the question of whether natural resources *in themselves* possess moral value. That is, whether natural resources are intrinsically valuable. Considering this question plays an important role in establishing the proper moral relationship between agents and non-agent resources.

My reply to this question, likely to the dismay of many environmentalists and nearly all proponents of the deep ecology movement, is that natural resources (or ecosystems) *in themselves* possess no moral value and are not, again in themselves, subject to considerations of justice.[16] Justice, in the sense I have been employing the term, is reserved for the duties that agents owe to one another. To illustrate this idea with a stark example, imagine that all agents decide to throw one last big party and destroy or seriously degrade all the natural resources in the world. *All* agents in the world agree to this in an informed and voluntary fashion, and there are no beings in the world such as children, fetuses, embryos, or non-human agents that will ever become agents in this world, nor are there future generations of agents that will occupy the world after the presently existing generation of agents ruin it. I maintain that the partying agents have done nothing unjust because their actions do not violate a claim owed to anyone. The agents are at moral liberty to throw the party described above.

Natural resources and the broader environment which they constitute are extremely instrumentally important because of the vital impact that they have in the lives of agents, but they are not intrinsically valuable in themselves. Natural resources simply fail to possesses the feature(s) that would demarcate some thing as having moral value in itself. Natural resources, for instance, lack both moral agency and sentience. (Here I put aside the real possibility of sentient natural resources. If, in fact, a natural resource is sentient, then an argument could be made for the claim that the intrinsic value of this sentient natural resource is grounded in the sentient nature of the natural resource.)

One pressing difficulty with maintaining that a tree (even a grand and majestic tree) or a stream of running water possess moral value in themselves is to offer some criteria which plausibly grounds the intrinsic moral value of these non-agent resources but does not, at the same time, erroneously ground the intrinsic moral value of human artifacts such as hammers and watches. I assume that, no matter how beneficial to human pursuits, watches and hammers are not the types of things that are not morally valuable in themselves.

What feature then could ground the intrinsic value of natural resources without, at the same time, falsely establishing that hammers, watches, and other such artifacts possess intrinsic value?

One proposal is that what grounds the intrinsic moral value of at least some natural resources, that would not proliferate such a designation to watches and hammers, is the feature of being alive. Although this feature would not apply to most natural resources, it would apply to a good number of natural resources such as trees and other flora. This feature of "being alive," however, is not a vey promising feature to ground intrinsic moral value. Bacteria is a living organism, but that does not seem like a good reason to think that bacteria are morally valuable in themselves. It seems highly dubious to maintain that an agent does anything unjust or more broadly morally wrong by killing bacterium unless perhaps when this destruction of bacterium harms another agent. Arguably any view that implies bacteria has intrinsic moral value has a ready built *reductio ad absurdum* for the view.

Another proposal that might be offered here is to suggest that natural resources are part of an ecosystem and that anything which is part of an ecosystem (as well as an ecosystem itself) is morally valuable in itself. There are two problems with this view. The first is that the "problem of bacteria" rears its head again. Bacteria is part of an ecosystem, in fact, frequently an important part of an ecosystem. But just as before, it is difficult to swallow the view that bacteria is intrinsically, opposed to being solely instrumentally, valuable.

The second problem is that there is no clear reason to morally distinguish a "natural" ecosystem over an unnatural artifact-driven system that supports the lives, well-being, and autonomy of agents. We can label such a system an *artisystem* as opposed to an *ecosystem*. Imagine that agent, much like us exist in a world with no natural resources but instead only possess technologically advanced artifacts that were left behind by some now extinct group of beings. These technologically advanced artifacts are functionally equivalent to the natural resources on Earth, and as such, the artisystem(s) that supports life on its planet are functionally equivalent with the ecosystems that support life on Earth. If an ecosystem has intrinsic moral value, then so too presumably would the functionally equivalent artisystem. There might be an argument for why this presumption is wrong, but it not clear what form such an argument would take or if any such argument could be successfully made. The artisystem described above does not have intrinsic value because the artifacts that comprise the artisystems are valuable only in so far as they advance the good of agents. But then why not think the same thing is true of an ecosystem? Unless a moral distinction can be drawn between an ecosystem and the artisystem described above, then the same lack of intrinsic moral value ought to apply to both.

None of this is to deny the awe-inspiring capacity of natural resources and the natural world, although the agents who live with the artisystem described above would likely be similarly inspired by the advanced artifacts and artificially driven world that they inhabit. I am sympathetic, in the same way as influential deep ecologist Warren Fox is, to the idea that there is often an intuition that develops (or is somehow released) when an agent experiences the wonders of natures that tend to suggest the "unity of nature."[17] For many agents, an intuition suggesting the "unity of nature" would be difficult to suppress (or odd not to experience) under the gaze of a star-filled sky perched on a ledge at some secluded spot in Yosemite National Park or marveling under the amazing splendor of a giant sequoia more than two millennia old towering more than three hundred yards toward the sky. I am, however, unconvinced that deep ecologists and others have successfully made the argumentative leap from the intuition that some type of unity of nature exists to the claim that non-agent resources are valuable in themselves.

The issue of whether natural resources, or more generally ecosystems, are valuable in themselves is complex and controversial. I do not take my brief thoughts to offer anything approaching a definitive resolution of the issue. These thoughts, albeit refutable, do however offer reasons for thinking that it is plausible to maintain that natural resources are only morally valuable in so far as they advance the good of agents. This finding is important because, if true, it suggests that there is no genuine moral tension or conflict *between* natural resources and agents. Agents are morally valuable in themselves, whereas natural resources are valuable because they advance the good of agents. Any moral conflict surrounding the removal of natural resources involves how such a removal by an agent or group of agents *impacts the lives of other agents*.

Focusing on the destructive and degrading removal of natural resources illuminates three clear environmentally centered ways in which an agent can substantially impact the lives of other agents. These are:

1. By using natural resources that belong to another in a destructive or degrading fashion.
2. By using unappropriated natural resources in a destructive or degrading fashion.
3. By using one's own privately held natural resources in a degrading fashion that will eventually, but not immediately, destroy or degrade the property of others at some future time.

Note a common feature that the above categories of environmentally problematic removal share. They are all problematic instances of *use*. This is because the appropriation of natural resources does not, in itself, have any environmental implications whatsoever. By appropriating a natural resource, an agent comes to have a certain set of moral rights with respect to the resource, and this leaves open how she uses the resources and in turn what impact she will actually have on the environment. Environmental impacts are brought about by using natural resources and not by appropriating them.

In the case of (1) assuming that an agent did not receive permission from the private owner of the natural resource(s) that she used in a destructive or degrading fashion, then she engaged in a clear violation of property rights that ought to trigger considerations of compensatory justice. While instances that fall under (1) are important cases of environmental injustice they do not concern the removal of natural resources from the commons. Unlike (1), the type of removal made explicit in (2) represents clear cases in which an agent removes from the commons in a fashion that harms others because of the damage that she does to the environment that she shares with others. Examples of this, both hypothetical and real, have been peppered throughout this work and have included the Toxic Jack scenario discussed in chapter 5 along with the pollution of the atmosphere and the oceans discussed in chapter 2.

Cases that fall under (3) bring with them a new and intriguing set of moral issues. Unlike (1) and (2), the agent in (3) uses *her own* natural resources in a fashion that will destroy or degrade the property of others in the future, possibly even in the very distant future. The destructive or degrading use of (1) and (2) clearly invoke concerns of justice—that is to say, an agent has a right against others from using natural resources in the ways described in (1) and (2). This is because in (1) and (2) an agent degraded or destroyed a resource that *belonged to others* either privately or in some shared common fashion. But the use of natural resources in (3) is trickier given that in such cases an agent uses her own natural resources in a way that will eventually, but not immediately, result in the destruction or degradation of another's property.

An appropriator of natural resource(s), recall from the discussion in chapters 4 and 6, gains the liberty right to use her appropriated resource(s) without needing the permission of others, but this is not an unqualified right to use in any way that the appropriator desires. An appropriator cannot use *her resources* in a fashion that violates the rights of others. Agents, on this score, have a right against those who privately own natural resources from using their privately held resources in a manner that will, in temporally open-ended fashion, non-consensually destroy or degrade the property of others, including property in the self. A private property owner is not at liberty to use her property in a fashion that will result (even at some time in the distant future) in the non-consensual destruction or degradation of another's property. Here I assume that another's property includes either the private property of another or unappropriated natural resources that belong to everyone. The above proposal is controversial but not radical. The justification for the above right already exists in the well-accepted claim of a property owner against the non-consensual use of her property by another. The right proposed above merely offers a temporal extension of this already well-accepted right.

It is not difficult to see how a private owner might use her property in a fashion that violates the right proposed above. An agent could, for instance, appropriate a parcel land so that she may bury toxic chemicals in the land. When she buries the chemicals they *only* destroy or degrade *her land*. But over time, maybe over a long period of time, the buried chemicals begin to release a chemical into the atmosphere that destroys or degrades the property of others. Others have a moral claim against the initial act of "burying the chemicals" that *initiated a sequence of events* that directly lead to the destruction or degradation of their property. The fact that this sequence of events took a good deal of time to matriculate does not speak against the clear nature of the rights violation.

A comparison to a violation of self-ownership is apt here. If an agent places a bomb in the car of a rival that is set to explode in six years and *will* explode in six years killing her rival, then she has violated the self-ownership rights of her rival. The rival plausibly has a claim right against others from initiating a sequence of events that will directly lead to a gross violation of the property rights that she has in her self.

If the above reasoning is correct, then those who appropriate have a duty not to use their property in ways that will, in non-consensual fashion, destroy or degrade the property of others. This suggestion has significant implications concerning those that initiate a sequence of events with their own property that will result in the degradation of the destruction of another's property. Those who destroy or degrade the environment, at least where this harm involves the property of others, are not shielded by the claim that this harm resulted from a use of their own private property.

Another way to approach the environmental injustice of agents using their own private property in ways that will, at some time in the future, destroy or degrade the property of others is to invoke the Lockean Proviso. The Lockean Proviso risks being ineffective if the duty to leave others enough and as good is not understood in a broad temporal fashion. This is because the Lockean Proviso is not meant to provide "moral cover" for the cunning agent who reasons as follows—oh yes, I will leave others enough and as good today, but tomorrow I will initiate a sequence of events that destroys or degrades what I have left in a few years. The possibility exists that those who use natural resources in a fashion that initiates a sequence of events that degrades or destroys the property of others could not do this with resources that they have appropriated because their disregard for the Lockean Proviso prevented them from appropriating in the first place. The Lockean Proviso, viewed in this light, would be a duty that applies to removers of natural resources not merely at the point of removal but on an on-going basis. This possibility tends to suggest that ultimately category (3) might collapses into category (2).

The proposed Lockean left-libertarian theory of justice strongly encourages conservation efforts. Agents, acting in a self-interested fashion, will desire to make their payment of competitive value to others as small as possible. This goal of reducing one's competitive value payment to others can manifest itself in a number of different ways, but the basic strategy will be the same—*remove less (either by using less or appropriating less)* from the commons.

The idea of mandating that removers of natural resources pay the full competitive value of their removal offers a strong incentive for agents to conserve and preserve natural resources for present and future generations of agents to use and benefit from. If an agent conserves and removes less of the world, then, holding other considerations constant, she has a duty to leave others less than if she had removed more of the world. The proposed Lockean left-libertarian theory of justice heavily incentivizes, through economic self-interest, the conservation of natural resources. The above suggestion that economic self-interest can greatly impact behavior toward the removal of natural resources should come as no surprise. An agent is more likely to ride her bike to work or take public transportation when the price of gasoline rises and is more likely to pursue such options the higher the price rises.

Many municipalities in the United States have suffered greatly because of oppressive drought conditions during 2012. The typical way in which local governments cope with drought is to place restrictions, sometimes very severe restrictions, on the use of water. That is, they mandate the conservation of water through legal force. In some cases, the shortage of water not only is the result of drought but is exacerbated by the frivolous and overuse of water. This type of use is often, though not always, a consequence of water being priced well below its competitive value. Given the extremely low cost of removing water, agents in the United States and in many parts of the world have virtually no economic incentive to conserve water. If agents had to pay the full competitive value for their removal of water, then it is highly plausible that many communities would be better suited to handle the next drought.

The strong economic incentive of the proposed Lockean left-libertarian theory of justice to conserve natural resources has implications concerning the use of renewable as opposed to non-renewable resources. Non-renewable resources, given their nature, are subject to conditions of scarcity in direct proportion to their use. The more non-renewables are used up, the more scarce they become. This rule of thumb holds technological advancement constant. As non-renewables become increasingly scarce, it stands to reason that their competitive value will rise accordingly. This rise in the cost of removing non-renewables as they become increasingly scarce serves as a way to encourage the conservation of these resources.

A worry, however, is that the way in which the competitive value of many non-renewables is presently established, largely through (global) commodity trading, grossly underestimates the genuine, morally sensitive competitive value of non-renewables. This is because the present way of establishing competitive value is insensitive to moral considerations that would, if factored in, generally increase the competitive value of natural resources. The present process for establishing competitive value is simply to let those that have economic resources (however this came about) to bid their preferences and in so doing establish a market clearing price for these resources. But this customary means of establishing competitive value leaves many agents effectively shut out, typically because they are impoverished or because of various practical limitations, from genuinely participating in the processes that establishes the competitive value of natural resources. This exclusion means that the market clearing price of removing natural resources, through less actionable demand, is (much) less than it would be if all agents could effectively participate in the establishment of competitive value. If, for instance, the competitive value of non-renewables were established using a procedure approximating the hypothetical auction explored in chapters 5 and 6 in which agents operate under conditions of *fair bidding power*, then the competitive value of natural resources would be greater than it is under the present day morally insensitive conditions.

It is difficult to say with any great precision exactly what the true moral cost (made an economic cost) of removing non-renewable natural resources would be under the proposed theory of justice in which agents have fair bidding power to establish the competitive value of natural resources. One promising method here might be to use computer simulations to help approximate what results the proposed hypothetical resource auction discussed in chapters 5 and 6 would yield in terms of the competitive value of natural resources. It is safe to assume that this competitive value would be substantially higher than it presently is for removing non-renewables and, as such, would foster greater efforts to conserve.

One consequence beyond the conservation of non-renewable natural resources that would result from mandating that removers of non-renewables leave the genuine moral cost of their removal is that the use of renewable natural resources would be greatly encouraged. This is because, given considerations of scarcity, a renewable natural resource will always, or nearly always, have a (much) lower competitive value than a non-renewable natural resource. There will even be cases in which the effective liberty to use a *renewable* natural resource has *no* competitive value at all because the resource is not removed from the commons in any discernable sense. If a natural resource is not removed from the commons, which is the case with at least certain renewable resources, then agents have no reason to bid for the effective liberty to use the resource. This is because in such a case others could not remove the resource and prevent the prospective bidder from using it. A bid, under such circumstances, for an effective liberty to use a natural resource that cannot be removed from the commons would be a wasted because the agent (and all others) already possess the effective liberty to use the resource that cannot be taken away or removed by others. Bidding for the effective liberty to use such a thing would yield the bidder nothing.

Consider, for instance, the use of the sun or solar power. Although given that the sun is not physically impinged upon, it is not clear that it is actually subject to use as opposed to simply being a natural resource that agents can benefit from, but I invoke the notion of use here for sake of demonstration. The use of the sun does not remove in any interesting sense the sun, or the value of the sun, from the commons, and as such, its use is arguably not subject to the Lockean Proviso. That is to say, an agent who uses or benefits from the sun does not owe a duty to *leave* enough and as good for others, because they have *not removed it*, in any interesting sense, from the commons.

Now I turn to address an objection that one concerned about the protection of the environment might make in respect to the proposed Lockean left-libertarian theory of justice. The proposed theory of justice allows in principle for the removal of *any* natural resources from the commons, including removals that could destroy or degrade the environment. After all, the effective liberty to use a natural resource in a destructive or degrading way has a competitive value, and nothing in the proposed account bars an agent from paying this price of removal in a fashion that promotes equal initial opportunity for welfare. The agent who leaves enough to pay for such a use could then proceed to exercise her justly acquired effective liberty and destroy or seriously degrade natural resources. As such, the proposed theory of justice ought to be rejected because it allows for the serious degradation of the environment.

This is a shrewd and troubling objection that deserves attention. My reply to this objection is to first acknowledge that the proposed theory of justice does allow, in principle, exactly what the objector reasonably fears. The proposed theory of justice allows agents to bid on all possible effective liberties to use unappropriated natural resources, including effective liberties that allow for destructive and degrading use. There is, however, good reason to think that the effective liberty to use natural resources in destructive or seriously degrading ways (particularly when such uses impose serious harms on others) will demand the leaving of a great deal of competitive value. This is because agents will often have a strong interest in bidding a great deal to block or prevent others from gaining the effective liberty to use natural resources in destructive or degrading ways.

We could imagine, for instance, that the effective liberty to use, in a specified polluting fashion, the sole water source in a desert community is up for bid in a Georgist resource auction. Agents could pool their resources together and collectively purchase the effective liberty to use, in a specified polluting fashion, the sole water source as a means to prevent such pollution. The removal of natural resources in a destructive or degrading fashion, under this proposal, could be kept in check by the cooperative bidding power of agents.

Agents would have the opportunity to act cooperatively by pooling their bidding power to remove certain natural resources from the commons for the express purpose of protecting and preserving such resources. Note that agents in the proposed Georgist auction possess fair bidding power, and as such, there is ample opportunity for agents to determine the fate of how natural resources are removed in a socially cooperative or democratic fashion. There is no Mr. Burns of *Simpsons* fame to sweep in with his bags full of dubiously gained money and thwart the will of agents acting collectively to preserve and protect natural resources. The arrangement detailing how agents who pool their bidding power together to protect and preserve natural resources could be made explicit through contractual agreement among members of a "resource preservation cooperative."

These resource preservation cooperatives could purchase the effective liberties (or private ownership rights) that create "environmental sanctuaries." These environmental sanctuaries could function in similar ways as existent Marine Sanctuaries, National Parks, or other environmentally protected areas. The extent to which agents pool their bidding power and protect natural resources is at their discretion. My hope would be that under conditions of fair bidding power and cooperative agreements agents would, for instance, pool resources that created a Marine Sanctuary that encompasses more than the one percent of ocean area in the actual world that carries this designation at present. But there are no guarantees of this and the proposed theory, admittedly, allows agents discretion to protect and preserve the environment to the extent that their preferences dictate.

Further, the proposed left-libertarian account embraces the reality that non-negligible amounts of non-renewable natural resources will be destroyed or degraded, e.g., trees will be destroyed to make toilet paper, and land will be bulldozed in order to make way for houses and apartments. The focus ought to be on how those who remove in such a fashion pay for their removal of natural resources that belong to everyone, not upon a presently infeasible utopic vision where non-renewable natural resources are never, or almost never, destroyed or degraded. This idea of making those who degrade or destroy natural resources pay the true cost of what they remove is the idea behind carbon credits. In many parts of Europe and California, as of January 2013, industrial facilities that release large amounts of carbon and as such degrade the atmosphere—a natural resource that belongs to everyone—must purchase credits to pay the cost of their degradation. The state of California generated nearly 300 million dollars in revenue from its first sale of carbon credits in early 2013. The state is committed to using the money from the sale of carbon credits to fund clean energy research and initiatives. Even though the carbon credit sale in California gets nowhere close to demanding that those who degrade the atmosphere pay the full competitive value of this removal, it is a good start. The sale of carbon credits is a promising idea because it provides a model by which those who remove the commons must pay for what they take. The owners of the commons—all of us—should demand no less.

In this chapter, I defended the view that the Lockean left-libertarian theory of justice developed and endorsed throughout is sturdy enough to tackle two of the gravest moral problems confronting humanity: the desperate poverty of roughly a billion agents and the ruin of the environment. These problems, no doubt, can seem so monumental that it is easy to take a defeatist attitude toward solving them. This understandable sense of defeatism should be combated, but at the same time blurry-eyed idealistic optimism in respect to these problems can also be counterproductive if it fails to appreciate that powerful individuals and groups have a strong economic interest in these problems not being solved. Frances Moore Lappé has offered the apt suggestion of being a "*possibilist*" when it comes to confronting the challenges of environmental degradation and global poverty.[18] It is possible to eliminate global poverty and save the earth from ruin, but this possibility can only be realized if agents take action to bring these changes about.

This is where Lois Gibbs and the "Love Canal People" rise again. Recall from the introduction that Lois Gibbs was the head of the Homeowners Association of Love Canal that took two members of the federal EPA hostage. The "Love Canal People," after suffering years of horrendous health problems brought about by the environmental degradation of their community and getting the run-around from local, state, and federal government officials, took the drastic step of holding government officials hostage until their demand to be relocated from Love Canal was met. There are many lessons to be learned from the events at Love Canal, but to conclude I want to focus on the lessons that tend toward what motivates agents to bring about change.

The "Love Canal People" acted out of a sense of desperation but not only from desperation. They also acted out of anger, an anger driven by the denial of what they felt they had a rightful claim toward, namely their land, health, and lives. The "Love Canal People" acted in an extreme fashion. Their anger, however, at being denied what they felt they had a rightful claim to is an ordinary response. Agents tend to get upset and react accordingly when they sense that what they have a rightful claim to is being threatened or undermined. Herein lies the potential pragmatic punch of the revolutionary idea that natural resources belong to everyone.

The vast majority of agents are confronted with a profound sense of injustice when they step back and contemplate the desperate poverty that besieges so many around the world or the increasing degradation of the environment that their children will inherit. This sense of injustice is frequently suppressed and does not manifest into direct action because it is not accompanied with the moral idea that such injustice takes away what everyone (including themselves) have a moral claim to. But the feeling of injustice is not a waste; it is the kindling needed for direct action. The spark to light the fire of direct action, I maintain, with either be desperation, the type of desperation experienced by the "Love Canal People," or it will be a very powerful idea that persuades people that what they have a rightful claim to is under assault. One of the best candidates for such an idea is the belief that natural resources belong to everyone and that some of the most serious injustices in our world are the direct result of this truth being disregard and trampled upon.

When agents come to believe and appreciate that it is not just "the atmosphere" that is polluted, but it is "their atmosphere" that is polluted, then change will be afoot. When agents come to believe and appreciate that most of the wealth in the world today was created, at some stage in history, through the unjust use and expropriation of natural resources that belong to everyone, then change will be afoot. When agents come to believe and appreciate that no one has a greater initial claim to the world and its value than another, then the possibility of a better world can be made a reality. We can only hope that this possibility is brought about with the genuine appreciation of ideas as opposed to the violence that all too often accompanies desperation.

NOTES

1. For a compelling account of the mountain of the empirical evidence that suggests the world is subject to vast amounts of environmental degradation see Frances Moore Lappé, *EcoMind: Changing the Way We Think to Create the World We Want* (New York: Nation Books, 2011). For a compelling accounts of the vast magnitude of global poverty see Peter Singer, *The Life You Can Save: How to Do Your Part to End Global Poverty* (New York: Random House, 2010); Jeffery Sachs, *The End of Poverty: Economic Possibilities for Our Time* (New York: Penguin Group, 2006).

2. This data is drawn from "The State of Food Insecurity in the World 2012" report of the Food and Agriculture Organization of the United Nations (FAO). The full report can be found at www.fao.org/publications/sofi/en/.

3. Paul Colliver, *The Bottom Billion* (Oxford: Oxford University Press, 2008).

4. This estimate is drawn from, "The State of the World's Children 2006: Excluded and Invisible" report of UNICEF. The full report can be found at www.unicef.org/sowc06/fullreport/full_report.php.

5. There is a strong case to be made for the claim that those who have *benefited* from the historical injustice created by others historically failing to leave enough and as good for others should in some fashion pay to rectify the injustice that they benefit from. The idea is that agents should not only rectify injustice when they have caused them but also when they benefit from them. Or alternatively, agents could refuse any benefit from historical injustice. I greatly suspect, however, that the vast majority of agents in developed countries would see their wealth plummet if they refused any benefit derived from historical injustice.

6. Thomas Pogge, "A Global Resource Dividend," in *Ethics of Consumption: The Good Life, Justice, and Global Stewardship*, eds. David Crocker and Toby Linden (Lanham, MD: Rowman and Littlefield, 1998): 501-536.

7. A recent anthology of work has been devoted to discussing the Alaska Permanent Fund Dividend, see *Alaska's Permanent Fund Dividend: Examining Its Suitability as a Model*, eds. Karl Widerquist and Michael Howard (New York: Palgrave Macmillan, 2012).

8. The precise historical information of dividend payouts can be found out by consulting information provided by the Alaska Permanent Fund Corporation which oversees the Permanent Fund that provides for the dividend at http://www.apfc.org/home/Content/dividend/dividendamounts.cfm.

9. The state of Alaska provides this and other information about the dividend payment at http://pfd.alaska.gov/.

10. See Singer, *The Life You Can Save*.

11. Allen Buchanan, *Justice, Legitimacy, and Self-Determination: Moral Foundations for International Law* (Oxford: Oxford University Press, 2004), 27.

12. For an attempt to interpret how the Natural Duty of Justice is limited and in this context as a limited duty applies to real world agents, see Eric Roark, "Moral Duties and International Justice: Developing Allen Buchanan's Natural Duty of Justice," *Review Journal of Political Philosophy* 4: (2006): 113-132.

13. The complete UDHR as well as other related resources can be found on the United Nations website at www.un.org/en/documents/udhr/index.shtml.

14. The ECHR maintains a repository of case law, highlights pending judgments, issues press releases, and offers webcasts of selective hearings from their website to be found at www.echr.coe.int/ECHR/homepage_en.

15. The full text of the European Convention for the Protection of Human Rights and Fundamental Freedom (as well as all amended protocols) can be found at www.echr.coe.int/ECHR/EN/Header/Basic+Texts/The+Convention+and+additional+protocols/The+European+Convention+on+Human+Rights./

16. For two of the best known and influential rejections of the view I endorse see Aldo Leopold, *A Sand County Almanac: With Essays on Conservation from Round River* (New York: Ballantine, 1986); Arne Naess, "The Shallow and the Deep, Long Range Ecology Movement. A Summary," *Inquiry* 16: 1973: 95-100.

17. Warren Fox, "Deep Ecology: A New Philosophy of our Time," in *Environmental Ethics: An Anthology*, eds. Andrew Light and Holmes Rolston III (Malden, MA: Blackwell Publishing, 2003): 252-261.

18. Lappé, *EcoMond*, 2.

Appendix: Defining Use

At first glance, the concept of use seems intuitive and easy to grasp, but further reflection proves that glance mistaken. Jimmy uses his Little League bat when he steps up to the plate and swings in the hope of hitting a home run. No doubt, examples like this could be given *ad naseum* to illustrate the concept of use. But it is desirable to go beyond an intuitive treatment of use given the important role that the concept of use plays within the bundle of rights that constitute private ownership. In what follows, examining the concept of use will be restricted to the use of natural resources or other physical objects.

Consider the following two plausible accounts of using a natural resource.

1. An agent uses a natural resource X if and only if she physically impinges on X.
2. An agent uses a natural resource X if and only if she makes X part of her plans and projects.

Note that the physical impingement account of use can address clear cases of use where a person sends a physical signal in order to use an object at a far distance. When an agent, for instance, fires a bullet into a target, the shooter uses the target because she sent a physical signal that physically impinged on the target. The plans and projects view can also account for how the shooter uses the target by maintaining that by firing the bullet at the target the shooter makes the target part of her plans and projects.

Both accounts of using a natural resource have plausibility and will often yield a plausible treatment of cases. Imagine an agent walking along a trail in the woods. The agent is using the trail. The agent physically impinges on the trail. The agent has also made the trail part of her plans and projects. It is likely that a comprehensive evaluation of cases will yield the result that both the physical impingement and plans and projects accounts of use are generally plausible. But general plausibility aside, there are a wide range of cases that offer strong challenges to both accounts of use.

Consider the following case as a counterexample to the physical impingement account of use.

> Jill takes cover from a passing storm under a tree with dense leaves and branches. The tree's canopy offers Jill protection from the storm, but she does not physically impinge on the canopy.

The above example, as well as many other similarly spirited examples that could be modeled from this example, challenge the thought that an agent uses a natural resource only if she physically impinges on the resource. The intuition that Jill uses the tree canopy even though she does not physically impinge on the tree's canopy is the result of an association between use and benefit. The use of a physical object can occur when an agent takes steps to benefit from the object and indeed does benefit from the object, even if this design does not include physically impinging on the object.

Counterexamples that involve *viewing* an object also pose a significant challenge to the physical impingement account of use. Imagine a simple case where Jill watches television. Jill's watching of the television seems to be a use of the television even though she is not physically impinging on the television or sending any physical signal to the television. It seems odd to suggest that Jill only uses the television when she physically moves it into her living room or sends a physical signal with a remote control or otherwise physically impinges on the television set. To claim that the only uses of a television occur when the television is being physically impinged upon seems like a desperate attempt to save the physical impingement account of use from what should be a fairly non-controversial counter-example. It is true that the television is an artifact as opposed to a natural resource, but with little work a multitude of cases involving natural resources could be constructed using this viewing inspired challenge.

> Consider yet another example that challenges the physical impingement account of use. Jill and her friend Mary are walking along a trail on a very windy day. A sudden gust of wind forces Jill to grab onto a tree to avoid being blown away. Mary then grabs onto Jill to avoid the same fate.

Jill can be said to be using the tree by physical impinging on it. But what should be said about Mary's use in this example? It seems true that Mary is using Jill by physical grabbing her to avoid being blown away by the wind. But it is also plausible that Mary is using the tree that Jill is latching onto. The tree keeps both Jill and Mary from being blown away and they both seem to be using the tree even though Jill is the only one physically impinging on the tree.

One might try to rescue the physical impingement view from this counterexample by arguing that Mary is indirectly physically impinging on the tree because her physical impingement on Jill is, while mediated by Jill's body, physically impinging on the tree. But this attempt at rescue demonstrates a significant problem with the physical impingement view. Our current best physics tells us that in some way, *all* physical objects, at an atomic level, interact with each other. Thus, if the current physics is right, all physical objects in some way, however small, physically impinge upon one another. Every physical object then would be physically impinging on all other physical object and under the physical impingement account of use it would be impossible, in a strict sense, to distinguish cases of using natural resources from cases of non-use.

Although the physical impingement account of use is flawed, there still seems to be some intuitive appeal to the idea that a person uses a natural resource when she physically impinges on the resource. The worry from physics can be addressed by adding a "non-negligible physical impingement" clause. This would require some work to distinguish negligible physical impingement from non-negligible physical impingement, but it seems like a task that could be accomplished. Physical interaction at the atomic level, for instance, could be put to the side and counted as negligible.

Additionally, the examples of Jill taking cover under a tree or watching television suggest that non-negligible physical impingement is not necessary for use. Neither example, however, speaks against the idea that non-negligible physical impingement is sufficient to use a natural resource. I do not anticipate that any convincing counterexample can be given to show that non-negligible physical impingement is not sufficient to mark the use of a natural resource. This view might be challenged with the reply that an agent could *unintentionally* physically impinge on a natural resource and in so doing not use the resource, but this is mistaken. An agent who makes a cake while sleepwalking still uses flour and sugar even though she is not aware of using these things. An agent need not be aware that they are using something to use it.

The plans and projects account of use is by no means immune from criticism, but nonetheless it has the potential to augment the non-negligible physical impingement sufficient condition of using natural resources. One difficulty with the idea that an agent uses a natural resource whenever she makes the resource part of her plans and projects is that this approach has the potential to explode and trivialize instances of use. An agent with a vivid imagination, for instance, could devise all sorts of fantastic plans with all kinds of natural resources. This agent could have the delusional plan to use the entire world by spinning the world on her index finger. But to suggest that an agent is using the entire world because of a delusional plan would trivialize what it means to use a natural resource.

A proponent of the plans and projects account of use must find some way to exclude use brought about by delusional or fantastically impossible plans and projects. This task can be accomplished. A plans and projects account of use, for example, can require that an agent have some *relevant connection* to the natural resources that are said to be part of her plans and project. Consider, for example, the following proposed sufficient condition of use. An agent uses a natural resource if she makes the natural resource part of her plans and projects in such a way that there is a reasonably strong probability that the resource will materially impact her well-being. The restricted plans and project sufficient condition of use specified above would suggest that Jill uses the tree canopy (even though she does not physically impinge on it) because she makes it part of her plans and projects in a way that stands a reasonably strong probability of materially impacting her well-being.

This revised plans and project account of use offers a promising sufficient condition of use, but it fails to be a complete analysis of use. One reason for this is because an agent can engage in use without any coinciding plan or project. Consider, for example, an agent who sleepwalks and simply travels up and down stairs in her slumber. The agent plausibly uses the stairs, but they are not part of any plan or project. Plans and projects require some sort of conscious and intentional planning and use can be done absent these elements. A full account of using natural resources that combines the best elements of both the physical impingement and plans and projects accounts can be summarized as follows:

> *An agent uses a natural resource X if she physically impedes on X in a non-negligible way, or if she makes X part of her plans and projects in such a way that there is a reasonably strong probability that X will materially impact her well-being.*

Bibliography

Alexander, Bob. 2011. *Rawhide Ranger, Ira Allen: Enforcing Law on the Texas Frontier.* Denton, TX: University of North Texas Press.

Arneson, Richard. 1989. "Equality and Equality of Opportunity for Welfare." *Philosophical Studies* 56: 77-93.

_____. 1991. "Lockean Self-Ownership: Toward a Demolition." *Political Studies* 39: 36-54.

_____. 1992. "Property Rights in Persons." *Social Philosophy and Policy* 9: 201-230.

Arrhenius, Svante. 1896. "On the Influence of Carbonic Acid in the Air upon the Temperature on the Ground." *Philosophical Magazine and Journal of Science* 41: 237-276.

Attas, Daniel. 2001. "Freedom and Self-Ownership." *Social Theory and Practice* 26: 1-23.

Becker, Lawrence. 1976. "The Labor Theory of Property Acquisition." *The Journal of Philosophy* 73: 653-664.

Berlin, Isaiah. 1969. *Four Essays on Liberty.* London: Oxford University Press.

Brands, Henry W. 2003. *The Age of Gold; The California Gold Rush and the New American Dream.* New York: Random House.

Brody, Brauch. 1983. "Redistribution without Egalitarianism." *Social Philosophy and Policy* 1: 71-87.

Buchanan, Allen. 2004. *Justice, Legitimacy, and Self-Determination: Moral Foundations for International Law.* Oxford: Oxford University Press.

Chartier, Gary. 2013. *Anarchy and Legal Order: Law and Politics for a Stateless Society.* Cambridge: Cambridge University Press.

Christman, John. 1986. "Can Ownership Be Justified by Natural Rights?" *Philosophy and Public Affairs* 15: 156-177.

_____. 1994. *The Myth of Property: Toward an Egalitarian Theory of Ownership.* Oxford: Oxford University Press.

Cohen, G. A. 1986a. "Self-Ownership, World-Ownership, and Equality." In *Justice and Equality Here and Now*, ed. Frank Lucash. Ithaca, NY: Cornell University Press. 108-135.

_____.1986b. "Self-Ownership, World-Ownership, and Equality, Part II." *Social Philosophy and Policy* 3: 77-96.

_____. 1989. "On the Currency of Egalitarian Justice." *Ethics* 99: 906-44.

_____. 1995. *Self-Ownership, Freedom, and Equality.* Cambridge: Cambridge University Press.

Colliver, Paul. 2008. *The Bottom Billion: Why the Poorest Countries Are Failing and What Can Be Done About It.* Oxford: Oxford University Press.

Diaz, Robert and Rutger Rosenberg. 2008. "Spreading Dead Zones and Consequences for Marine Ecology." *Science* 321: 926-929.

Dworkin, Ronald. 1981. "What Is Equality: Part II Equality of Resources." *Philosophy and Public Affairs* 10: 185-245.
Fressola, Anthony. 1981. "Liberty and Property: Reflections on the Right of Property in the State of Nature." *American Philosophical Quarterly* 81: 315-322.
Ford, K. Lacy. 2009. *Deliver Us From Evil: The Slavery Question in the Old South.* New York: Oxford University Press.
Fox, Warren. 2003. "Deep Ecology: A New Philosophy of Our Time." In *Environmental Ethics: An Anthology*, ed. Andrew Light and Holmes Rolston III, Malden, MA: Blackwell Publishers. 252-261.
Gard, Wayne. 1947. "The Fence-Cutters." *The Southwestern Historical Quarterly* 51: 1-15.
Gauss, Gerald. 1994. "Property, Rights, and Freedom." In *Property Rights*, ed. Ellen Paul, Fred Miller and Jeffrey Paul, New York: Cambridge University Press. 209-240.
George, Henry. [1879] 1955. *Progress and Poverty.* Reprint. New York: Robert Schalkenbach Foundation.
Gibbard, Allen. 1976. "Natural Property Rights." *Nous* 10: 77-86.
Gibbs, Lois. 1998. *Love Canal: The Story Continues.* Gabriola Island BC, Canada: New Society Publishers.
Gorr, Michael. 1995. "Justice, Self-Ownership, and Natural Assets." *Social Philosophy and Policy* 12: 267-91.
Grotius, Hugo. [1609] 1916. *The Free Sea.* New York: Oxford University Press.
_____. [1625] 1901. *The Rights of War and Peace.* ed. A.C. Campbell. New York: M. Walter Dunne.
Grunebaum, James. 1987. *Private Ownership.* New York: Routledge & Kegan Paul.
Hardin, Garrett. 1968. "Tragedy of the Commons." *Science* 162: 1243-48.
Hohfeld, Wesley. 1919. *Fundamental Legal Conceptions.* ed. W.W. Cook. New Haven: Yale University Press.
Honoré, A.M. 1961. "Ownership." In *Oxford Essays in Jurisprudence*, ed. A. G. Guest. London: Oxford University Press. 107-147.
Hornbeck, Richard. 2010. "Barbed Wire: Property Rights, and Agricultural Development." *The Quarterly Journal of Economics* 125: 767-810.
Jones, Peter. 1986. "Private Property and Public Order: The Hippy Convoy and Criminal Trespass." *Journal of Law and Society* 13: 343-370.
King, Stephen. 1987. *Misery.* New York: Signet.
Kirzner, Isreal. 1978. "Entrepreneurship, Entitlement, and Economic Justice." *Eastern Economic Journal* 4: 9-25.
Konkel, Lindsey. 2012. Jan 27, 2012, "The Great Escape: Gene-Altered Crops Grow Wild." Environmental Health Services. www.environmentalhealthnews.org/ehs/news/2012/gm-crops-escape-and-grow-wild.
Kropotkin, Peter. 1909. *Anarchism: Its Philosophy and Ideal.* London: Freedom Pamphlets.
Kymlicka, Will. 1990. *Contemporary Political Philosophy.* London: Oxford University Press.
Lappé, Frances. 2011. *Ecomind: Changing the Way We Think to Create the World We Want.* New York: Nation Books.
Leopold, Aldo. 1966. *A Sand County Almanac: With Essays on Conservation from Round River.* New York: Ballantine.
Levine, Andrew. 1988. "Capitalist Persons." *Social Philosophy and Policy* 6: 39-59.
Locke, John. [1690] 1998. *Two Treatises of Government.* ed. Paul Laslett. New York: Cambridge University Press.
_____. [1690] 1986. *The Second Treatise of Government.* ed. Thomas Peardon. New York: Macmillan.
Lyons, David. 1970. "The Correlatively of Rights and Duties." *Nous* 4: 45-55.
Mack, Eric. 1990. "Self-Ownership and the Right of Property." *Monist* 73: 519-43.
_____. 1995. "The Self-Ownership Proviso: A New and Improved Lockean Proviso." *Social Philosophy and Policy* 12: 186-218.
_____. 2010. "The Natural Right of Property." *Social Philosophy and Policy* 27: 53-78.
Magnell, Thomas. 2011. "The Correlativity of Right and Duties." *The Journal of Value Inquiry* 45: 1-12.

Marx, Karl. [1867] 1992. *Capital: Vol. 1: A Critique of Political Economy*. ed. New Left Review. London: Penguin.

Mazor, Joseph. 2009. "A Liberal Theory of Natural Resource Property Rights." Ph.D. diss. Harvard University.

McKean, Margaret. 1992. "Success on the Commons: A Comparative Examination of Institutions for Common Property Resource Management." *Journal of Theoretical Politics*, 4: 247-281.

Miller, David. 1989. *Market, State, and Community*. London: Oxford University Press.

Naess, Arne. 1973. "The Shallow and the Deep, Long-Range Ecology Movement. A Summary." *Inquiry* 16: 95-100.

Narveson, Jan. 1988. *The Libertarian Idea*. Philadelphia: Temple University Press.

_____. 1996. "The Anarchist's Case." In *For and Against The State*, ed. John T. Sanders and Jan Narveson. Lanham, MD: Rowman and Littlefield. 195-216.

_____. 1999. *Moral Matters*. Ontario: Broadview.

Neeson, J.M. 1996. *Commoners: Common Right, Enclosure, and Social Change in Europe, 1700-1820*. Cambridge: Cambridge University Press.

Nozick, Robert. 1974. *Anarchy, State, and Utopia*. New York: Basic Books.

Orwell, George. 1968. *The Collected Essays, Journalism, and Letters of George Orwell Vol. 3*. ed. Sonia Orwell and Ian Angus. New York: Harcourt, Brace, and World Inc.

Ostrom, Elinor. 1990. *Governing the Commons: The Evolution of Institutions for Collective Action*. Cambridge: Cambridge University Press.

Otsuka, Michael. 2003. *Libertarianism Without Inequality*. London: Oxford University Press.

Pogge, Thomas. 1998. "A Global Resource Dividend." In *Ethics of Consumption: The Good Life, Justice, and Global Stewardship*, ed. David Crocker and Toby Linden. Lanham, MD: Rowman and Littlefield. 501-536.

Proudhon, P.J. 1970. *What Is Property?* trans. Benjamin Tucker. New York: Dover Publications.

Pryor, Frederic. 1973. *Property and Industrial Organization in Communism and Capitalistic Nations*. Bloomington: Indiana University Press.

Pufendorf, Samuel. [1672] 1994. "*On The Law and Nature of Nations*." In *The Political Writings of Samuel Pufendorf*. ed. Craig L. Carr. Oxford: Oxford University Press.

Rachels, James. 1975. "Passive and Active Euthanasia." *New England Journal of Medicine* 292: 78-80.

Rawls, John. 1971. *A Theory of Justice*. Cambridge: Harvard University Press.

Roark, Eric. 2006. "Moral Duties and International Justice: Developing Allen Buchanan's Natural Duty of Justice." *Review Journal of Political Philosophy* 4: 113-132.

_____. 2008. "Using and Coming to Own: A Left-Proprietarian Treatment of the Just Use and Appropriation of Commons Resources." Ph.D. diss. University of Missouri-Columbia.

_____. 2012. "Applying Locke's Proviso to Unappropriated Natural Resources." *Political Studies*, 60: 687-702.

Roberts, Callum. 2007. *The Unnatural History of the Sea*. Washington D.C.: Shearwater Books.

_____. 2012. *The Ocean of Life*. New York: Penguin.

Romley, John, Andrew Hachbarth, Dana Goldman. 2012. *The Impact of Air Quality on Hospital Spending*. RAND Corporation. www.rand.org/pubs/technical_reports/TR777.html

Rothbard, Murray. 1978. *For a New Liberty: The Libertarian Manifesto*. New York: Libertarian Review Foundation.

_____. 2003. *The Ethics of Liberty*. New York: NYU Press.

Rose, Carol. 1994. *Property and Persuasion: Essays on the History, Theory, and Rhetoric of Ownership*. Boulder: Westview Press.

Rousseau, Jean Jacques. [1755] 1950. *Discourse on the Origin and Basis of Inequality Among Men*. trans. G.D.H. Cole. Reprint. New York: E. P. Dutton.

Ryan, Alan. 1998. *Property*. Minneapolis: University of Minnesota Press.

Sachs, Jeffery. 2006. *The End of Poverty: Economic Possibilities for Our Time*. New York: Penguin Group.

Schmidtz, David. 1990. "When Is Original Appropriation Required." *Monist* 90: 504-518.

Sen, Amartya. 1980. "Equality of What?" In *The Tanner Lecture on Human Values Vol. 1.* Cambridge: Cambridge University Press. 197-220.

Simmons, John. 1992. *The Lockean Theory of Rights.* Princeton: Princeton University Press.

_____. 1993. *On the Edge of Anarchy: Locke, Consent and the Limits of the State*. Princeton: Princeton University Press.

_____. 1994. "Original-Acquisition Justifications of Private Property." *Social Philosophy and Policy* 11: 63-84.

Sindermann, Carl. 1996. *Ocean Pollution: Effects on Living Resources and Humans*. Boca Raton, FL: CRC Press.

Singer, Peter. 2010. *The Life You Can Save*. New York: Random House.

Smith, Robert. 1981. "Resolving the Tragedy of the Commons by Creating Private Property Rights in Wildlife." *Cato Journal* 1: 439-468.

Spencer, Herbert. 1851. *Social Statics*. London: John Chapman.

Steiner, Hillel. 1994. *An Essay on Rights*. Cambridge: Blackwell Publishers.

Steiner, Hillel and Peter Vallentyne. 2009. "Libertarian Theories and Intergenerational Justice." In *Justice Between Generations*, ed. Alex Gosseries and Lukas Meyer. Oxford: Oxford University Press. 50-76.

Stirner, Max. 1907. *The Ego and Its Own*. ed. David Leopold. Cambridge: Cambridge University Press.

Temkin, Larry. 1993. *Inequality*. Oxford: Oxford University Press.

The Corporation. Directed by Mark Achbar and Jennifer Abbott. 2003; New York: Zeitgeist Films, 2004, DVD.

Thomson, Judith Jarvis. 1986. "Some Ruminations on Rights." In *Rights, Restitution, and Risk*, ed. William Parent. Cambridge: Harvard University Press. 49-65.

Thompson, E.P. 1966. *The Making of the English Working Class*. New York: Vintage.

Tideman, Nic. 2000. "Global Economic Justice." *Geophilos* 00: 134-146.

UNICEF. 2006. *The State of the World's Children 2006: Excluded and Invisible*. www.unicef.org/sowc06/fullreport/full_report.php.

United Nations. 2006. Human Development Report 2006, *Beyond Scarcity: Power, Poverty, and the Global Water Crisis*. http://hdr.undp.org/en/reports/global/hdr2006/.

_____. 2007. *IPCC Fourth Assessment Report: Climate Change 2007.* http://www.ipcc.ch/publications_and_data/publications_ipcc_fourth_assessment_report_synthesis_report.htm.

_____. 2012. *The State of Food Insecurity in the World 2012*. www.fao.org/publications/sofi/en/

Vallentyne, Peter. 2000. "Introduction: Left-Libertarianism-A Primer." In *Left-Libertarians and its Critics: The Contemporary Debate*, ed. Peter Vallentyne and Hillel Steiner. New York: Palgrave. 1-17.

_____. 2002. "Brute Luck, Option Luck, and Equality of Opportunities." *Ethics* 112: 529-557.

_____. 2007. "Distributive Justice." In *Companion to Contemporary Political Philosophy*, eds. Robert Goodin, Philip Pettit, and Thomas Pogge. Oxford: Blackwell Publishers. 548-562.

_____. 2009. "Left-Libertarianism and Liberty." In *Debates in Political Philosophy*, eds. Thomas Christiano and John Christman. Cambridge: Blackwell Publishers. 137-151.

Vallentyne, Peter and Nic Tideman. 2001. "Left-Libertarianism and Global Justice." In *Human Rights in Philosophy and Practice*, ed. Bruton Leiser and Tom Campbell. London: Ashgate. 443-457.

Vallentyne, Peter and Hillel Steiner. 2000a. *Left-Libertarianism and Its Critics: The Contemporary Debate*. Hampshire: Palgrave.

_____. 2000b. *The Origins of Left-Libertarianism: An Anthology of Historical Writings.* Hampshire: Palgrave.

Valletnyne, Peter, Hillel Steiner, and Michael Otsuka. 2005. "Why Left-Libertarianism is not Incoherent, Indeterminate, or Irrelevant: A Reply to Fried." *Philosophy and Public Affairs* 33: 201-215.

Van Parijs, Philippe. 1995. *Real Freedom for All*. London: Oxford University Press.

Waldron, Jeremy. 1979. "Enough and As Good for Others." *The Philosophical Quarterly* 117: 319-328.

_____. 1983. "Two Worries About Mixing One's Labor." *The Philosophical Quarterly* 33: 37-44.

_____. 1988. *The Right to Private Property*. Oxford: Clarendon Press.

_____. 1991. "Homelessness and the Issue of Freedom." *UCLA Law Review* 39: 295-324.

Watkins, J.G. 1947. "Antisocial Compulsions Induced Under Hypnotic Trance." *Journal of Abnormal Social Psychology* 42: 256-259.

Wellman, Christopher. 1996. "Liberalism, Samaritanism, and Political Legitimacy." *Philosophy and Public Affairs* 25: 211-237.

Wells, W.R. 1940. "Ability to Resist Artificially Induced Disassociation." *Journal of Abnormal Social Psychology* 35:261-272.

_____. 1941. "Experiments in the Hypnotic Production of Crime." *Journal of Psychology* 11:63-102.

Wertheimer, Alan. 1996. *Exploitation*. Princeton: Princeton University Press.

Wheeler, Samuel. 1980. "Natural Property Rights as Body Rights." *Nous* 16: 171-93.

"Who Shot Mr. Burns? (Part 1)." *The Simpsons*. First broadcast May 21, 1995 by FOX. Directed by Jeffrey Lynch and written by Bill Oakley and Josh Weinstein.

Widerquist, Karl and Michael Howard. 2012. *Alaska's Permanent Fund Dividend.* New York: Palgrave Macmillan.

Wolf, Clark. 1995. "Contemporary Property Rights, Lockean Provisos, and the Interests of Future Generations." *Ethics* 105: 791-818.

World Wildlife Fund. 2012. *2012 Living Planet Report.* wwf.panda.org/about_our_earth/all_publications/living_planet_report/ *2012_lpr/.*

Yarrow, Andrew. 1992. Feb 2, 1992. "U.S Denies Role in Toxic Dumping." New York Times. www.nytimes.com/1992/02/02/nyregion/us-denies-role-in-toxic-dumping.html.

Index

Academy Awards, 71–72
adverse possession, 69, 86n6
Alaska Permanent Fund, 152, 153, 169n7–169n9
Alexander, Bob, 22
appropriation, xiii, 14, 70, 73, 82, 106, 109–110, 111, 121, 162; claiming, 140–142, 148n10, 148n8; definition of, 24n15, 70; of the commons, xi, xiii, xv, xvi, 10–11, 43, 44, 85, 89, 95–96, 98, 102, 104, 105–106, 106, 107–108, 108, 112, 135–147, 149
Arneson, Richard, 65n18, 132n27, 136–137
Arrhenius, Svante, 36
artifacts, 2, 28–29, 30–31, 33–34, 79, 81–82, 141, 158–159
Attas, Daniel, xiv

barbed wire, 21–22, 24n35
Berlin, Isaiah, 49, 55
brainwashing *see* psychological manipulation
Brands, Henry, 24n34
Brody, Brauch, xi, 140
Buchanan, Allen, 154; Natural Duty of Justice, 154–155

California Gold Rush, 21
carbon credits, 166
charity, 60, 152–154, 155, 155–156
Chartier, Gary, 39n9
Christman, John, xviiin15, xvin7, 66n32, 67, 68, 71, 86n7
Cohen, G.A., xi–xii, xviin15, 54, 66n21, 132n27
Colliver, Paul, 151
common ownership, 92–93, 93, 95
commons, 8, 15, 15–17, 89, 95, 107, 131, 143, 150, 151, 157, 161, 165, 166; enclosure of, 17–22; moral analysis of, xi, xiii, 10–12, 96; tragedy of, 13–15, 17, 108–110

deep ecology movement, 158, 160
disability payments, 126
Dworkin, Ronald, 132n25, 132n28

ecosystem, 7, 158, 159–160
egalitarianism, 3, 125–126
environmental degradation, xi, xvi, 147, 149–150, 157, 167, 168; air pollution, 36, 76; climate change, 35–36; drought, 163; oceanic dead zones, 37
environmental sanctuaries, 166
European Convention of Human Rights, 156, 169n15
European Court of Human Rights (ECHR), 156, 157, 169n14
exploitation, xiii, 35, 130

Fence Cutters War, 22

first claimant *see appropriation*
Ford, Lacy, 66n36
Fox, Warren, 160
Fressola, Anthony, 131n2
future generations, 97, 108, 110, 131n4, 152, 158, 163

Gard, Wayne, 24n36
genetically modified crops, 74–75, 86n15
George, Henry, xi, 29–30, 50–51, 53, 63, 64, 83, 97, 111–112, 121, 132n16, 132n20
Georgism, 112, 114; competitive rent, 112, 114–115, 115, 125, 126, 128, 129; competitive value, 112–113, 115, 120, 121, 127, 128–130, 132n18, 149, 151–152, 163, 163–164; cooperative bidding power, 166; equal opportunity for welfare Georgism, 120, 126–131, 135, 143–144, 149; equal share Georgism, 120–122; fair bidding power, 115–120, 164, 166; Rothbard's critique of Georgism, 145–147
Gibbard, Alan, xi–xii, 23
Gibbs, Lois, ix, x–xi, 167
global poverty, xi, xiv, xvi, 147, 149–152, 157, 167, 168; the bottom billion, 151, 153; UNICEF, 168n4
Grand Canyon, 6
greenhouse effect, 36
Grotius, Hugo, xi, xii, 8, 46, 63
Grunebaum, James, xi

Hardin, Garrett, 24n18
Hartsock, Michael 86n17
homelessness, 84, 87n23
Honoré, A.M., 66n28, 67
Hornbeck, Richard, 24n35

Industrial Revolution, 17, 20

Jefferson, Thomas, 63
joint-ownership, xii, 44, 57, 91–92, 131n2, 145
justice, xiii–xv, 41–42, 45, 64, 82, 95, 100, 126, 128, 149–150, 158, 161, 165, 169n5; compensatory justice, 153, 161; enforceable justice, 152–154

Kamen, Dean, 87n20
Kant, Immanuel, 55, 137
Kierland, Brian, 38n3, 132n15, 148n8
King, Stephen, 49
Kirzner, Israel, 6–8, 23n6
Kropotkin, Peter, 18
Kymlica, Will, xi

Lappé, Frances Moore, 167, 168n1
Law of the Sea Treaty, 16, 24n21, 37
Leopold, Aldo, 169n16
libertarianism, xiv, 52–53, 54, 58, 82, 95, 137, 150; differences between left and right libertarianism, 52, 62–63, 64
left-libertarianism *see Lockean Left-Libertarianism*
libertarian creed, 58–60, 62, 137
Lockean left-libertarianism, xi, xiii, xv, 41, 62–64, 89, 127, 149, 157, 163, 165, 167; right-libertarianism, xv, 63
Locke, John, xi, 2, 53, 63, 96, 150; treatment of natural resources within the commons, xii, 8–9, 10, 17; equal and independent moral status, xiii, 47–48, 60–62, 64, 97, 98, 109, 125, 129, 130, 140, 149, 150; labor mixing account of property, 138–140; natural rights approach, 9–10; spoilage principle, 138; state of war, 9; views of punishment, 65n11
Lockean Proviso, xv, 62, 89, 95–100, 101, 102, 103–104, 105, 105–106, 106, 107, 108, 108–111, 121, 123–124, 125, 127, 129, 131, 137–138, 143, 147, 149, 151, 152, 154, 154–155, 156, 157, 162, 165
love canal disaster, ix–xi, xiii, 167–168; health impacts, ix, x; possible government involvement, x
Lyons, David, 65n5

Mack, Eric, xviin21, 50, 55, 86n18, 101
Magnell, Thomas, 65n5
marine sanctuaries *see environmental sanctuaries*
Marx, Karl, 20–21; marxism, xiv, 11, 41, 64, 109
Mazor, Joseph, xi
McKean Margaret, 17
might makes right thesis, 1, 59

Miller, David, 148n7
monopoly pricing, 130
moral standing, 27

Naess, Arne, 169n16
Narveson, Jan, 53, 57, 60, 63
national parks *see environmental sanctuaries*
natural resources, 27, 28–29, 79, 83, 85, 89–90, 92, 94, 97, 98–100, 100–110, 113–114, 115–120, 121–122, 123–124, 127–131, 138, 147, 151, 152, 157, 158, 160–161, 165; conservation of, 163–165; consumption of, 34, 94–95, 100, 111; equality of natural resources thesis, xi, xv, 2–5, 30, 35, 102, 103, 112, 119, 149, 151, 152, 154, 165; importance for agents, xiii, 4, 34–37, 123, 157, 158, 160; intrinsically valuable, 158–160; perishable, 94–95, 111; rights in respect to, xiv, 62, 82, 83, 84, 142
Neeson, J. M., 19
Nozick, Robert, xv, 10, 33, 42, 47, 53, 63, 95, 138; account of appropriation, 12–13

Occupy Movement, 69
open field system, 17, 18
Orwell, George, 19–20
Oscar Award *see* Academy Awards
Ostrom, Elinor, 24n20
Otsuka, Michael, xi, xviin15, 55–56, 61, 62, 66n21, 66n40, 95, 122, 127–130, 133n33; egalitarian proviso, 127–128

pacifism, 10
paternalism, 58–59
phytoplankton, 6–7
Plato, 47
Pogge, Thomas, 152
private ownership *see property rights*
privatization of water, 35
prosthetic body parts, 79–82, 84, 87n21
Proudhon, Pierce-Joseph, xi, 86n7
Pryor, Frederic, 66n27
psychological manipulation, 49
Pufendorf, Samuel, xi, 63, 142

Rachels, James, 87n24
Rawls, John, 33, 132n24; veil of ignorance, 33, 117, 119
re-foresting, 93
rights, 42, 54, 60–61, 91, 95, 98; basic human rights, 154–157; correlated with duty, 45; Hohfeldian account, 43–45; natural rights, xiii, 47; of access, 67, 76–78, 102; of squatters, 69, 86n4; proliferation of, 47, 68; property rights, xv, 6, 28, 46–47, 67–78, 86n17, 86n3, 97, 102, 107, 109, 112, 136–137, 147, 149, 161–162; protective from domination, 51; protective of, 45; stringency of, 46–47, 54; to destroy, 72–73
Ring of Gyges *see Plato*
rivalrous good, 90, 131n1
Robert's Rules of Order, 131n7
Roberts, Callum, 39n19
Rose, Carol, 86n6, 148n9
Rothbard, Murray, 57–58, 63, 66n21
Rousseau, Jean Jacques, 17

Sachs, Jeffery, 168n1
Schmidtz, David, 108–110
self-ownership, xiv, xv, 53–58, 58, 60–62, 64, 67, 91, 99, 117, 128, 140, 157, 162; access to self, 78–85; rejection of, xiv, 99; suicide, xiv, 51; voluntary slavery, xiv, 51
Sen, Amartya, 132n23
Simmons, John, xviin13
Sindermann, Carl, 39n18
Singer, Peter, 168n1, 169n10
slavery, 58
Smith, Robert, 4
Spencer, Herbert, xi, 4, 53, 58, 63
Stanley Cup, 72
Steiner, Hillel, xi, xviin15, 45, 62, 65n5, 66n21, 66n40, 68, 95, 121, 132n20, 132n25, 132n28, 140
Stirner, Max, 53

Temkin, Larry, 132n26
The Simpsons, 35, 166
Thompson, E.P., 19
Thompson, Judith Jarvis, 60–61
Tideman, Nic, 132n20

Tomhave, Alan, 97, 131n8, 131n9

United Nations, 35, 39n10, 155, 168n2
Universal Declaration of Human Rights (UDHR), 155, 169n13
Use, xi, xv, 74, 85, 89, 90, 91–92, 92–93, 95, 96, 98, 136, 160; definition of, 74, 171–174; destructive use, 4, 9, 93, 100, 105, 106, 132n17, 158, 160–162, 165–166; degrading use *see destructive use*; monopolistic use *see overuse*; overuse, 4, 10, 13, 15, 101, 108, 132n17; of natural resources *see natural resources*; restrictive use, 101–103, 105, 132n17

Vallentyne, Peter, xi, 28, 42, 54, 62, 66n21, 66n40, 82, 87n21, 87n22, 125, 126
Van Parijs, Philippe, xi, xviin15
vickery auction, 115, 116–117, 132n19
Vince Lombardi Trophy, 72

Waldron, Jeremy, 18, 87n23, 131n3
Wells, W.R., 65n15
Wellman, Christopher, 65n18
Wertheimer, Alan, xviin11
Wheeler, Samuel, 87n19
Wolf, Clark, 131n4

Yosemite National Park, 160

www.ingramcontent.com/pod-product-compliance
Ingram Content Group UK Ltd.
Pitfield, Milton Keynes, MK11 3LW, UK
UKHW041843031026
15587UKWH00002B/966

9 780739 174685